WITHDRAWN

WITHDRAWN

LITERARY STRUCTURES
Edited by John Gardner

THE
CONSTRUCTION
OF
Paradise Lost

By

Burton Jasper Weber

Foreword by John Gardner

Southern Illinois University Press
Carbondale and Edwardsville

Feffer & Simons, Inc.
London and Amsterdam

For Mrs. Augusta Gottlieb

Contents

Foreword

BURTON Weber presents in this book a careful structural analysis of *Paradise Lost*. Everyone knows, including of course Mr. Weber, the hazards involved in such criticism. As Joseph Summers points out in *The Muse's Method: An Introduction to "Paradise Lost"* (London, 1962; pp. 113–15), systematic structural criticism may limit the critic's vision, causing him to miss what lies outside his scheme and to distort the poem to fit the scheme; and he adds that such criticism may prove merely tedious to the reader. Real as these dangers are, the critic can circumvent them only if he values richness before orderliness as an aesthetic quality. For the man who loves order (as Milton did), the risks are worth taking. Mr. Weber has a mind uncommonly penetrating and orderly. The scheme he discovers as the logical structure of *Paradise Lost* is so neat, and essentially so simple, that some readers will perhaps be outraged by it. Nevertheless, the scheme seems right: it explains what has not been explained before. Once one has understood the scheme and recognized how carefully Milton follows it, one can return, with new insight and pleasure, to the richness of language and symbolism with which Milton fleshes the skeleton of argument.

Mr. Weber teaches at Regina, Saskatchewan (Canada). He is presently working on, among other things, a study of Milton's *Paradise Regained*.

John Gardner

Carbondale, Ill.
January, 1971

[ix

Preface

THIS reading of *Paradise Lost* presents a scheme for explaining the structure of the poem—where its major divisions fall, how its two plots are related, what place the minor characters have, how the prophecy relates to the rest—and for explaining how plots, minor characters, and episodes relate to the poem's meaning. Since my exposition of this scheme is not very orthodox, let me begin by explaining my procedure.

My reading is detailed and slow-paced: I pursue ideas through almost every speech and incident in the work, instead of making a generalization and then illustrating it by analysis of selected passages. I have adopted this procedure partly because of the nature of the poem—a work Milton thought out with care—but chiefly because of the nature of my concern. A man discussing Beethoven's treatment of the ninth chord can classify the occurrences and the resolutions of the chord, draw conclusions, and illustrate by selected examples, with the understanding that the points he makes apply equally to other members of the same subclass. But a man explaining the structure of a movement of a Mozart concerto has not explained that structure when he says that the first exposition consists of a first theme, a transition, a false second subject, and a first coda. The structure of the second exposition, the development, and the recapitulation remain unaccounted for. Nor has he finished his job when he notes that the false second subject appears in the first exposition, the development, and the recapitulation. The ordering of other elements remains untreated. Structural analysis requires a discussion of all the sections of the work with regard to all their principal elements. So with the structural analysis of a narrative. If the critic

[xi

is to discuss the structure at all (if he believes that in a given work the structure is worth his celebration) , he has no choice but to think out and discuss all the basic elements as they appear throughout the work.

The question of structure is an empirical one, and any structural theory must appeal to the criteria of neatness, consistency, and applicability by which other empirical hypotheses are verified. As for neatness, I have begun with assumptions which I have justified, I hope, in my Introduction. I have assumed that, since Milton's poem is a narrative, its main constituent is its story, and that the major divisions of the work will coincide with the divisions of the narrative—the places where changes occur in the conditions of the protagonists. I have assumed that, in a plot avowedly concerned with right and wrong relationships to God, the sorts of changes that will be most significant are changes in moral status—that primary attention should be paid to the moral significance of behavior, rather than to, say, psychological causation; and I have assumed that the standards for judging this behavior must be deduced from or at least judged against the actions and pronouncements of God. Since the poem has a double plot, I have assumed that the two plots may be supplementary— augmentative where parallel, complementary where divergent— and that they may be structurally analogous, since this sort of treatment is relatively common in double plots. I have assumed that minor characters may have some significance relative to the issues raised by the two plots, and perhaps some supplementary connections with those plots; and I have assumed that (epic convention or not) the prophecy ought to be examined for connections with the ideas and structure of the work, since without these qualities the minor elements would lack relevance. Finally, I have assumed that the "meaning" of the poem is that abstraction which is illustrated primarily by the fates of the protagonists of the poem's actions, but which the minor elements may also support. Though these assumptions can of course be disputed, they are not farfetched, as far as I can see, and I have built on them as neatly as I could, tracing a few basic points throughout the poem and tying its various elements together. In addition, I have tried to be consistent, and where there are gaps between logical expectation and the facts of the poem, I have noted them. The discrepancies may be signs of the faultiness of the theory, or they may be illogicalities in the poem. The third quality of the theory, its applicability, is obviously the crucial question, and so I have offered at length what is, after all, the only proof which can be brought for such a theory. My reason for abandoning selectivity is, then, the necessity of proving my case.

I apologize for this excursion into theory. I did not undertake this reading in order to exemplify an aesthetic system, but rather to end my own questionings about the structure and meaning of *Paradise Lost*—questions which I found I could not answer (nor could anyone else, it seemed to me) from examinations that used the traditional method of generalization and illustration.

This reading may seem severely limited. Accustomed to such usual topics as the rhetoric of *Paradise Lost,* or characterization, or the philosophical basis of the poem, the reader may feel that I touch upon all these things without going thoroughly into any of them—that I sometimes discuss the structure of speeches but never examine rhetorical figures, that I discuss the character of Adam and Eve but never mention the characterization of God, that I discuss some metaphysical issues but never handle such matters as the degree of orthodoxy in the treatment of the Trinity. Or, again, the reader may feel that I have shirked what would be a logical application of my materials, a discussion of the ethical utility of *Paradise Lost*. But the limitations are necessary. I began with a single aesthetic question: What is the structural scheme of *Paradise Lost*? In answering this question I was forced, obviously, to touch upon many topics usually treated in other connections, but my treatment of these topics has been confined to their bearing on my subject.

I WOULD like to express my thanks to Jarvis Thurston, for teaching me criticism, and to Samuel Monk, for his example and for kindnesses done me during the writing of this book.

Because my subject requires no examination of the original spelling and punctuation, I have chosen to use a modernized text of *Paradise Lost* as less distracting to the reader. I have used

The Poems of John Milton, Second Edition, Edited with Introduction and Notes by James Holly Hanford   Copyright 1953   The Ronald Press Company, New York. I thank the publishers for permission to quote from this edition.

Burton J. Weber

Regina, Saskatchewan
December, 1970

Introduction

THERE is, of course, nothing new about trying to account logically for the structure of *Paradise Lost*. Not only various attempts, but various kinds of attempts have been made. Lately critics have tried to explain the poem's structure in terms of leitmotifs. Joseph Summers asserts that the construction of *Paradise Lost* consists of the repetition in the settings of hell, heaven, and Eden of five motifs: "love, creation, battle, fall, and praise." [1] Summers does not develop this thesis in detail, however, his book (a fine one) being devoted to poetic texture rather than to structure, and so the primary exponent of the theory must remain Jackson Cope, who treats *Paradise Lost* in terms of its imagery of light and darkness and of rising and falling.[2] His study probably needs no comment here. It is inherently improbable that a seventeenth-century epic poem be structured by image patterns, and the proof which Cope offers is not convincing (I discuss his case in note 4 to chapter 3).

An older approach, that of blocking out the poem's parts into consecutive sections, seems at first more promising. E. M. W. Tillyard mentions two theories of this sort; he associates them with Denis Saurat and Sir Walter Raleigh.[3] Saurat's theory is that the poem falls into two halves, one concerned with the fall of Satan, the other with the fall of man.[4] This theory has been modified and developed by B. Rajan, who argues that each half of the poem subdivides into a "destructive" and a "creative" action, the latter balancing and atoning for the former.[5] The fall of Satan, Rajan says, is countered by the creation of the world, and the fall of Adam and Eve by the Son's atonement.[6] The theory is plausible enough at first glance, but unconvincing when examined

[xv

in detail. In the first place, God is the principal figure in the part
of the poem devoted to the creation, but he is only a subordinate
figure in the part devoted to the regeneration of Adam and Eve,
the part which Rajan connects with the atonement. Adam and
Eve are the subjects of the atonement section, but the character
analogous to them, Satan, does not even appear in the crea-
tion episode. Thus the two "creative" actions are hardly analo-
gous, and Rajan can find only a few incidental connections be-
tween them. He cites as evidence such passages as the hymns to
the Son during the creation scene (7. 182–91, 613–19) and
Adam's exclamatory reply to Michael's account of Christ's mis-
sion (12. 469–73).[7] The weakness of this evidence Rajan partly
admits: "The similarities between the creative phases are," he
says, "less numerous" than those between the "destructive"
phases.[8] A second problem in this theory is its inability to account
for the development of Satan, principal character, according to
the theory, in the first of the poem's two main divisions. Though
the fall of man and the atonement do mark the two major turn-
ing points in the development of Adam and Eve, the fall of Satan
and the creation do not differentiate the stages of Satan's decline.

In his *Milton,* E. M. W. Tillyard elaborates the theory of Sir
Walter Raleigh, that everything in *Paradise Lost* leads up to the
fall of Eve;[9] but Tillyard revises and partly repudiates this ac-
count in his later *Studies in Milton.*[10] In the earlier account,
Tillyard divides the poem into four "movements" which he as-
sociates with hell, heaven, paradise, and the fall of man. These
sections he divides at Books One, Three, Seven (with an antici-
pation at Book Four), and Nine.[11] In his later account Tillyard ar-
gues that the climax of the poem is not the fall but the redemp-
tion of man, and that this climax occurs not at Book Nine but in
a broad area in Books Nine and Ten.[12]

Unfortunately, the division at Book Seven undermines Till-
yard's account. Tillyard begins with the assumption that Milton's
invocations mark stages of the narrative.[13] The first two of these
invocations coincide with changes of place, but the third major
change in scene, the change to earth, occurs at Book Four, which
is headed with only a brief prologue, while the third great in-
vocation heads a book which marks no change of scene, but only
a change of subject in Raphael's narration. In order to account

for this fact, Tillyard argues that the invocations coincide with the places "where the reader imagines himself to be situated"— "not necessarily," he adds, "where the action is taking place."[14] It seems offhand not very probable that Milton would divide his narrative according to changes in the reader's vantage point rather than according to changes in the characters' nature or fortune, the central considerations in a narrative. But, more important, the proof that Book Seven does accomplish a crucial shift in the reader's vantage point is unconvincing. Tillyard argues that the reader is gradually transferred to earth by the transition from the external perspective of the creation episode to the terrestrial perspective of Adam's question about the stars.[15] The trouble with this is that in Books Three and Four there is a similar transition from the external perspective of Satan's approach to earth to the terrestrial perspective of Eve's question about the stars.

A further objection to Tillyard's account of the poem's structure is that his sectional division does not illuminate the poem's action. The original version of the theory has the disadvantage of establishing a comparison of Satan after the fall with Adam and Even during the fall—a fault which Tillyard acknowledges in his later analysis.[16] The revised version has two other disadvantages. In order to prove that Satan in hell is compared with the repentant Adam and Eve, Tillyard feels obliged to demonstrate that the fall of man is not a significant stage in the narrative, and that there is a continuous movement from the fall to the repentance. He argues, therefore,[17] that man's fall begins early in what he calls the state of "nominal innocence,"[18] and that the regeneration begins before Adam and Eve are aware of it, during the judgment scene, when the Son clothes the pair.[19] These arguments blur the two main turning points in the development of Adam and Eve, their change from innocence to guilt, and their change from alienation to renewed piety. Furthermore, Tillyard's "movements" in their revised form do not correspond with the divisions derived from the placement of the invocations. Tillyard divides the actions into two parts, "the motives prompting revolt, and the positive lines of action afterwards."[20] If the poem were sectioned according to this plan, it would have divisons at Book Four and in the center of Book Five, the points at which the expositions of motives begin, and the division at Book Nine would mark the regeneration of man, the "positive line of action" in the story of Adam and Eve.[21] Instead, the "movements" which Tillyard derives from the invocations begin at Books Three and Seven, and the subject announced by the invocation at Book Nine is clearly the fall of man:

> *No more of talk where God or angel guest*
> *With Man, as with his friend, familiar used*
> *To sit indulgent, and with him partake*
> *Rural repast, permitting him the while*
> *Venial discourse unblamed. I now must change*
> *These notes to tragic. . . .*
>
> (9. 1–6)

The defects in the two theories that rely upon division of *Paradise Lost* into consecutive sections suggest that these sections do not account for how the poem's materials are structured and do not cast light upon the division of the poem's actions.

The structural approach that I have adopted is the narrative one. Other critics who have adopted it have come up with two alternative ways of looking at *Paradise Lost,* some treating the work as having a single plot, some as having a double plot. The major difference is the role assigned to Satan. According to one reading, Satan is a minor character in the central action. When Addison demonstrates that the action of *Paradise Lost* is entire, he says that it is "contrived in Hell, executed upon Earth, and punished by Heaven" [22]—a reading which gives Satan the role of villain in a plot whose main characters are Adam and Eve. According to the other reading, Satan is the central character of a secondary plot. In his demonstration that *Paradise Lost* has a unified action, Addison comments that the resemblance of the fall of the angels to that of man is "the same kind of beauty which the critics admire in *The Spanish Friar, or the Double Discovery,* where the two different plots look like counterparts and copies of one another." [23] In this account Satan is, of course, the protagonist of an independent action.

Although (as Addison's treatment shows) these two views of the narrative can be confused, they have quite different structural consequences. In the first view, Satan is one of the two figures

flanking Adam and Eve: his role (in the orthodox reading) is that
of villain, and he is the direct antithesis of God. In the second
view, Satan is parallel to Adam and Eve; he is a central character,
and he does not contrast directly with God. Satan may be treated,
in the first view, as a static character; in the second he must be
treated as a changing one. In one view Satan may be seen as pri-
marily an abstract figure, a personified abstraction or a type; in
the other, Satan's character and its development are emphasized,
and abstraction is subordinated. Thus Douglas Bush, who ap-
proaches the poem as if it had a single plot,[24] assigns Satan the
"functional role" of "villain." [25] Though at one point Tillyard
similarly describes heaven and hell as fighting for Adam and
Eve,[26] nevertheless in his *Studies in Milton* he does treat the poem
as having a double plot,[27] and when he does so he compares
Satan's story section by section with that of the human pair.[28]
Bush mentions in passing a decline in Satan,[29] but when char-
acterizing him [30] he does not treat the subject as if it were a major
or even significant topic. Tillyard, on the other hand, divides
Satan's story into two parts, "the motives prompting revolt, and
the positive lines of action afterwards," making the subject of
Satan's development a central matter. When Bush describes the
war in heaven as a "macrocosmic illustration of, and background
for, Milton's real theme, the war between good and evil in the
soul of man," [31] he makes Satan a semi-allegorical embodiment
of evil. Tillyard, however, argues that Milton does not make his
devils primarily representations of "essential evil"; instead, he
says, Milton humanizes them.[32]

The Satanist versions of these two approaches to the narrative
contrast in the same way as their orthodox counterparts. Sir
Walter Raleigh may be taken as the Satanist analogue to Bush.
Raleigh sees *Paradise Lost* as having a single action, for in sum-
ming up his view that the poem is a monument to Milton's own
genius and habits of thought,[33] Raleigh adapts Addison's formu-
lation of the action, describing the poem as "Milton's Paradise
Lost, lost by Milton's Adam and Eve, who are tempted by Milton's
Satan, and punished by Milton's God." [34] Thus when he says that
Satan is the hero of the poem,[35] he means not that Satan is a
protagonist but that he is the most sympathetic minor character,
the figure who is contrasted with the poem's villain, God. Raleigh

treats Satan's character without discussing his development—in
fact, he dismisses the idea that Satan develops; [36] and he treats
Satan, if not as an allegorical figure, at least as a type, the Prome-
thean bringer of freedom.[37]

William Empson, on the other hand, may be taken as the
Satanist analogue to Tillyard. He treats Satan not as an antithesis
to God but as a rebellious creature parallel to the rebellious Adam
and Eve, making one main point about all three characters, that
their fall is justified.[38] Empson carefully outlines Satan's develop-
ment,[39] and he approaches Satan and his followers as literal rather
than symbolic figures, as "angels who have become convinced that
their God is bad." [40]

The existence of analogies between the stories of Adam and
Eve, on one hand, and Satan, on the other (analogies of the sort
noted by Tillyard [41]), suggests that *Paradise Lost* does have a
double plot of the kind Addison described. And so the structural
approach that treats Satan as a protagonist is clearly preferable
to the alternative reading. To treat him otherwise would be as
misleading as to treat Gloucester as a counselor to Lear, a foil
to the nobler Kent, and to ignore the fact that his story parallels
the king's. In fact, Milton takes pains to play down those theo-
logical issues which would interfere with the parallel—for in-
stance, the difference between man's and angel's access to grace,
and the difference between the circumstances of man's fall and
the angels'. Milton indicates that angels do not receive the grace
available to man (3. 131–32), but he points out that men can put
themselves in Satan's position if they do not heed God's call
(3. 198–202). He distinguishes between the circumstances of the
two falls when the theological point is required (3. 129–31), but
when he narrates the fall of the angels, he does not concentrate
on Satan's invention of heresy, so as to emphasize by contrast the
extenuating circumstance in man's fall, nor does he stress the
distinction between Satan's persuasion of his fellows and his out-
witting of Eve, but instead likens the two sets of heresies.

From the view that Satan is the protagonist of a secondary plot
—the view adopted in this book—comes a view of God's function
in the action. If Satan is seen as the villain of the main plot, then
God must be seen as an active figure in that plot, an antithetical
champion of good. This is the place Addison gives him when he

declares "the Messiah" to be the "hero" of the poem; [42] and Bush adopts this view when he sees God as the opponent of Satan in a "macrocosmic illustration of . . . the war between good and evil in the soul of man." (Raleigh presents the analogous Satanist position when, calling God a "whimsical Tyrant," [43] he assigns him the role of villain, opponent to the heroic Satan.) But if, on the other hand, Satan is a protagonist, then he is not a semi-allegorical antithesis of God, but simply a disloyal creature who contrasts with other, loyal creatures, the unfallen angels. God in this case is not needed for a counterpoise, and his role can be viewed as merely that of expositor: creatures are judged by their opinions about God, and God tells what opinion those creatures ought to hold.

These are, I think, the structural premises of *Paradise Lost*. Before developing them further, let me turn to the problem of determining the poem's theme.

The difficulty criticism encounters in delimiting the theme of *Paradise Lost* comes down, in effect, to the problem of choosing between two theories of Milton's purpose. In justifying God's ways to man, is it Milton's object to celebrate God's generosity to those who respond properly to him, and to legitimate his rather unpleasant way of dealing with those who, like Satan, hate him? —or is it to analyze the ethical nature of those who please God and the ethical failure of those who do not? To put the question another way, is Milton's focus on God or on man? One theory justifies God directly, the other indirectly, one focusing on God's relation to his creatures, the other on the creatures' relation to God. The first theory is the currently fashionable felix culpa theory. The second is the older ethical view, voiced by Addison when he said that the "one great moral" of *Paradise Lost* was "that obedience to the will of God makes men happy, and that disobedience makes them miserable." [44]

One trouble with the felix culpa reading is that that doctrine cannot be proved to exist within the poem. As Dick Taylor, Jr., notes,[45] God does not speak as though what he had originally planned for man were inferior to what he plans for those of the fallen who accept salvation. After the repentance of Adam and Eve, the Father says that it would have been "Happier" for man "had it sufficed him to have known Good by itself, and evil not at all" (11. 88–89) . Furthermore, the passages that are cited as expositions of the doctrine are inconclusive. The passages usually mentioned are Michael's promise of a "Paradise within" (12. 585–87) and Adam's assertion that the Son's sacrifice makes him stand "full of doubt . . . Whether [he] should repent [him] now of sin . . . or rejoice / Much more, that much more good thereof shall spring" (12. 469–78) . But, as Lawrence A. Sasek points out, when Michael says that Adam will "not be loth / To leave" Eden, but will find a "Paradise within [him], happier far," he is preparing Adam for the departure from Eden, comparing the happiness to be derived from the Garden with the happiness which comes from faith in God; he is not comparing Adam's final state with his original innocence.[46] And, as Taylor observes,[47] Adam's joyful exclamation about the Son's sacrifice is only an emotional reaction to Michael's announcement, not a reasoned doctrinal assertion, for Adam ends his speech with a question which qualifies the earlier optimism, a question about the persecution of Christ's followers (12. 479–84) . (William G. Madsen eschews the usual texts, but his case for the doctrine is even less persuasive.[48])

A more important, if less tangible, objection to the view that *Paradise Lost* asserts the doctrine of the fortunate fall is the discrepancy between that doctrine and the poem's subject. The problem is noted by A. O. Lovejoy, who says that the idea of the felix culpa "undeniably place[s] the story of the Fall, which [is] the subject of the poem announced at the outset, in a somewhat ambiguous light." [49] The ambiguity is pressed by Empson, who says that in his exclamation over the Son's sacrifice, Adam is saying to God, "Oh, so you did want us to eat the apple, after all? Well, I'm pleased to hear that, because Eve rather thought you did, at the time." [50]

In order to get around this conflict in judgment, those who support the felix culpa reading argue that in handling the fall Milton does not place emphasis upon its unfortunateness. Millicent Bell, for example, claims that Milton undercuts the horror of man's loss by never showing him in any but a fallen condition.[51] She argues that "Adam's case has never been other than our case," that "the Redemption" has always been "his only real hope . . . of Paradise," and that "the upward motion that begins in Book

Ten with the repentance of Adam and Eve is the first real change in direction taken by the plot." [52] William H. Marshall argues that Milton lightens the fall with ironic indications of man's destined salvation. Claiming that throughout the first nine and a half books of *Paradise Lost* the reader is made "constantly aware" of the irony that God will bring good out of Satan's evil acts, Marshall argues that the fall creates "a kind of catharsis"; and he adds that "if anything remains of the central action of the Fall, it is merely to give dramatic emphasis, by Satan's return to hell in the tenth book, to the irony which has been implicit in the action leading to his apparent victory." [53]

These arguments of course badly misrepresent the materials of the poem. However many anticipations of the fall are granted to Mrs. Bell (instances are disputed in notes 2, 3, and 12 to chapter 3) , it should not be overlooked that the dominant impression made by the opening scene in the Garden is markedly different from that made by the scene which follows the eating of the forbidden fruit. If on his first visit to earth Satan had come upon an Adam who was admonishing his wife, "Wilt thou not hearken to my words, and stay / With me?" (see 9. 1134–35) , and if he had come upon an Eve who was replying, "Am I never to be parted from thy side? / As good to grow there still a lifeless rib!" (see 9. 1153–54) , it is not likely that he would have responded as he does when first viewing the pair:

> *Ah gentle pair, ye little think how nigh*
> *Your change approaches, when all these delights*
> *Will vanish and deliver ye to woe.*
>
> (4. 366–68)

Milton does represent a change of mankind from happy innocence to unhappy guilt, and he marks that change with an explicit announcement of a "change in direction" in the plot:

> *No more of talk where God or angel guest*
> *With Man, as with his friend, familiar used*
> *To sit indulgent, and with him partake*
> *Rural repast, permitting him the while*
> *Venial discourse unblamed. I now must change*
> *These notes to tragic; foul distrust and breach*

Disloyal on the part of man, revolt
And disobedience; on the part of Heaven
Now alienated, distance and distaste,
Anger and just rebuke, and judgment given,
That brought into this World a world of woe,
Sin and her shadow Death, and Misery
Death's harbinger.

(9. 1–13)

Nor is it true, as Marshall claims, that Milton undercuts his repre-
sentation of the fall with irony. Marshall, first of all, treats the first
nine and a half books of *Paradise Lost* as if their action were
Satan's war against God and as if Adam and Eve were only sec-
ondary characters in that action, the objects of contention; only
under these conditions is the reader "constantly aware" of God's
defeat of Satan, and does he think of the fall of man primarily as
an incident in Satan's war. If, noting Milton's opening declaration
(1. 1–5), he believes that the action of the first three quarters of
the poem is "Man's . . . disobedience," not Satan's war, and that
man's moral change ("first disobedience") rather than his turn
of fortune ("loss of Eden") is central, the reader directs his
attention to the initial moral innocence of Adam and Eve, to the
limitations which prefigure their fall and the warnings given
them, to the steps by which they transgress and the spiritual re-
sults of the transgression; his primary interest is not the irony that
Satan's victory is a temporary one. Furthermore, nothing in
Milton's treatment of the fall itself contributes to the effect that
Marshall describes, the demonstration that, ironically, man is not
really doomed. What the commentary and description assert is
simply the seriousness and pathos of the fall:

O much deceived, much failing, hapless Eve,
Of thy presumed return! event perverse!
Thou never from that hour in Paradise
Found'st either sweet repast or sound repose;
Such ambush, hid among sweet flowers and shades,
Waited with hellish rancor imminent
To intercept thy way, or send thee back
Despoiled of innocence, of faith, of bliss.

(9. 404–12) [54]

All arguments that Milton does not treat the fall as an "infinite disaster" (the words are Mrs. Bell's) must clash with the facts of a poem in which, as A. J. A. Waldock says, the words "disobedience" and "woe" are "paired a hundred times."[55] Lovejoy is thus much more accurate than his followers, for he says that Milton portrays the fall as a "deplorable" event and that, reserving the idea of the felix culpa for the end of the poem, he does not permit it to "intrude" earlier.[56] It should be noted, however, that this account constitutes a strong argument against pressing the view that certain passages in the poem describe the fall as fortunate. For if passages in a work are susceptible of two interpretations, and if one of these interpretations is not only inconsistent with the rest of the material in the work but tends to contradict that material, then common sense, it seems to me, urges the critic to pursue the alternative reading.

But even if the evidence for the theological approach to *Paradise Lost* were stronger than it is, there would be reason, I think, for pursuing a moral approach, for it is this approach that accounts for what is most impressive about Milton's poem. The problem is like that one meets in formulating the theme of *Macbeth*. It is possible to view *Macbeth* either as a tragedy in the fall-of-princes tradition or as a demonstration of the cumulativeness of evil: the former view emphasizes the events of the play; the latter focuses on the characterization. The latter view, I believe, is preferable, for what is most impressive about *Macbeth* is not its demonstration of ambition's fall but its portrayal of spiritual decline. In the case of *Paradise Lost,* the view that the poem illustrates the doctrine of the felix culpa emphasizes the events in the plots, the turns of fortune themselves, while the view that the poem shows the effects of accepting or rejecting God emphasizes the characterization of the central characters. That stressing characterization gets nearer to the heart of the poem than stressing events can be seen from specific examples of the two critical approaches. Marshall, treating the scene of Satan's return to hell (10. 410–584) as it relates to the fortunate fall, argues that the scene emphasizes Satan's defeat in victory,[57] and he appends the comment that the "observation of A. J. A. Waldock [is] very much to the point, that the technique of the poet—to raise Satan to expectation of success 'and then to dash him down'

—is *'exactly* that of the comic cartoon.' " [58] With regard to the
same scene, Arnold Stein—whom Cope rightly terms an "essayist
in psychology" [59]—comments that in the course of Satan's develop-
ment, Satan comes to experience his own failure. "The develop-
ment of [his] realization begins," Stein says, "in Book I, with the
evidences of inner conflict. It concludes in Book X with the short-
lived triumph of Satan's return to hell—with the histrionic mount-
ing of the throne incognito; with the distorted emphasis of his
report, as if it were to his credit to have turned the trick with an
absurd apple; with the final mass metamorphosis of all the devils
into serpents." [60] Surely there is no question as to which of these
two accounts comes closer to doing justice to the poem.

Many of the critics who adopt, as I do, the ethical approach to
Paradise Lost use the well-known principle of hierarchy as their
moral key—the principle that everything in the universe has a
proper role and rank. Taken by itself, this approach does not, I
believe, lead to satisfactory interpretation of the poem.

Those critics who adopt this alternative either apply the con-
cept of hierarchy microcosmically, whereupon the interpretation
centers on the hierarchy of reason and passion, or they apply it
macrocosmically, whereupon it centers on the creature's adher-
ence to his place in the chain of being; or, if the critic faces the
problem of relating the two realms, he applies it literally to one
realm and makes it the basis of symbolism in the other.

One obvious disadvantage to the microcosmic application is
its inapplicability to large portions of the poem. B. Rajan, for
instance, treats Adam as an example of passion unruled by rea-
son,[61] and Eve as an example of defective reason.[62] The results of
man's fall he sees as epitomized in the "Usurp[ation]" by "sensual
Appetite" of the rule which belongs to "sovran Reason" (9. 1127–
31).[63] Rajan does not, however, apply this approach to Satan, and
the reason is that material is lacking: Milton focuses his account
of Satan's fall on Satan's theological arguments, not on his psychic
processes (see note 2 to chapter 2). A second disadvantage of the
approach is that it makes God seem morally abominable. Bush
argues that because Milton turns the arbitrary prohibition of
Genesis into a test of reason, God is saved from the charge of
tyranny.[64] A. J. A. Waldock, however, notes Tillyard's argument
that Adam falls through "gregariousness" [65] and Eve through

"mental triviality," [66] and Waldock asks, "[I]s levity a better cause for [the pair's] awful doom than outright disobedience? Has Dr. Tillyard helped matters by looking beneath the disobedience and finding—gregariousness?" [67] The same objection can be raised to Bush's argument that "Eve falls through weakness of reason, Adam through weakness of will": [68] it does not make God seem less tyrannical to argue that he punishes man not for an act of disloyalty but for a logical error and a lapse in self-control, especially when the penalties for these rational errors are death for the offenders and death for all their children.

One version of the macrocosmic application of the idea of hierarchy has been attacked by Waldock. He notes that when Charles Williams attempts to interpret *Paradise Lost* in terms of pride, he can account for Satan well and Eve less well, but Adam not at all. [69] The same objection can be raised to the interpretation of Bush, who says that "the theme of *Paradise Lost* is the conflict between human pride and religious humility," [70] but who can apply these key concepts only to Satan and Eve, [71] not to Adam. [72]

Rajan does apply the concept of degree to all three central characters. After connecting Satan's fall with the scale of nature, [73] Rajan argues that Adam and Eve both violate the principle of hierarchy by abnegating their superior positions, Adam by obeying Eve, Eve by obeying a snake. [74] One trouble with this argument, however, is that it does not fit the poem very well. In the first place, it runs counter to the material which convicts Eve of aspiring above her place—Satan's resolve to tempt men to "Aspir[e]" to be "Equal with gods" (4. 522–27), Eve's speculation on whether eating the fruit will bring divinity (9. 773–75), Eve's later belief that she is "growing up to Godhead" (9. 874–77). In the second place, Eve is nowhere condemned for obeying a subhuman creature. Rajan makes his claim on the basis of a quotation from Godfrey Goodman's *Fall of Man*, [75] a quotation which speaks of the impropriety of "the basest creature['s]" giving "advice and direction to the best, in the highest point of religion." But in *Paradise Lost* Eve is not blamed for a breach of degree analogous to Adam's; the Son asks Adam, "Was [Eve] thy God, that her thou didst obey / Before his voice" (10. 145–46), but he asks Eve no parallel question about the serpent; the Son begins his sentencing of Adam with "Because thou hast hearkened to the voice of thy wife" (10. 198), but Eve's sentence begins simply "Thy sorrow I will greatly multiply" (10. 193).

A second objection to Rajan's theory is that it creates structural and thematic problems by weakening the analogies between the poem's two plots. In this respect his theory is inferior to that of Stein, who parallels the falls of the central characters (Stein's theory is discussed in note 6 to chapter 3).

An additional problem arises from the use of both the microcosmic and macrocosmic explanations. Hierarchical critics often refer to more than one kind of hierarchy, and Rajan, at least, is aware of the fact, for he mentions the possibility of "follow[ing] the book of homilies and identify[ing]" the violation of degree "with revolt," of "follow[ing] the political theorists and attempt[ing] to relate it to the Law of Nature," and of "treat[ing] it in terms of faculty psychology." [76] Once an interpretation sets out to use several aspects of the same world view, however, it is obliged to establish connections between these aspects. One obvious possible connection is causality, and sometimes Rajan, for example, does mention causal connections. For instance, he links Adam's overestimation of Eve with the overriding of reason by passion.[77] In general, however, the users of the hierarchical principle seem to assume that different aspects of the same world view may be used as alternative modes of explanation, simply because they rely on the same basic concept. Thus Rajan discusses Satan's apostasy in terms of the law of nature,[78] Eve's apostasy in terms of faculty psychology,[79] and the repentance of Adam and Eve in terms of repudiated revolt;[80] and Bush connects the fall of Eve with the macrocosmic concept of "ambitious pride" and the fall of Adam with the microcosmic concept of "sexual love." [81] The resultant interpretations are only deceptively comprehensive, for though they may account for all the events in the poem, they account for them according to different sets of ideas; and they are only deceptively coherent, for though the different sets of ideas may have a common base, nevertheless they involve different phenomena and different criteria—unwary reason is not, after all, synonymous with pride.

Denis Saurat's interpretation of *Paradise Lost* has the great virtue of uniting macrocosmic action with microcosmic psychology. Following Blake's famous analysis,[82] Saurat makes Satan a symbol of passion [83] and Christ an embodiment of reason; [84] their conflict thus reproduces what Saurat sees as a conflict between reason and passion in Adam and Eve, the latter of whom falls because her feelings rule her inferior intellect, and the former of whom falls because he allows the passionate Eve to rule him, who is the "representative of reason." [85] This theory presents many difficulties, however. The allegorization of Satan ignores the emphasis in Milton's presentation (see note 2 to chapter 2); the account of the fall inaccurately describes Eve; [86] and the structural pattern inadequately accounts for the development of Satan.

Although the principle of hierarchy is not sufficient, by itself, to account for what actually happens in *Paradise Lost,* it need not be dismissed as totally irrelevant. The alternative is to view hierarchy as a premise of the ethical system which Milton develops rather than as an ethical standard in itself. To adopt this position is to assess in a new way the evidence used by hierarchical critics, giving a less central place than they do to the concept of pride and denying entirely the importance of faculty psychology. Most of what the hierarchists interpret as pride can be seen as evidence of the creature's defiance of God's authority (sometimes a matter of pride, sometimes not). Such defiance is part of a creature's defection from God, but it need not be taken as the whole of that defection. As for faculty psychology, it simply does not seem to me to be focal. I do not think, first of all, that the famous passage in which "sensual Appetite" is described as "Usurping" the rule of "sovran Reason" (9. 1119–31) is a key philosophical explanation of the meaning of man's fallen state. The passage is descriptive rather than explanatory; its point is that now that the "exhilarating vapor bland" has been dissipated (9. 1046–49), Adam and Eve are depressed; the method of description includes a scientific description of the turbulent mind; the purpose of the description is to introduce the recriminations of Adam and Eve (9. 1131–89) which prove their lack of wisdom in rejecting God's pattern for human relationships. As for the other psychological passages, Raphael's warning against passion (8. 561–94) and Adam's explanations of how man's reason can be deceived (9. 351–63), neither of these passages makes faculty psychology a subject of independent interest. Raphael treats passion only in terms of its effect upon Adam's judgment of Eve, and that subject he relates to Adam's love for God and loyalty to him (8. 633–43). Adam treats the fallibility of reason as part of a reply to Eve's praise of unaided trial; the subject is significant insofar as it reveals Eve's failure to acknowledge Adam's superiority. In these cases, not psychology but the creatures' responsibility to God or to other creatures is the subject under discussion.

My argument in this book, then, is that *Paradise Lost* is a unified defense of God, a defense made through moral analysis of God's creatures. The major points I have to make about the elements of the narrative are these: First, with regard to the central characters, I argue that the stories of Adam and Eve and Satan constitute supplementary defenses of God. Since God is not a central character, the defense of him which the poem offers is not primarily a direct one—a defense based on God's treatment of his creatures—but an oblique defense based on the relationship of creatures to him. The story of Satan dramatizes the decline that results from the denial of God, in Milton's view, and the story of Adam and Eve shows the elevation that can be attained by renouncing this denial and returning to obedience and love. In other words, Milton defends God both positively and negatively, showing both the good effects of following him and the bad effects of rejecting him. The two plots are related in structure, and the parallels and antitheses between them serve to intensify the points presented by each plot alone, underlining the gravity of rejecting God and setting off the merit in accepting him. With regard to the minor characters, I have tried to show that these characters, the loyal and disloyal angels, contribute both directly and indirectly to God's defense. The loyal angels demonstrate what sort of life God's creatures are intended to have, and the disloyal angels reinforce the negative defense presented through Satan's decline. In addition, these characters suggest by their resemblance or their dissimilarity to Adam and Eve what moral judgments are to be made of the human pair, and in this way they help to clarify the defense of God which is offered through the poem's main plot. Finally, I try to show that the poem's expository episode, Michael's prophecy, contributes both indirectly and directly to God's defense. The structure of the prophecy relates it to the main concerns of the poem, being drawn, primarily, from the secondary plot and the poem's theological premises. Because the points which the prophecy makes are versions of the two main defenses of God offered through the double plot, the episode bears directly on the poem's theme.

My reading begins with an outline of the theological premises of *Paradise Lost,* then takes up the elements of the narrative one by one, first the major elements—the secondary plot and the main plot—then the minor ones—the minor characters and the expository episode. The final section is a demonstration of the structural and thematic connections between the separate elements.

THE CONSTRUCTION OF *Paradise Lost*

1

The Premises

GOD is neither a central character in *Paradise Lost* nor a minor character in the same sense that the loyal and the defecting angels are. As he is in a separate category from the other characters with regard to his nature, since he is not a creature, so he is in a separate category with regard to his function, for his basic function in *Paradise Lost* is not to participate in the action but to lay down the premises about himself and his creatures by which the actions of the other characters can be judged.

One of these basic premises concerns God's attributes.[1] Milton assigns him two principal attributes in *Paradise Lost,* authority and goodness, the first of these comprising God's rule and his claim to divine superiority, the second his love and his wrath. These two attributes are demonstrated in all of God's offices, the second basic premise of the poem being that God has four offices in relation to his creatures. The first of these is the office of creator and lawgiver. In this capacity God is shown as making and ordering creation with the ultimate aim of rewarding his creatures by elevating them to a closer union with himself. This office is God's original one; it is the only one which he would have performed had his creatures not fallen and the only one which he does in fact perform toward the unfallen angels. The second office assigned to God is that of judge, whereby God is shown as meting out punishment to those of his creatures who, having broken his laws, rebel against him. The third office is that of giver of grace.

In this capacity God allows his fallen creatures the possibility of repentance and reform, giving them the ability, lost in the fall, to acknowledge his authority and goodness. God is shown as exercising this office with regard to fallen man alone; grace is denied the fallen angels. The last office assigned to God is that of savior. In this office God is seen as granting reconciliation and salvation to those of his fallen creatures who, having repented and reformed, accept his gift. This office too is exercised only with regard to mankind; the fallen angels are again refused. These two fundamental premises about God's attributes and offices are established through God's acts and pronouncements relative to Satan and mankind.[2]

God's authority as creator and lawgiver to Adam and Eve is demonstrated first in the rule which he exercises over them. God assigns man the duty of tending Eden (8. 319–20), in order, as Adam sees, to show his supervision of man:

> *Man hath his daily work of body or mind*
> *Appointed, which declares his dignity,*
> *And the regard of Heaven on all his ways.*
>   *(4. 618–20)*

As God tells Adam, he makes one central command, the prohibition of the tree of knowledge, in order to test Adam's obedience to his rule (8. 323–28) ; and the test which he makes of Adam's rationality is intended to prove that he means man to obey him. When God tells Adam to content himself with the company of animals (8. 369–75), he tempts Adam to identify himself with creatures that have no duties; for, as Adam explains to Eve, "of [the] doings [of animals] God takes no account" (4. 622). When God holds up his own solitude as a model for Adam (8. 399–411), he tempts Adam to identify himself with the being who is the source of laws. Thus, testing whether Adam can "judge of fit and meet" (8. 448), God tests whether Adam knows his place, because it is that particular place which makes man subject to divine command. God's rule is asserted not only by his commands, however, but also by his pronouncements on freedom. When God says that he made man "Sufficient to have stood, though free to fall" (3. 98–99), he indicates that the ability to obey or disobey is meant not as an exemption from law, but rather as a necessary

condition for willed obedience. This freedom, enabling and oblig-
ing man to obey, is contrasted with the kind of freedom attrib-
uted to God; when God says, "what I will is Fate" (7. 173), he
indicates that he is subject to no ruling force, but is the maker of
the laws by which the universe is governed.

The authority of God is also demonstrated through his claims
of divine superiority. God's right to rule derives from his power
as creator; as Raphael explains, God when he set out to create
man assigned him his place in the universe, complete with privi-
leges and duties (7. 505–16). Furthermore, divine control is
maintained over man's place, for God possesses the power to ele-
vate his creatures. This power is asserted when God announces
his plan for elevating the not-yet-created race of man (7. 150–61);
and Adam refers to it when in reply to God he says, "[Thou]
Canst raise thy creature to what height thou wilt / Of union or
communion, deified" (8. 430–31).

God's rule as creator and lawgiver to angels is established by
his test of angelic obedience, the duty assigned to the angels of
obeying the Son as their head (5. 600–608), and by his applica-
tion to the angels of the same definition of freedom applied to
man. Announcing that he created man free to choose obedience or
disobedience, God continues,

> *Such I created all the Ethereal Powers*
> *And spirits, both them who stood and them who failed;*
> *Freely they stood who stood, and fell who fell.*
>
> (*3. 100–102*)

God's divine superiority is established through his joke about
Satan's defection (5. 719–24, 729–32). By the words "what an-
ciently we claim / Of deity or empire," God ironically suggests
that he is not the creator who gave the angels their place, but
merely a temporal creature ruling by custom; by the words "with
what arms / We mean to hold . . . empire," he suggests that he
is not the source of all angelic strength, but merely one angelic
warrior among the rest; and by his proposed muster of troops, he
suggests that he is not an omniscient and omnipotent creator, but
merely another finite creature. The irony establishes the point
made by Raphael with regard to mankind, that God is not a
creature, and that his right to rule is based upon his power as

creator to assign his creatures their proper roles in the universe. And as God maintains the power of elevating his creatures, so, Milton says, he maintains the power of degrading them – that "regal power" by which the Son proposes to "subdue" the defecting angels (5. 739–42).

In his office of creator and lawgiver to Adam and Eve, God's second principal attribute, his goodness, is demonstrated. His love is shown through the fact that he gives man the means of happiness and through the fact that he rewards man's goodness. God gives man Eden (8. 319–22); his plan for the world includes a reward for man's virtue, an elevation entailing closer union with himself (7. 150–61); and even the nature of his test is to be taken as a sign of his love for man, since, God says, man would have been happier experiencing only good than learning of good through the experience of evil (11. 86–89). By God's threat that Adam, disobeying, would be "expelled . . . into a world / Of woe and sorrow" and would die (8. 328–33), the second aspect of God's goodness, his wrath, is manifested – the hatred of evil complementary to his love of good.

God's goodness as creator and lawgiver to angels is demonstrated first of all in his love, analogous to his love for man. The banquet in heaven described by Raphael (5. 627–41) shows heaven to be an Eden for angels; and God's command to the angels is meant to show, like his plan for mankind, God's intention to reward his creatures' virtue. His aim is best expressed in Abdiel's explanation to Satan, that the angels are elevated by the union of God with their order (5. 841–45), but it is also implied in God's command itself:

> Under [the Son's] great vicegerent reign abide
> United as one individual soul
> For ever happy.
>
> (5. 609–11)

God's command, like his prohibition to man, is a test whose completion is to be rewarded with the happiness of a closer union of his creatures with himself. As with mankind, God's wrath is demonstrated by a threat of punishment for disobedience – in this case, the punishment of expulsion from heaven and exile into hell (5. 611–15).

God's second office, that of judge, is displayed in his response to his creatures' rebellion. In this second office also, divine authority and goodness are demonstrated—though, because the cases of the angels and mankind differ, the attributes appear in differing forms.

In the judgment of Adam and Eve, there is a direct assertion of divine rule. The Son begins by rebuking Adam's neglect of duty:

> *I miss thee here,*
> *Not pleased, thus entertained with solitude,*
> *Where obvious duty erewhile appeared unsought.*
> *(10. 104–6)*

Thus he establishes that Adam, having duties to God, is subject to God's judgment of his failures. And by the ease with which he proves Adam's disobedience from Adam's own words ("That thou are naked, who / Hath told thee?" [10. 121–22]), the Son indirectly rebukes Eve's belief in the wisdom gained by eating the forbidden fruit (9. 863–66) —a rebuke the effectiveness of which is seen in the fact that later Eve implies that she was mistaken in her belief (10. 159–62). But though he asserts his rule by condemning disobedience, the Son does make allowances for the extenuating circumstances in man's fall. In judging, the Son refrains from anger in accusing Adam (10. 118). This lack of anger is meant to betoken the mercy which both the Father (10. 58–59) and the Son (10. 77–79) pledge in the divine colloquy preceding the judgment scene—a pledge which in turn recalls the opening assembly in heaven, where both the Father (3. 130–34) and the Son (3. 150–55) propose that man be shown mercy because of the push that was partial cause of his fall.

The second aspect of God's authority, his divine superiority, is also demonstrated in God's office of judge to mankind. In the opening scene in heaven, the Son is endowed in his dual nature with supreme power (3. 305–20) —the means by which, the Father says, the descent of the incarnation is kept from "lessen[ing] or degrad[ing]" his divinity (3. 303–4). Later, when the Father sends the Son to judge mankind, he recalls this scene: "to thee I have transferred / All judgment, whether in Heaven, or Earth, or Hell" (10. 56–57). The reference contrasts divine power with human presumption: man has depreciated the power of God

(9. 805-7) and (as will be shown) has believed himself raised, while the Son has willingly accepted humiliation, and in so doing has been raised in his humanity. Not only is God's power of judgment directly asserted, however, but even his mercy in judgment is presented as evidence of divine superiority. Milton's statement that, in judging, the Son covers man's "inward nakedness" with his "robe of righteousness" (10. 220-23) can only refer to God's mercy as preventing full blame from falling upon man; but the power of God in his office of savior to justify mankind is also suggested by the image: mercy is made possible only by the savior's justification of man. This assertion of the Son's unique ability to show mercy is also implied in the divine colloquy preceding the judgment scene, where the Father stresses the fact that man's judge is to be his savior (10. 58-62) and where the Son similarly connects these roles (10. 71-79).

God's rulership in his office of judge of angels is asserted in the scene in which the Son faces the rebel angels. The principle of rule is stated earlier, when the Father, commending the faithful Abdiel, indicates that the creature must answer to God, whatever laws his fellow creatures may form, and that the creature has a duty to uphold God's laws against deniers (6. 29-43). The Son, facing the rebel angels, denies their claims to independence according to that principle; for, in explaining why the rebels have chosen a trial by combat, the Son is also rejecting their claims. The statements that the rebels are "emulous" of no "excellence" but strength (6. 820-22), and that they do not "care who them excels" (6. 822) form a rejection of Satan's claim that angels have the right to make their own laws (6. 150-57). The first statement blames the angels for rejecting what is one of the criteria of heavenly worth, the "zeal" to uphold divine commands (5. 592-94) —the trait which is characteristic of Abdiel (5. 805-6). The second statement blames the angels for disregarding the judgment of God in their assertion of angelic rights. The Son's statement that the rebels "by strength . . . measure all" (6. 820-21) denies Satan's claim to uphold his laws by force (6. 153-54), for the Son here differentiates the use of force in upholding divine laws from the use of force in opposition to law. The divine superiority of God, the second aspect of his authority as judge, is asserted, first, in the divine colloquy preceding the judgment scene, where the Father gives to the Son the power to enforce his judgment (6. 700–718), and, second, in the confrontation itself. There the Son asserts God's divine superiority against its deniers by attributing "Kingdom and power and glory" to God (6. 814–15) and by stating that the "godless" merit God's "indignation" (6. 810–12); and when the Son says that the rebel angels have "despised, / Yet envied" him (6. 812–13), he blames them for the unwarranted claim to divinity revealed by their envy, and for the denial of God's superiority displayed in their despising.

God's goodness as judge is shown first of all in the love shown Adam and Eve. There are indirect assertions of this love—ironic contrasts between God's worth and man's erroneous views of what has value. Eve rejoices in the Experience (9. 807–10) which means the suffering of evils (9. 1070–73) instead of loving the God who comes to mitigate those evils (10. 75–77); Adam praises the excellence of the Eve (9. 1017–21) who has discovered the means for his moral ruin (9. 1073–78) instead of loving the God who is man's "friend" (10. 60). God's love is also directly demonstrated in the mercy which he shows in judging. In the judgment scene, the Son blames Adam for the excessive love of the creature (10. 145–56) which entails an insufficient love for God. But despite man's moral debasement, the Son shows mercy to Adam and Eve by softening their punishment: he delays death (10. 209–11) and alleviates the physical evils (10. 211–19) which are death's forerunners. His act in clothing Adam and Eve with skins is an act of mercy in judgment, like his clothing of their inner nature, but, like that covering, it also suggests God's office of savior. The fact that the Son's action is compared to Christ's washing of his disciples' feet (10. 215) shows that this act of mercy is intended to prefigure the Son's redemption of mankind, just as the washing does; for it is the Son's redemption which makes mercy in judgment possible. The second aspect of God's goodness, his wrath, is shown when the Father, in the dialogue preceding the judgment scene, announces the necessity for punishing sin (10. 47–53), and when the Son pronounces sentence on Adam and Eve (10. 193–208) in fulfillment of God's threats.

Since there is no mercy extended to the rebellious angels, because there is no extenuating circumstance in their fall, God in judging cannot show them love. It is, however, suggested that God

shows his love through the secondary function of judgment, the
protection of the good; for the Son explains that in removing the
evil angels, he acts to restore the harmony of heaven:

> *Then shall thy saints, unmixed, and from the impure*
> *Far separate, circling thy holy mount,*
> *Unfeigned halleluiahs to thee sing,*
> *Hymns of high praise, and I among them chief.*
>   (*6. 742–45*)

God's purpose here serves, furthermore, to defend his goodness
through comparison with the rebellious angels, who, as Satan says,
value aggressive war, "The strife of glory" (6. 288–90), rather
than the peace and love which are the aims of God. God's wrath
is shown in the Son's proclamation of hatred for the rebels
(6. 734–41), and in his execution of God's earlier threat
(6. 824–66).

The third office of God, that of giver of grace, is announced in
God's reply to Satan's plot against mankind and is later demon-
strated in God's contribution to the repentance of Adam and Eve.
But God refuses to exercise this office with regard to Satan, whose
acts after his expulsion are to be viewed as resulting from his
ungraced state.

As in his other offices, God's authority is demonstrated in his
rule. Giving grace to man, God shows his rule by calling men to
obedience (3. 185–88), and by restoring to them the power to
obey. By the statement that creatures are "free . . . / Till they
enthrall themselves" (3. 124–25), God indicates that once crea-
tures fall, they lose the ability to obey. Thus, if men are to obey
him, God must restore to them their initial power of mind and
will; this he does, "clear[ing]" (as he says) "their senses dark"
and "soften[ing] stony hearts / To pray, repent, and bring obe-
dience due" (3. 188–90). The fact that God gives men the chance
to repent does not mean that repentance is automatic. As God ex-
plains, men may still choose to reject him, to "neglect and scorn"
his "day of grace" (3. 198–99). In the divine colloquy which fol-
lows the repentance of Adam and Eve, this general principle is
applied by the Son to the earthly pair:

> *See Father, what first-fruits on Earth are sprung*
> *From thy implanted grace in Man, these sighs*

> And prayers, which in this golden censer, mixed
> With incense, I thy priest before thee bring,
> Fruits of more pleasing savor from thy seed
> Sown with contrition in his heart, than those
> Which his own hand manuring, all the trees
> Of Paradise could have produced, ere fallen
> From innocence.
>
> (11. 22–30)

The Son affirms here that the pair's repentance is the product of God's imparted power, but he also implies that the pair have acted to accept this power. The comparison of grace to sown seed implies that Adam and Eve could have rejected grace as a stony soil rejects seed; and this implication is reinforced by the image of cultivation, which suggests that Adam and Eve have labored at their repentance in order to achieve their final penitent state, just as they tended God's trees in order that these might bear fruit.

God's authority as giver of grace is also asserted by his claims of divine superiority. The general principle is given in the opening assembly in heaven, where the Father states that he can strengthen men, and therefore that men must credit him for delivering them from evil (3. 173–82) —credit (so the logic would seem to be) in the sense that his grace is the sine qua non of their repentance. This principle is applied to Adam and Eve in the divine colloquy following Adam's prayer, in which the Father credits himself with the pair's repentant state ("My motions in [Man]"), contrasting that state with their weakness when unaided ("[Man's] heart I know, how variable and vain / Self-left") (11. 90–94).

God's refusal to restore lost abilities to the fallen angels through grace means that they are denied the ability to repent and acknowledge God's authority. Thus when Satan fails to give up his claims to be ruler of angels (4. 86–92), he does so because God has refused to call him and to give him the powers whereby to respond with allegiance. And when Satan refuses to retract his defiance of God's omnipotence (4. 81–86), he does so because God has denied him the aid which alone could give him sufficient strength to recant past error. In hanging his scales in the heavens to prevent battle between Satan and the angels who are guarding earth (4. 990–1004), God demonstrates that Satan's defiance is not a positive thing, a display of power, but a negative one, a lack of insight. By warning Satan to depart, God refutes Satan's boasts of monarchical power, both his expressed belief in his prowess (4. 935–40) and his unexpressed intention to rival God's rule (4. 110–12). The fact that God allows Satan to try to deceive the angels with his account of his purpose for being in Eden but prevents him from doing battle is analogous to the limits which God places upon Satan's activities toward Adam and Eve, his prohibition of violence but not of "deceit and lies" (5. 238–43). Satan's guile is permitted to exist not because it deceives God, but because God allows his creatures to be tested by it, and God's intervention indicates that the test is over, the angels having defeated Satan. In addition, as Gabriel notes (4. 1006–10), God refutes Satan's boast that he is able to overcome the loyal angels in battle (4. 972–76).

In his office of giver of grace to mankind, God's love is shown in the fact that he allows man to reform. As Raphael says, there is no happiness without love (8. 621), and thus God allows man the possibility of happiness when he restores, through grace, man's faculty of conscience (3. 194–97), the faculty which enables him to love good and hate evil.[3] God's wrath is shown in the increased punishment which he decrees for those who reject grace: he withdraws from them the possibility of regeneration, and leaves them to natural deterioration (3. 198–202).

God's refusal to extend grace to the fallen angels means that they are denied the ability to reform. When Satan feels unable to overcome hate and to avert punishment by repenting (4. 93–102), he does so because God has refused to restore his conscience, with its powers of love and awe; and Satan also senses God's denial: "as far / From granting he, as I from begging peace" (4. 103–4). Though God does not show love to the "self-depraved" angels, he does take care to protect the victims of their spiteful actions, showing his love for those victims in the same way that in his capacity of judge he protected the loyal angels. In the opening assembly in heaven, the Son protests that if the product of Satan's failure to reform, his plan to destroy man, is fulfilled, God's goodness will be circumvented (3. 156–58); the Father replies with his offer of grace to counter the effects of Satan's plan on all men who accept divine aid (3. 173). Logically, perhaps, since God does not offer Satan grace he should not display his wrath, punishing Satan for impenitence; nevertheless it is clear that God does decree increased punishment for Satan's rejection of the punishment allotted him and his choice of revenge (3. 80–86).[4]

As in the case of his third office, God's closely related final office, that of savior, is displayed only in connection with mankind. This office, like the preceding one, is announced in the opening assembly in heaven; it is demonstrated in God's final actions toward Adam and Eve. But in regard to this office, God's refusal as well as his action is made explicit: both the Son's pronouncement on the serpent's fate and the transformation which the Father inflicts upon the fallen angels serve to reveal the degeneration which is the lot of those who are denied salvation.

The first aspect of God's authority as savior, his rule, is demonstrated in his requirement that men accept the justification offered by him. In the opening assembly in heaven, God explains that the savior's virtue frees men from their state of guilt (3. 290–91); man is thus restored to the state of acceptability which he lost by his disobedience. For this restoration, however, God requires that men "renounce / Their own both righteous and unrighteous deeds" (3. 291–92); they are justified not by their deeds but by their acceptance of God's gift of merit. In the divine colloquy which follows the repentance of Adam and Eve, this principle is applied to Adam and Eve, though in a modified way, when the Son pleads for man:

> *Now therefore bend thine ear*
> *To supplication, hear his sighs though mute;*
> *Unskilful with what words to pray, let me*
> *Interpret for him . . . .*
>   *. . . [L]et him live*
> *Before thee reconciled, at least his days*
> *Numbered, though sad.*
>   *(11. 30–33, 38–40)*

The ignorance that the Son mentions refers to Adam and Eve's lack of doctrinal knowledge. Since the Son pleads for reconciliation, however, and since he "interpret[s]" for the pair, he must know them to be in a state of humiliation and trust, the state of implicit faith which can precede instruction in doctrine. Thus God accepts Adam and Eve as proselytes, afterwards revealing to them what they must believe. God also requires, in addition to acknowledgment of his justification of man, that men demonstrate fidelity in the face of trial. In the divine colloquy, the Father mentions that man's life is to be "Tried in sharp tribulation" (11. 62–63) ; and before making his revelations, Michael speaks of these revelations as providing training in the endurance needed in living: in the "True patience" and the steadiness which can bear prosperity without overelation and adversity without, presumably, distrust (11. 358–66) —can bear both, thus, without loss of piety.

God's divine superiority is demonstrated in his ability as savior to absolve man. In the opening assembly in heaven, the Father explains the conditions under which man can be absolved—that the merit of the savior must be credited to man; that in order for the merit to be credited, the savior must be made man (3. 281–89) ; and that the merit must be won by the savior's being "just the unjust to save" (3. 215), by his fulfilling the laws broken by man in the fall. That God alone is capable of undertaking the office of savior is demonstrated by the fact that all the angels are unable to accept the responsibility (3. 217–19), that only the Son accepts it (3. 222–26). This power is later asserted in reference to Adam and Eve; the Son requests that his merit be credited to the pair (11. 34–36), and the Father grants the request on the grounds that it accords with his earlier pronouncement: "all thy request was my decree" (11. 46–47).

God's refusal to act as savior to the fallen angels, to grant them reconciliation and to require in return their acceptance, is made explicit in the revelations he gives to them. Whereas in the prophecy delivered by Michael, God informs Adam of the nature of justification and acquaints him with divine power, preparing him for his restoration, the Son in his "oracle" (10. 182) informs Satan of his final defeat. Because of Satan's renewed rebellion, the Son pronounces him totally "accurst" (10. 175–76) ; he refuses him the justification extended to mankind. And because God does not exert himself for Satan, Satan is degraded instead of saved. In the gloss which is appended to the "oracle," the groveling which the Son predicts (10. 177–78) is connected with

Christ's sight of Satan's fall (10. 183–85) – a reference to Luke which is to be taken as itself referrring to Satan's unsuccessful temptation of Christ (this connection is suggested in *Paradise Regained* as well, where after making his final temptation, Satan falls). As in expelling Satan from heaven, the Son defeated him, demonstrating his power as judge in the face of Satan's defiance, so (the lines suggest) with Satan's new fall, Christ in the office of savior defeats him by fulfilling God's law in the face of Satan's temptation, thereby absolving mankind, but leaving the fallen angels without redemption. The final transformation scene in hell also serves to enlighten Satan, along with his followers; whereas God sends Adam forth restored, he shows the fallen angels their degeneracy. The hissing of Satan by the fallen angels is explained as showing that Satan's supposed triumph is in fact a shameful act (10. 545–47), and the spread of snakiness from Satan to his followers (10. 532–45) indicates that as a ruler, Satan has led his followers into a state of cursedness. As Satan's triumph is false, so is the boasted prowess by which he accomplished it (10. 468–69); the fact that Satan is unable to speak (10. 517–19) is a sign of his loss of mentality, and the fact that he is eminent as a dragon (10. 528–32) shows the depravity of his strength. In addition to showing the status of those who do not receive and accept God's reconciliation, God shows the necessity of his power to save. By his forcing Satan to grovel (10. 511–15), God shows that only his aid can raise the creature, the aid which he has denied to Satan, and by repeating the degradation yearly (10. 572–77), God demonstrates the unending nature of his rejection.

God's goodness as savior is demonstrated first in his love for mankind. God restores to man the elevation which was the aim of creation and which, lost by the fall, could not, as God explains, be restored by any change in man, not even by his reform (3. 203–9). In the opening assembly in heaven, God explains that in order for man to be saved from death, the savior must suffer death in his stead (3. 210–12), an act of love of which even angels are shown to be incapable (3. 220–21) but which the Son chooses to perform (3. 222–26), and an act which entails sacrifice by the Father for man, as he says (3. 274–80). In the divine colloquy which follows the repentance of Adam and Eve, the Son's atonement

(11. 34–36) and the resultant redemption of man (11. 40–44) are invoked relative to Adam and Eve. To God's sacrifice, man is expected to respond with love and with deeds which reflect this love; God in the divine colloquy mentions the "faith and faithful works" expected from man (11. 63–64), and Michael after his prophecy places stress on the love and deeds which are required of Adam (12. 581–85). God's wrath is shown in his withdrawal of salvation from those who fail to accept his gift and sacrifice; in the opening assembly in heaven, God notes that not all men will be redeemed (3. 287–89). But in addition, it is shown that salvation itself is intended only to limit, not to obliterate, the punishment decreed for man's fall. In the dialogue which follows the repentance of Adam and Eve, the Son indicates that his redemption of mankind is not meant to undo the death decreed for man, but only to make that death temporary (11. 40–41); and the Father, noting that death is needed as a "final remedy" to the "woes" ordained as punishment for man's fall (11. 57–62), banishes Adam and Eve from the Garden in order to prepare them for that death (11. 48–57).

The revelations God makes to the fallen angels announce his refusal to show them love by saving them from the death of eternal damnation. Whereas God sends Michael to reveal to Adam God's redemption of mankind (11. 112–16), the Son in his oracular curse informs Satan of God's denial. The predicted bruising of the serpent's head (10. 179–81) has two glosses appended to it. The first refers to Christ's resurrection and ascension (10. 185–89), the means whereby God protects the victims of Satan's spite, leaving Satan unredeemed. In addition, whereas God sends Adam away in faith, he informs Satan in the transformation scene of the falsity of everything valued by the unredeemed, tempting the transformed angels with apples which are beautiful but ashy (10. 547–67). Though again God should not, logically, display his wrath, he is shown as damning Satan for the deeds which Satan has accomplished in his dissoluteness. A second gloss is appended to the predicted bruising of the serpent's head: "[H]e shall tread [Satan] at last under our feet; / Even he who now foretold his fatal bruise" (10. 190–91). These lines refer to the final shutting of hell described earlier in relation to the Son's capacity as judge (3. 330–33). By this prediction, the

Son indicates that the death of eternal damnation is the punishment allotted for Satan's depravity. Whereas God sends Adam away in a state of awe whereby he fears to offend God, in the transformation scene God informs Satan of his dissolute inability to shun evil from fear of punishment, repeatedly tempting the transformed angels to eat, even when they know that ashes will be their reward (10. 567–70).

Consistently and repeatedly, then, Milton establishes it as one basic premise about God that he acts in four distinct offices toward Adam and Eve—creator and lawgiver, judge, giver of grace, and savior—while toward Satan he acts in the first two capacities but refuses to act in the latter two. Milton's second premise is that in all his offices, God demonstrates two basic attributes, his authority —which comprises his rule and his claim to divine superiority— and his goodness—which comprises his love and his wrath.

2

The Secondary Plot

GOD'S two principal attributes provide the basis for judging Satan's relationship with God. In recognition of God's authority, Satan is supposed to be dutiful, that is, to follow God's rule and acknowledge his superiority. In response to God's goodness, he is supposed to be virtuous, that is, to return God's love, and to hold his wrath in awe. He is judged by his failures in these requirements, and the four offices of God are correlated with the four stages of his decline.[1] The first stage is that of the fall, during which Satan breaks the laws of God the creator and lawgiver. The second is that of rebellion, during which the arguments broached by Satan during his fall become dogmas, established truths by which he and his followers live; these God answers in his capacity as judge. The third stage is that of relapse. In this stage, Satan sees the error and fault of his fall, but because God has denied him grace, he is unable to choose repentance and reform, and, in choosing defiance and evil, he repeats his fall, this time on a lower level. The final stage of Satan's development is his deterioration: repeating his rebellion—this too on a lower level—Satan ends by losing what touches remained of former insight and virtue, sinking into a degenerate state from which God refuses to save him.

Satan's fall occurs during the assembly which he calls in heaven to protest God's command of obedience to the Son.[2] During this assembly Satan refuses duty—first of all by denying God's rule. Denouncing God's command, he argues that angels "without law

/ Err not" and that they are "In freedom equal" to God (5. 794–99). By the first of these arguments he denies the idea that angels ought to obey God, claiming for angels an inherent perfection, rather than a value measured by adherence to law. By the second argument he denies God's definition of angelic freedom, claiming God's freedom from external control in the place of the creature's freedom to choose whether or not to obey. The refusal to accept rule is Satan's principal sin. He falls, as Raphael suggests, because he overestimates his place in the universe (5. 659–65). In addition to disobeying, however, Satan also denies God's authority by doubting his divine superiority. Driven by Abdiel's arguments into spelling out the corollary to his denial of God's rule, Satan denies God's power as creator to assign angels their roles, claiming that neither Father nor Son is creator (5. 853–55) —God ridicules this argument before it is advanced—and he denies God's ability to degrade his creatures, claiming independent and equal strength (5. 864–66).[3]

Failing in goodness as well as in duty, Satan fails to love God. In his soliloquy upon Niphates, Satan remembers that before the fall he begrudged God the love which he owed him, resenting "The debt immense of endless gratitude, / So burdensome still paying, still to owe" (4. 46–53). In his address in heaven Satan rationalizes this lack of love, converting it into a doubt of God's goodness. In his opening outburst, Satan argues that the motive behind God's command is the desire to deprive the angels of their proper honor (5. 772–84) —a motive which is in fact the opposite of God's desire to elevate his creatures by union with himself. Satan also fails to hold God's wrath in awe. He chooses to threaten God with siege (5. 866–69) because entrapment is the contrary of God's threat of expulsion—Satan is of course daring God—and he allows Abdiel to convey the threat (5. 869–71) as a sign that he does not fear God's wrath.

The birth of Sin (2. 747–61) sums up the first stage of Satan's development, the origination of evil; it also serves as a decisive sign of his fall. In the assembly in heaven, Abdiel assumes in his rebuttal that Satan and his followers can still remain unfallen by rejecting the proffered arguments against God's authority and goodness (5. 846–48). The birth of Sin does not occur until Abdiel has left, his counterstatement rejected; it signifies that the defecting angels have progressed from speculation to the affirmation of heresy.

The second stage of Satan's development, in which he becomes confirmed in his heresies, occurs during the war in heaven.[4] This stage, the stage of rebellion, is divided into two parts, the rebellion proper and the judgment scene—the first two battles of the war making up the former, the third battle the latter.

During the first battle, Satan develops his earlier heresies. With Abdiel Satan argues the subject of divine authority (6. 150–59, 164–70). First of all, by his argument here, Satan expands his previous denial of God's rule. By his reference to the "synod" of angels, Satan asserts that angels make their own laws; and by the epithets "seditious" and "Inspired with contradiction" which he applies to Abdiel, he asserts that obedience is owed not to God but to fellow angels. These arguments expand Satan's previous denial of divine monarchy; and Satan also expands his previous denial of God's definition of angelic freedom. He calls the decision to obey God "servility," and by his boast that he will defeat Abdiel, he claims that angels are able to uphold their laws by force. The refutation of this set of arguments appears in the Son's explanation of why the rebels have chosen a trial by combat. And Satan also denies divine superiority. He openly denies that God is omnipotent, and by claiming that angels have "Vigor divine," he denies the derivation of angelic power from God—contentions which are to be measured against the claims of power later defended by the Son, and against the fact that even the Son receives power from the Father.

With Michael Satan argues the subject of divine goodness:

> *Err not that so [i.e., with my defeat]*
>   *shall end*
> *The strife which thou call'st evil, but we style*
> *The strife of glory; which we mean to win,*
> *Or turn this Heaven itself into the Hell*
> *Thou fablest; here however to dwell free,*
> *If not to reign.*
>
>   (*6. 288–93*)

Michael has blamed Satan for replacing love with war and hate (6. 262–71); Satan's reply develops his earlier ingratitude and doubt. The words "The strife which thou call'st evil" develop the doubt of God's motives into a doubt of the values which God has established. The words "The strife which . . . we style / The strife of glory" imply that angels have the ability to determine by experience what is good, and by this theory Satan can make a virtue of the hatred of God which has developed from his previous ingratitude. Michael has also reminded Satan of God's promised punishment (6. 271–80); Satan's reply reaffirms his lack of awe. By his threat to turn heaven into hell, Satan claims for himself an ability to punish equal to that claimed by God; and by his dismissal of hell as a fable, as well as by his assumption that he will remain in heaven, Satan doubts God's threat.

To this heresy Satan adds, in the second battle, an overweening confidence in his cause, expressed in the riddling puns by which he orders his cannons fired (6. 558–67) and in the triumphant ironies with which he celebrates the results (6. 609–19).

Satan's judgment closes this stage of his development; to the judgment he and his followers come rebellious, and reveal in their behavior the chief cause of their fall. Before the third battle, the rebels' trial by combat, the Son restores the trees uprooted in the second battle (6. 781–84). This action is said to be a "sign" to "convince the proud" (5. 789), that is, a proof that God is indeed ruler of the universe, since even its trees obey him. Furthermore, the action is said to be a "wonder" to "move the obdurate to relent" (6. 790), that is, a warning to angels, who can only throw trees (6. 662–69), that God excels them. Thus, by their refusal to be taught (their "despair" brings them "hope" [6. 786–87]) and by their refusal to be softened (they stand "obdured" [6. 785]), the rebellious angels repeat that denial of God's authority which was the chief factor in their fall.

This second stage in Satan's development is summarized in the second stage of his relationship with Sin. The fact that after the birth of Sin, Satan becomes "enamored" of her (2. 761–67) represents the fact that during his rebellion, Satan becomes confirmed in the heresies originated during his fall.

The third stage of Satan's development extends from his awakening on the burning lake through his first visit to earth. This stage, the stage of relapse, falls into two major parts. In the second of them—it consists of Satan's encounter with the angels guarding Eden—Satan ratifies the decisions made during the first part, which is the relapse proper. This part contains two scenes, Satan's exploration of hell and his exploration of earth, and in both of them there is a repeated pattern of insight, decision, and descent: Satan *sees* the error of his fall and rebellion, but because God has denied him grace, he is unable to repent and reform, and in his refusal of duty and goodness, he falls again, and falls lower.

In hell Satan sees evidences of God's authority. In his opening address to Beelzebub on the burning lake, Satan acknowledges God's strength and his own previous ignorance of it:

> [S]*o much the stronger proved*
> *He with his thunder, and till then who knew*
> *The force of those dire arms?*
> (*1. 92–94*)

Later, in his first glimpse of hell, Satan's appalled question, "Is this the region . . . That we must change for Heaven . . . ?" (1. 242–45) is an admission that Satan has been degraded against his will, and Satan follows the admission with an acknowledgment of the supremacy of God, who, "sovran," can (he says) "dispose and bid / What shall be right" (1. 245–47). And later still, Satan reveals his awareness of God's authority in addressing his overwhelmed troops:

> *Princes, Potentates,*
> *Warriors, the flower of Heaven, once yours, now lost*
> *If such astonishment as this can seize*
> *Eternal spirits; or have ye chosen this place*
> *After the toil of battle to repose*
> *Your wearied virtue, for the ease you find*
> *To slumber here, as in the vales of Heaven?*
> *Or in this abject posture have ye sworn*
> *To adore the conqueror, who now beholds*
> *Cherub and Seraph rolling in the flood*
> *With scattered arms and ensigns, till anon*
> *His swift pursuers from Heaven gates discern*
> *The advantage, and descending tread us down*
> *Thus drooping, or with linkèd thunderbolts*

Transfix us to the bottom of this gulf.
Awake, arise, or be for ever fallen!

(*1. 315–30*)

In his ironic reference to his followers' "abject posture" as a sign of their obeisance to God, Satan calls for disobedience, but his statement is also an indirect acknowledgment that God has forced recognition of his monarchy; and Satan's reference to possible annihilation at the hands of the loyal angels is, when taken in connection with the later-narrated events of the rebellion, an admission of the falsity of Satan's defamation of these angels as servilely weak. In his rebuke that the angels' conduct shows that they are not divine and that they will not be able to regain heaven, Satan is appealing to the angels' pride, but his statement is also a recognition that in fact the angels' "astonishment" does place in doubt their claim to divine eternalness, with its concomitant denial of God's creativity; and Satan's sarcastic comparison of sleep in heaven with that on the burning lake is not only an attempt to rouse, but also a recognition of the angels' forced degradation. Behind the exhortations lies Satan's pained awareness that his former denials of God's authority are false.

But in each case, after Satan sees his errors, he voices his refusal to repent and reaffirms his old heresies, despite their absurdity; for it is one thing to deny God's authority before it is proved, and another to deny in the face of indubitable evidence. In continuing his address to Beelzebub, Satan announces that his mind (1. 94–105) and will (1. 105–11) are unchanged; and he goes on to reembrace defiance. He refuses to seek pardon, "To bow and sue for grace" (1. 111–12), an act which would acknowledge God's rule; and he claims the ability to defeat God by strength of arm or mind (1. 118–24), a boast which reasserts his former claim of freedom from control. He refuses to acknowledge that God is God (1. 112–14), and he claims power independent of God's, arguing that fate guarantees his strength (1. 116–17). Satan's admission of divine superiority in glimpsing hell is followed by his proclamation of the unalterability of his mind (1. 249–55) and by his acceptance of hell on grounds which defy God. He denies obedience, preferring to "reign in Hell" rather than "serve in Heaven" (1. 261–63) and rejoicing in his freedom

(1. 258–60) ; and he denies divine superiority, claiming that force is no proof of God's superior status, that he himself is "all but less"—anything but less—than the God "Whom thunder hath made greater" (1. 256–58). After his exhortation to his troops, Satan, viewing the assembled force, loses his sense of defeat, for "his heart / Distends with pride, and hardening in his strength / Glories" (1. 571–73). And though remorse overpowers the pride for a while (1. 604–21), and softens the opening lines of Satan's address, the pride returns, and Satan repeats to his troops the intentions expressed to Beelzebub. Arguing that no one could have foreseen their failure and that no one can doubt their future success (1. 622–37), he proclaims the inability of proof to alter belief. He refuses obedience, decrying submission (1. 659–62) and proposing a war by guile (1. 645–49). And by attributing God's rule to custom (1. 637–40) and to force which should not be attacked in aggressive war but need not be feared in a defensive one (1. 641–45), Satan repeats the denial of divine superiority made during his fall; he denies God's inherent right as creator to determine his creatures' roles, and he denies in addition God's omnipotence.

It is true that in all these denials of divine authority, Satan is not telling what he thinks. Consciousness of error is foremost in his thought, for in his speech to Beelzebub and in his speech upon viewing hell, Satan reveals this consciousness spontaneously, then hurries to conceal it; and in his address to his engulfed troops, admissions of error lie just beneath the surface of his exhortations. The element of concealment on Satan's part is explicitly stated: "So spake the apostate Angel . . . / Vaunting aloud, but racked with deep despair" (1. 125–26). But the fact that Satan does not reveal his thoughts is itself proof of his beliefs, for behind the concealment lies Satan's belief that he ought to keep his followers from repentance. In the absence of God's call, which would enhance the vividness of insight, and in the absence of effort on Satan's part, which would enhance the depth of the impression made by the insight, Satan's consciousness of error cannot lead him to change his beliefs, and in choosing to encourage impenitence by a pose of defiance, Satan is truly choosing impenitence and truly affirming disproved beliefs.

During Satan's exploration of hell, his relation to God's au-

thority is shown; his relation to God's goodness is treated during
the scene of his exploration of earth; for on earth Satan finds
reminders of God's love. First viewing Adam and Eve, Satan is
struck dumb (4. 356–57) and feels admiration and love because
of the "divine resemblance" in the pair (4. 358–65), reacting,
thus, to God's goodness through its manifestation. Later, when
Satan confronts Zephon, he is reminded of the virtue he has lost,
his former state of love:

> *Abashed the Devil stood,*
> *And felt how awful goodness is, and saw*
> *Virtue in her shape how lovely; saw, and pined*
> *His loss.*
>
> *(4. 846–49)*

But in the absence of the divine gift of conscience, and in the
absence of spiritual effort on Satan's part, such love cannot over-
come his hatred of God; therefore he refuses to reform and to
love God; but whereas previously Satan doubted God's goodness,
now, in accordance with his earlier words to Beelzebub (1. 162–
68), he embraces evil *knowing* it to be evil.

The moral descent is evident in Satan's two speeches about
Adam and Eve. After its opening tribute to good, Satan's first
speech (4. 366–92) follows a downward course. Satan recalls his
destructive aim, and though his response to the goodness seen in
Adam and Eve is at first strong enough to cause him to pity the
pair, it is not strong enough to cause him to alter his plans. Then
pity vanishes as Satan justifies his act as according with God's
value of love; he calls his action "amity" and views himself as a
guest or host of the pair. Then Satan concedes the evil in his plan,
the pain caused Adam and Eve, but he blames this evil upon God
for creating hell, and contrasts his own generosity in offering hell
with God's niggardly gift of a garden. Next Satan admits that not
only is his plan evil in effect, but that it is evil in intention, a
"revenge" upon God, and therefore an intended hurt to man; but
he blames this evil upon God as instigator. And finally he at-
tributes the evil not to God's evil, but to his own aim of con-
quest, the value which he established in his rebellion in oppo-
sition to God's value of love. Thus in the course of the speech,
Satan turns from love to pretended love, from pretended love to

acknowledged evil blamed on others, and finally from evil blamed on others to evil blamed on himself but justified.

The second speech (4. 505–27) follows the same downward course, but it begins lower, and it ends lower. In the beginning Satan is for a second time distracted from his purpose, but this time he thinks not of God's goodness seen in Adam and Eve, but only of the happiness of the pair's life, and instead of loving them momentarily, aware of their goodness, he envies them their lot, contrasting it with his own. Then he recalls his purpose, but instead of his previous pity for his unsuspecting victims, here there is only a neutral reference to their lack of suspicion: "[L]et me not forget what I have gained / From their own mouths." Next Satan blames God and foresees man's "ruin," but whereas before he claimed good intentions and blamed God for bad results, here he acknowledges his evil intentions without excuse, so overjoyed is he at having discovered the means of using against God what he considers to be God's evil; self-justification has given way to open spite. And finally, when Satan formulates his plan, he repeats his aspersions against God's "Envious commands," but here with a difference in aim: he is no longer blaming God, but is instead rehearsing the lies wherewith he hopes to deceive and kill Adam and Eve, for he ends with an open admission of this purpose. Satan ends by countering God's intentions even when he admits that these intentions are not evil; and in embracing evil knowing it to be evil, he fulfills the principle mentioned in the dialogue with Beelzebub, completing his second fall. It is in answer to this plan that God extends his offer of grace to mankind.

In Satan's later encounter with goodness, his confrontation with Zephon, Satan relapses more easily. His memory of past goodness is tainted by selfish concern for the loss of his former beauty (4. 849–50); he is not deeply moved, as he was in his first view of Adam and Eve, for he is not distracted from his purpose even momentarily—he is able to appear "Undaunted" (4. 850–51); and he quickly expresses hostility (4. 851–54), his memory of goodness vanishing.

Satan's soliloquy upon Niphates is in a different category from the other speeches in this section of Satan's story; it is the key passage to the section. First of all, it epitomizes the section, containing a full range of insight, decision, and relapse. Secondly, it is the central episode in the section. In hell, Satan in his resolve to influence his troops does not seriously ponder God's authority, and on earth, Satan's rejection of God's goodness is influenced by the decision made earlier in this soliloquy; it is here that Satan seriously considers God's nature and chooses not to return to duty and goodness. Finally, this speech demonstrates God's refusal to give grace to the fallen angels, for here Satan rises as high as a fallen creature can without grace, and, being unaided, finds himself unable to obey God and to love and hold him in awe.

In the first section of the soliloquy (4. 32–78), Satan reveals his insight into the nature of God. In the opening apostrophe, Satan acknowledges God's authority. His comparison of the sun to God enthroned reveals his memory of heaven and serves to acknowledge God's monarchy, while his comparison of the stars to angels "Hid[ing] their diminished heads" suggests Satan's shame before God. Satan also admits the omnipotence of "Heaven's matchless King," and by his discomfort at being reminded of his former glory, he shows his consciousness of degradation. In the reminiscence and meditation which follow the apostrophe, Satan acknowledges God's love. Taken in connection with the later-narrated account of his fall, Satan's memory of the favors granted him constitutes a denial of his claim, made in falling, that God intended to deprive his creatures of their due; and his admission that praise and thanks are owed to God repudiates the protests he made against God's supposedly unendurable demands. Furthermore, Satan's following argumentation does not change this acknowledgment of divine love. Finally, in the lament which ends this section of the speech, Satan reveals his consciousness of God's wrath, and he responds with proper awe.

The effort required for these insights and responses is evident in Satan's meditation on God's love. After his admission of his past ingratitude to God, Satan shifts ground in an attempt to jusitfy himself; by wishing to have been created less high and therefore less liable to pride, Satan absolves himself from the charge of ingratitude by attributing ingratitude to pride, and pride to God's ordering of the universe. This lapse is followed by an exertion of mind in which Satan disposes of his sophistry; thus he is brought back to his starting point, and by asking what he

can blame besides "Heaven's free love," he admits that he must
take full blame for his ingratitude, since he cannot blame God's
rule and since it is absurd to blame God's love for his own lack
of reciprocation. This admission is followed by a sudden lapse
into spite: "Be then his love accurst." But again there is a re-
covery, a return to self-blame. The zigzag course of the argument
shows Satan, as a fallen creature, exerting the full force of his
mind and conscience against the tendencies to error and evil
which his fall has brought upon him.

In the second section of the soliloquy (4. 79–104), Satan,
having acknowledged God's nature, chooses between penitence
and impenitence. He faces the question of repentance directly,
and at this point his strength proves insufficient, and because God
refuses to give him the additional strength which would restore
his freedom to choose repentance, Satan decides irrevocably upon
continued opposition to God. He contemplates the misery which
accompanies that reign in hell which he has preferred to God's
service, but feels that he is unable to submit permanently to
God's rule. He describes his denial of God's divine superiority
as "vaunts" and boasts, but he is deterred from acknowledging
that superiority by his proud reluctance to admit before his
inferiors that he has erred. He feels that his "deadly hate" pre-
cludes a return to true love for God; and in fearing to repent
because of the punishment allotted for a second relapse, Satan
fails in awe, for he fails to fear sufficiently the punishment await-
ing his unrepentant acts. Pride and weakness of conscience win
out, and in the end, sensing that God has refused him as he has
God, Satan is partially aware of God's denial of the grace which
would strengthen his capacity for duty and his capacity for love
and awe.

In the third section of the soliloquy, Satan, having chosen,
repeats his fall by committing himself to his defiant course (4.
105–13). He challenges God's monarchy with his own; and in
casting out "remorse," he blots out his sorrowful memory of the
glory that he has lost, choosing to forget the cost of his last
defiance of God's omnipotence. In addition, Satan embraces evil
although he is conscious that it is evil, and rejects "fear," the
awe due to God's wrath. Having confirmed his choice in this
manner, Satan makes inevitable the punishment which God has
decreed for such a decision.

This stage of Satan's development ends with his ratification of his decisions. During the questioning by Gabriel which ends Satan's first visit to earth, Satan denies God's rule. He boasts of his prowess as leader in coming to earth as a spy for his army (4. 935–40), and he repeats his accusations that the loyal angels are servile. In one of these accusations, Satan, referring to the angels as minstrels (4. 941–45), clearly intends to recall his previous (though later-narrated) words to Abdiel during the first battle in heaven. In the other two aspersions, Satan refers to the events of the war itself, first scorning the loyal angels for needing divine aid (4. 925–29), then daring them to attack even with such aid (4. 971–76). By these statements, Satan seeks to hide his new role as man's tempter by causing the angels to think of him in his past role of warrior; he defies God in the old way in order to conceal his new resolve to defeat God by guile. Both the expressed and the secret defiance God answers by hanging his scales in the heavens. During the questioning, Satan also denies the love of God. He defends the credibility of his stated reasons for being on earth by twice invoking the theory that experience brings knowledge of values (4. 895–96, 930–31), the theory by which he denied God's values in his argument with Michael during the first battle in heaven. In addition, Satan denies awe, claiming to have fled hell in order to escape punishment (4. 888–94) and scorning God's failure to prevent his escape (4. 896–99). By pretending that he has reasons for being in Eden— reasons that seem cogent to a fallen creature—Satan allays suspicions that he has come to harm man, an intention which he denies (4. 900–901), and by challenging expulsion from the Garden, he diverts attention from the question of his purpose in being there; in short, he makes a display of old wickedness to conceal new spite and recklessness. By the protection that he gives his plan, Satan proves his devotion to his chosen course.

The third stage of Satan's development is summarized in Satan's reaction to Sin and Death in hell. Meeting them, Satan sees Death for what he is, "execrable" (2. 681–84), and Sin for what she is, "detestable" (2. 744–45); but he nevertheless allies himself with them (2. 817–26). Satan is unable to act upon the basis of his insight into his folly and evil, and thus he relapses.

The final stage of Satan's development extends from his second visit to earth through the final transformation scene in hell. In this stage, the stage of deterioration, Satan repeats his rebellion on a lower level, and loses whatever remained of his former insight and virtue, ending in a degeneracy from which God refuses to save him and which God makes known to him in the Son's oracular curse and in the transformation which the Father imposes. This section of Satan's story falls into three parts. The first, consisting of Satan's thoughts before his temptation of Eve, serves as a preliminary exposition of character. The second part, consisting of Satan's temptation speech to Eve, contains the depraved action which seals Satan's fate. The third part, Satan's return to hell, reveals his final inanity.

Satan's thoughts before the temptation of Eve clearly recall his thoughts while exploring earth on his first visit; and when his new soliloquy is compared to the Niphates soliloquy, and when his thoughts upon viewing Eve are compared to his earlier speeches about Adam and Eve, the contrasts that emerge reveal the extent to which Satan has already deteriorated as a result of his relapse. But the speeches in this preliminary scene also look forward; they provide a standard for measuring Satan's final state and for measuring the deterioration which results from the execution of his plot against man.

Satan's second soliloquy has three major sections. In the first (9. 99–123) Satan discusses earth; in the second (9. 124–57) he discusses his aims; and in the third (9. 157–78) he discusses his means of implementing his aims. This soliloquy lacks the conflict of the first, and contains a more feeble perception of duty and virtue as well as a new incoherence, the result of affirming an untenable position.

All these things—enfeeblement, contradiction, and lack of conflict—are evident in Satan's remarks on divine monarchy. In the first section of the soliloquy, Satan acknowledges God's rule in his apostrophe, comparing earth to God and the "danc[ing]" stars to serving angels; but whereas in the Niphates soliloquy the opening apostrophe was part of a sequence of thought leading to a consideration of God's nature, this apostrophe is part of a sequence leading to a consideration of the hierarchy of earth's living things. The thought of God has become less significant to Satan. In the second section of the speech, Satan casually mentions the possibility of "mastering Heaven's Supreme." There is no tension between this statement and the preceding one, for

Satan does not debate whether or not to obey, as he did in the first soliloquy. There is no interaction between the preceding acknowledgment and this denial of God's rule, as there was in the first soliloquy, in which Satan decided to establish his own sphere of rule. Nor is there even the step-by-step change of position which marked Satan's reluctant decision to destroy Adam and Eve. Opposing views of duty are simply stated, without any sense of contradiction. In the third section of the soliloquy, Satan's first allegorization of his imbrutement—his comment on the baseness inherent in ambition—recalls Satan's confession, in the first soliloquy, of the misery of reigning in hell; but here the idea induces no consideration of repentance; there is no struggle of insight with folly.

On the subject of freedom, Satan is also contradictory. Justifying his aim, Satan in passing boasts his strength in freeing angels, yet in discussing his imbrutement he notes his fear of detection by the loyal angels, an admission which at least tends to jeopardize both his aspersions on these angels' strength and his own claims of strength. (This fear, incidentally, explains why Satan imbrutes himself, rather than merely taking the form of a snake; for when he took the shape of a toad during his first trip to earth [4. 799–800],[5] the alert Ithuriel compelled him to return to normal form [4. 810–13].)

The statements about God's superiority are even less cogent than those about God's rule. In the first section, the apostrophe in which Satan praises earth as superior to heaven recalls the apostrophe in the Niphates soliloquy in which Satan blamed the sun for reminding him of his former heavenly state. The fact that Satan prefers the lesser creation, earth, to the greater shows that his memory of heaven has grown dim; and the deterioration which he has undergone is shown by the fact that in his earlier soliloquy he thought of the world only as a reminder of heaven. In addition to enfeeblement, Satan shows signs of incoherence. In the first section of the soliloquy, Satan credits God with improving upon his earlier creation (a statement, incidentally, which is doubly fallacious, since it blasphemously doubts God's omniscience, and since it confuses difference in status with difference in perfection, assuming that God's two creations must differ in degree of perfection when in fact they are two perfect examples different in kind). In the second section, Satan incidentally disparages God's later creative powers in comparison with his earlier, when he attributes the creation of man to God's loss of the ability to create angels; and, compounding contradictions, Satan adds in a parenthesis a repetition of his earlier doubt that God is the creator of angels. Finally, when, in the second section of the soliloquy, Satan declares that his aim is not to live on earth or in heaven, he shows himself unmoved by any conflict of the sort which marked his earlier refusal to repent.

In relation to the love of God, Satan also shows diminution of insight, of coherence, and of internal conflict. Satan ends the first section of his speech with the assertion that the beauty of earth brings him only pain. During his first soliloquy, Satan's love of good was strong enough to overcome at least temporarily his spite and his self-excuse, but now Satan's awareness of good is only theoretical: he has lost the ability to respond. The same loss is revealed later, in the second section, when Satan says that he destroys in order to distract himself from his misery—the misery that the inability to love entails. During the first soliloquy, Satan was inclined to evil only by the preponderance of his hatred for God, but now he has lost so much response to good that a much slighter motive, the desire for distraction, inclines him. Decline is also evident in Satan's identification of glory with destruction, the opposite of God's creativity. In first positing the value of glory, Satan connected it with conquest, which is at least the perversion of a good, specifically of the value of dignity of place; and in his first thoughts about Adam and Eve, Satan retained this definition of glory. Though Satan previously accepted the notion of destruction, he either thought of it as a means to the end of revenge, as in his first meditation upon Adam and Eve, or considered it apart from his values, as in his second meditation. And though Satan previously adopted evil on principle, his statements of the principle were abstract, as in his first soliloquy. Now Satan has so far deteriorated in his grasp of goodness that he can accept the concrete meaning of his former abstract resolution; that he can call destruction itself a good, and not merely consider it as an element of a plan, or as a means to an end; and that he can connect his value with the inversion of value, rather than with a perversion.

Incoherence appears in Satan's arguments on God's character —his attempt to justify his own spite by blaming God for spitefulness. In the second section of his speech, he repeats his initial doubt of divine intentions when he accuses God of degrading the angels by placing them in man's service, and of elevating man to replace the fallen angels. In order to make the charge, however, he is forced to credit God with care for the dignity of his creatures (he made man lord of earth) and with care for their happiness (he gave man a "Magnificent" universe). The generosity which Satan attributes to God in his treatment of mankind is incompatible with the malice attributed to him in his dealings with angels. Lastly, the ease with which, in the second part of his speech, Satan turns from his admission of the inability to find pleasure in good to his acknowledgment that he does not expect to find pleasure shows a resignation to evil which contrasts with Satan's earlier exploration of the question of repenting.

Finally, Satan's reactions to God's wrath show diminution both in insight and in tension. When in the third section of his speech Satan makes a second allegorization of his imbrutement, an acknowledgment of the self-defeating nature of revenge, the admission recalls his sense in the first soliloquy of the "lower deep / Still threatening to devour" him; but now Satan has lost the ability to respond with fear. And whereas in his first soliloquy Satan weighed the penalties that would result from his deciding upon repentance or impenitence, here in the second section of his speech Satan accepts the increased punishment that his plan entails, not even considering the possibility of an alternative choice.

The same deterioration which marks the second soliloquy is present in Satan's thoughts upon encountering Eve. Satan's distraction upon viewing Eve (he stands "abstracted . . . / From his own evil" [9. 457–66]) recalls his wonder upon first viewing mankind, and is the last instance of a reaction to goodness productive of conflict within Satan. It is fitting that his virtue rather than his dutifulness should retain the greater strength here, since disobedience rather than ingratitude was his principal sin. But the decline in Satan is nevertheless evident in the opening of his speech:

> *Thoughts, whither have ye led me, with what sweet*
> *Compulsion thus transported to forget*
> *What hither brought us, hate, not love, nor hope*

Of Paradise for Hell, hope here to taste
Of pleasure, but all pleasure to destroy,
Save what is in destroying; other joy
To me is lost.

(9. 473–79)

The sort of attraction displayed is decadent. The lover's oxy-moron, "sweet / Compulsion," indicates that what Satan feels is not a response to God's goodness seen in God's creatures (the response present in Satan's first speech about Adam and Eve), nor is it even a response to the pair's state as contrasted with his own (the response present in his second speech): disinterested-ness has disappeared from Satan's reaction. Furthermore, the re-turn to ill intent displayed here is more abrupt than formerly. Instead of turning from distraction to pity, as in his first speech, or from distraction to neutrality, as in his second, Satan here turns directly to hatred, restating the resignation to evil and the enjoyment of destroying broached in the second soliloquy. In addition, the statement of tactics with which Satan ends this speech (9. 479–93) contrasts in its directness with the apologetic air of his past meditations. The speech shows Satan's declining grasp of goodness and his habituation to evil.

After the exposition of character provided by this preliminary section comes the temptation of Eve, the action that seals Satan's fate. The temptation is analogous to the first battle in heaven, for it is Satan's second war against God (though here the arguments offered are not positions to be defended by force, but are instead the instruments of war). This later war takes place at a lower level than the earlier, however.

Satan's central temptation speech can be divided into three sections. The first is Satan's apostrophe to the forbidden tree (9. 679–83). The second section offers proof that it is wise to violate God's command (9. 684–702). The third section dispar-ages God's motive in making his prohibition (9. 703–32). The arguments offered in the speech are adaptations of the arguments which Satan used against Abdiel and Michael during the first battle in heaven.

Satan attacks divine rule in the second section of his speech, offering three direct arguments. Having repeated in his opening apostrophe his premise that the tree is efficacious, he argues that it is right to seek the "happier life" that the fruit would bring. By this argument he asserts the right of the creature to determine his own laws in defiance of the laws of God—the same right implied in the argument made to Abdiel that angels have the right to determine their own laws by vote. In arguing that either God does not deny Eve the fruit or that by denying he proves his lack of divinity, Satan suggests that man owes obedience to human law and not to divine, since he makes the former the test of the validity of the latter. The argument parallels Satan's condemnation of Abdiel according to angelic rather than divine law. Finally, in arguing that God will think disobedience a sign of bravery, Satan proposes the equivalent of his earlier proposition that obedience to God is servility.

Satan attacks the second aspect of divine authority, God's divine superiority, in the third section of his speech. He uses this attack in a supporting argument which backs up his assertion that God is maliciously degrading man; the argument defends the premise underlying the assertion, the premise that man can attain godhood by eating the fruit. The first argument that Satan offers is that if a beast can attain manhood, a man can attain godhood; this argument doubts God's control over the status of his creatures. His second argument is that the difference between man and God is only a matter of diet; in it Satan directly deprecates divinity: he doubts first God's creativity, then God's omnipotence (the tree could not give wisdom contrary to God's wishes, nor could such wisdom hurt him, if God were omnipotent, the argument runs) , and finally he doubts God's divinity itself ("can envy dwell / In heavenly breasts?") . Satan's arguments here against God's superiority directly parallel the denials of divine superiority and of angelic secondariness which he made to Abdiel during the first battle in heaven.

When in the third section of his speech Satan argues that God intends to degrade men by depriving them of their proper wisdom, the knowledge of good and evil, he attempts to undermine the first element of man's virtue, his love for God. The argument parallels the aspersions which Satan made during his fall; it also recalls the claim made to Michael that there is wisdom to be found by experiencing evil. The second element of man's virtue,

his awe, is assailed in the second section of the seduction speech.
There Satan offers an indirect argument for disobeying, a proof
not that disobedience brings good results, but that it does not
bring bad ones; in this argument, Satan questions God's wrath
by arguing that the serpent's safety proves the emptiness of God's
threats. The skepticism which Satan expresses here parallels those
doubts of punishment which Satan voiced to Michael during the
first battle in heaven.

The difference between the war in heaven and Satan's temp-
tation of Eve is that during the war Satan believed his arguments
and was willing to defend them in battle, but now Satan offers
his arguments knowing all of them to be false; for all are con-
tradicted in his soliloquy and his thoughts about Eve. When
Satan offers his first argument against God's rule, his praise of
the "happier life" attained by following the creature's laws
rather than God's, he knows into what baseness his own assump-
tion of rule has led. When he offers his second argument, that
duty is owed not to God but to man, he knows, as the apostrophe
of his soliloquy shows, that God is the ruler of the universe. When
he offers his third argument, on the bravery of disobedience, he
knows what weakness has come of his own defiant strength: he
has shunned the guardian angels, and has even confessed later to
the fear of Adam's power of mind and limb (9. 482–88). Simi-
larly, on the question of God's superiority, when he offers his
opening argument on the probability of man's ascent, Satan
knows of his own degradation, having surrendered the hope of
life in heaven or on earth; and when he denies God's attributes
he contradicts the acknowledgment of God's creativity which he
made during the soliloquy. Again, when Satan asperses God's
motives toward mankind he knows that God has been generous
to man, and when he recommends the wisdom gained through
knowledge of evil he knows that he, who sought this wisdom, has
lost the ability to respond to good. Finally, when Satan doubts
God's threats, he knows how inevitable God's punishment is; in
fact, his statement of the serpent's safety in "venturing higher
than [his] lot" is a bitter inversion of Satan's admission in his
soliloquy that his imbrutement is a symbol of the inevitability of
punishment.

The Son's oracle stands as the divine answer to this attack by
Satan. God's reply to Satan's knowingly false denial of his rule is

the curse whereby God denies to Satan the justification which
restores mankind to that state of acceptability lost by disobedi-
ence. God's answer to Satan's knowingly false denial of his supe-
riority is to defeat Satan at the temptation, absolving man but
leaving Satan unaided. God's answer to Satan's knowingly false
aspersions on his love for man is to save man at the resurrection,
leaving Satan unsaved. And God's reply to Satan's knowingly
false aspersions on his wrath is his threat of eternal damnation.

The final scene in this segment of Satan's story is his return to
hell. The opening of the scene somewhat resembles the first as-
sembly that Satan called in heaven, for Satan is here marking the
end of the struggle against God which began at that assembly,
and is announcing the triumph that he had planned to announce
after the war in heaven. In function, however, this part of the
scene resembles the second battle in heaven, in which Satan re-
vealed an erroneous confidence in his victory. The mistake here
is more serious in nature, however, in that it reveals Satan's com-
plete loss of awareness. For in his second soliloquy and in his
thoughts before the temptation, Satan showed some insight, even
though his insights were feeble and mingled with error; but
having denied these insights in tempting man, Satan loses them,
and is thus reduced to total unawareness.

In his speech to his assembled followers, Satan begins by de-
fying God's rule:

> Thrones, Dominations, Princedoms, Virtues, Powers,
> For in possession such, not only of right,
> I call ye and declare ye now, returned
> Successful beyond hope, to lead ye forth
> Triumphant out of this infernal pit
> Abominable, accursed, the house of woe,
> And dungeon of our tyrant. Now possess,
> As lords, a spacious World, to our native Heaven.
> Little inferior, by my adventure hard
> With peril great achieved.
>
> (10. 460–69)

Satan presents himself in the role of the ruler of earth, and by
comparing earth to heaven he establishes his claim to be a mon-
arch rivaling God; in addition, when crediting himself with lead-

ing his troops from hell, he boasts that he has defeated God. Satan has forgotten what he acknowledged in the apostrophe of his soliloquy, the sovereignty of God; and when he calls attention to his bravery in "adventure hard," he forgets what he admitted in avoiding the angels and Adam, that by asserting his freedom, he has lost rather than gained in strength. Returning to his defiance of God's authority at the end of his speech, Satan tells his followers to "up and enter now into full bliss" (10. 501–3); thus he claims the divine power of elevating the creature, "full bliss" even suggesting the divine communion which is the end of such elevation. In this claim, Satan forgets his former awareness of his degradation, a degradation which proves that the place of creatures is controlled by God.

In his description of his journey (10. 480–93), Satan disdains love for God. Satan's description of the perfection of the universe and his remark that man has been "Made happy" by the angels' "exile" recall the charge made during his soliloquy that God created a beautiful world for man in order to spite the defecting angels. The earlier argument, however, admitted God's generosity to man (if inconsistently for the argument), while the later makes no such acknowledgment: the beauty of the world is connected not with God, who made it, but with man, whom it effects; even the tangential perception of God's goodness has disappeared. Furthermore, the earlier argument justified the attack on man by appealing to God's spite, while this later one attacks man directly, and attacks man not for any intended hurt to the angels, but merely for being "happy" when the angels are not. In one more case Satan declines in moral grasp, passing from the greater motivation of hate to the lesser of malice, and from the pretense of moral excuse to the absence of even that degree of acknowledgment of divine values. The next part of the description, the part devoted to the seduction of Eve, recalls Satan's speech preceding that temptation, but now contempt has replaced Satan's last impure attraction to Eve, that final vestige of the love of the reflection of God's goodness in his creatures. The final part of the description returns to the soliloquy's treatment of the creation, for Satan is boasting here that he has upset the conditions that existed before the temptation: God's anger has replaced his favor to man, marauders attack those formerly guarded by the "flaming ministers," and man's servitude to the fallen angels has

replaced his lordship over earth. By this boast, Satan doubts the
constancy of that love which he previously acknowledged; and
when he ridicules God's anger at man's transgression, he shows
how much insight into virtue he has lost. For in Satan's first so-
liloquy, he recognized the thanks owed to God's goodness; in his
second, he mentioned God's goodness to man without considering
the question of man's reciprocal gratitude; now he laughs at the
idea that God should expect his love to be returned. Thus what-
ever faint traces of love remained to Satan before his temptation
of man have vanished; furthermore, when Satan, after his de-
scription of his journey, ridicules God's threat ("A world who
would not purchase with a bruise . . . ?" [10. 494–501]), he
shows that he has forgotten his former insight into the severity
of God's wrath.

The total unawareness of Satan's final state God exposes in his
transformation of the fallen angels. He refutes Satan's aspersions
on his rule by showing the cursedness of Satan's rulership and
leadership and the depravity of his boasted powers; he asserts
his superiority by demonstrating his power to elevate and to de-
grade; he shows the depravity which has obscured Satan's knowl-
edge of good and the folly of Satan's lack of awe. The ending of
this final scene in Satan's story parallels the third battle in
heaven; as the confidence of Satan's second battle was answered
by God's triumph in the third, so Satan's triumphant speech is
answered by this refutation.

The final encounter of Satan with Sin and Death sums up this
last stage in his development. In this encounter, Satan shows the
same love for Sin that he showed during his rebellion, but now
that love is more debased: now Satan thinks Sin in her revealed
foulness, "fair" (10. 384), and he loves her more strongly than
before, for he appoints her and her son his agents (10. 403–7)
in imitation of the Father's relationship with the Son. Thus, after
erroneous doubt, after erroneous conviction, and after the refusal
to reject error when error is demonstrated, Satan comes to that
state of complete moral degeneracy in which the most indubi-
table folly and evil can be taken for the true and the good.

The central matter in Satan's plot is clearly his relationship
with God—the story of his fall, rebellion, relapse, and deteri-
oration. Satan's relationship to other creatures is a secondary
matter, as its treatment shows: the personal relationship is

not developed so completely or carefully as the divine one, and it is dependent upon the divine relationship for its meaning. Nevertheless, Satan's relationship with his fellows is important, for it follows the same course as Satan's relationship with God, and therefore serves to reinforce the central concerns of the plot.

The bases for judging Satan's development in this secondary realm are the requirements governing the relationships of creatures—requirements which are derived from and parallel to the relationship of God and his creatures. With respect to his fellows, Satan holds a leader's authority: since he is himself a creature, his authority is delegated from God, and therefore he must frame his commands in accord with divine law; but he is also a superior, and as such, he is expected to exact obedience to his commands. Satan is expected to show a leader's virtue: he is to display a protective love for his followers, and to exercise the creaturely equivalent of God's wrath, the threat of displeasure that serves to induce virtue.

The first stage in Satan's development is analogous to the fall in his relationship with God; it is in this stage that Satan first violates the laws governing the relationships of creatures. The fall occurs during the conversation with Beelzebub which precedes Satan's first assembly in heaven.[6]

In that conversation, Satan first of all abuses his authority. His primary sin is the failure of obedience by which he calls a council not in conformity with God's law, but in dispute of it (5. 679–82). In addition, when framing his command, Satan abuses his rule. He orders his troops assembled for the purpose of, he says,

> *prepar[ing]*
> *Fit entertainment to receive [their] King,*
> *The great Messiah, and his new commands,*
> *Who speedily through all the Hierarchies*
> *Intends to pass triumphant, and give laws.*
> (5. 689–93)

The ambiguities in "Fit entertainment" and "Intends to pass" show that Satan is willing to deceive his followers; he asks obedience to what seems to be God's law but is not so.

Satan also fails in virtue. It is possible for Satan to feel discontent without his sinning, for Adam inclines to excessive love for Eve (8. 521–59) while still innocent. It is possible for Satan to reveal his weakness to another creature, for Eve confesses her excessive love of beauty to Adam (4. 449–91). But it is doubtful that Satan should reveal his weakness to an inferior, who would be more likely to succumb through his example than to help him against his weakness; it is to superiors that Adam and Eve confess. And it is clearly wrong that Satan, instead of seeking his friend's aid, tries to make him share his dissatisfaction, as he does when recommending his own discontented wakefulness: "Sleep'st thou companion dear, what sleep can close / Thy eyelids?" (5. 673–74). It is also wrong that instead of protecting his friend, Satan introduces him to ideas (5. 674–76) which he thinks it "not safe" to discuss (5. 882–83). In addition to perverting love, Satan, when coaxing Beelzebub, abuses his power to shame:

> *Thou to me thy thoughts*
> *Wast wont, I mine to thee was wont to impart;*
> *Both waking we were one; how then can now*
> *Thy sleep dissent?*
>
> (5. 676–79)

By playing on their closeness and by reproaching Beelzebub, Satan seeks to make his friend choose loyalty to a fellow creature before loyalty to God; he uses shame to encourage sin rather than virtue.

The second stage in Satan's development comprises the war in heaven. It resembles the rebellion against God in three respects: first, in that the violations of the law initiated in the fall become dogma; second, in that the new dogma leads to disorder; and third, in that the validity of the dogma is disproved. In this stage, the relation of Satan and his followers is examined under two conditions, prosperity and adversity. The first is touched on briefly in a reminiscence by Satan; the second is treated in the council that Satan calls after the first battle in heaven.

In his opening speech to Beelzebub on the burning lake, Satan in passing recalls the war in heaven, saying that he and Beelzebub were united then by "equal hope / And hazard in the glorious enterprise" (1. 88–90). They were thick as thieves, the phrase reveals—united not by concern for one another's good and happiness, but united in their pursuit of the same evil end. In good times, it is suggested, Satan's social principles lead to union through compatible vice.

These principles receive their test when pain, the foretaste of divine judgment, appears. In the council that follows the opening battle in heaven, Satan defends his violation of the first aspect of his leader's authority. He justifies his failure to frame his commands in accordance with God's law by arguing that his troops have been successful—"in arms / Not to be overpowered"— (6. 418–24) and that God has proved "fallible" in not defeating them (6. 425–30); he minimizes the significance of the pain that his disobedience has brought (6. 430–36). In addition, Satan continues to abuse his rule, exhorting his troops to continue against God (6. 437–45). But disorder results when Nisroch, one of Satan's captains, applies to Satan the principles that Satan has been applying to God. As Satan doubted God's authority on the grounds that he has mismanaged the war, so Nisroch questions Satan's wisdom. He denies Satan's pronouncements of success (if war continues under the same circumstances, he says, "Ruin must needs ensue" [6. 452–59]), and he denies Satan's minimizing of the importance of pain ("pain is perfect misery," he says [6. 459–64]). And as Satan perverted his rule, so Nisroch denies his duty to obey; he argues that anyone who can provide the needed power and defense deserves Satan's place as ruler (6. 464–68). The instability of Satan's government is proved by the fact that in order to prevent rebellion within his own camp, Satan must find new grounds, the invention of cannonry, to induce obedience (6. 493–95) and to defend his continuing rejection of God's law (6. 470–93). The suggestion is that once the divine pattern governing the relationship of creatures is broken, there is nothing that can provide a stable union of creatures in time of adversity. This lack of unity, finally, is used to demonstrate the falsity of Satan's social principles.

The third stage of Satan's development is treated in the opening scenes in hell. This stage resembles Satan's relapse in relation to God. First of all, in it Satan repeats his fall on a lower level. Second, a pattern of insight followed by reversion to evil appears in it. Third, the central characteristic of this stage, Satan's tyranny, is connected with the lack of reason and will characteristic of those to whom God has denied his grace. During his prophecy, Michael explains to Adam that God sends tyrants to enslave those who have lost rational control of themselves (12. 90–96). Michael's explanation applies to mankind, but it can be extended to the case of Satan, whose tyranny is the political equivalent and the result of failure to repent.

Satan's abuse of authority is treated in the council that Satan calls in hell. The first step in this abuse—which is Satan's tyranny —is his proclamation of elective monarchy at the opening of the infernal council (2. 18–40). Satan fails to acknowledge the delegated nature of his authority, but instead claims for himself the authority that belongs to God—a usurpation which is evident in the grounds to which he appeals. Comparison to the later-narrated account of his fall indicates that Satan now claims for himself the post that he previously denied to the Son. His appeal to "just right" correlates with his complaint that the Son could not "in reason . . . or right" assume rule over the angels (5. 794–95) ; his appeal to the "fixed laws of Heaven" correlates with his complaint that in elevating the Son, God was attempting to "introduce / Law and edict" (5. 797–98), that is, to change the old laws of heaven; his appeal to "free choice" correlates with his complaint that the Son's monarchy violated angelic freedom (5. 795–97) ; and his appeal to "merit" correlates with his denial of the Son's divine powers (5. 853–66). In addition, Satan violates his rule with his theory of democratic allegiance. When he argues that hell can have no disunity based upon rank because such rank entails danger and pain, Satan argues for obedience on grounds of self-interested consent, and when he argues that such union is superior to union in heaven, Satan openly challenges the validity of obedience based upon fealty.

In this disobedience and misrule, Satan repeats his fall, but on a lower level, for now he acts in the face of evidence, and on grounds which are patently absurd. First of all, the "merit" Satan claims "in counsel or in fight" is credit for having led his men to hell—sufficient reason to doubt the validity of his denial of God's authority. Secondly, his claim is disprovable internally; for one who claims that angels are above law (as Satan did in denying the Son) cannot appeal to that law for justification; and no one can claim election on the basis of the votes of a third of the electorate (even in his second soliloquy Satan never boasts the allegiance of more than "well nigh half / The angelic name" [9. 141–42]). Thirdly, Satan's grounds would indirectly justify the delegated authority which he denies, for they would prove the Son's monarchy before his own. If the "fixed laws of Heaven" have validity, they have validity as emanating from God, and therefore the law elevating the Son to King of Angels also has validity. If election determines rule, then the Son must be ruler, since he holds the votes of two-thirds of the electorate. And if "merit" is proved "in counsel or in fight," then the Son has the superior merit, for he has proved the folly of trusting in cannon to overcome God's "dreaded bolt" (6. 490–91), and has bested Satan in battle. As to Satan's theory of democratic allegiance, insubordination has already resulted from the adversity which is supposed, according to Satan, to guarantee unity; and the principle would justify obedience to the Son before obedience to Satan, since freedom from danger and pain can better be obtained by allegiance in heaven than in hell.

The proclamation of elective monarchy which opens the infernal council gives way to more open despotism in Satan's acceptance of the mission to earth at the end of that council (2. 432–66). That Satan is usurping the authority due to God is emphasized by the contrast between Satan's acceptance of his mission and the Son's acceptance of incarnation; but this contrast is not straightforward, and it is unintended by Satan, unlike the contrast present in Satan's opening address. One meaning is suggested by the fact that Satan replies to a proposition offered by Beelzebub (2. 402–16) but devised by himself (2. 378–80), while the Son replies to a question of the Father (3. 203–16). Since the Son is praised for his obedience to the Father (3. 266–71), the obedience of an inferior to a superior is contrasted with Satan's rejection of such obedience and his pursuit of self-devised policies. Also, despite the lack of analogy between the arguments and phraseology of the two speeches, a second meaning is suggested by the contrast in the way that Satan and the Son describe their missions. The trials and pains of the Son's mission are described for Adam by Michael:

[H]e shall live hated, be blasphemed
Seized on by force, judged, and to death condemned

A shameful and accursed, nailed to the cross
By his own nation.

(12. 411–14)

When the Son accepts this mission, however, he lists none of those trials and pains:

I for [Man's] sake will leave
Thy bosom, and this glory next to thee
Freely put off, and for him lastly die
Well pleased
Well pleased.

(3. 238–41)

Instead, he stresses his desire to bring grace to mankind:

Father, thy word is passed, Man shall find grace;
And shall grace not find means, that finds her way,
The speediest of thy wingëd messengers,
To visit all thy creatures, and to all
Comes unprevented, unimplored, unsought?

(3. 227–31)

Satan, on the other hand, lists in detail all the dangers of his coming expedition and stresses his payment for monarchical status. The Son's act of self-sacrifice, whereby he lowers himself for the benefit of his creatures, contrasts with Satan's monarchical usurpation, in which he claims for his own benefit a status above that of his fellows, the status of monarch which belongs to God alone.

The contrast between this closing speech and the opening speech of the council shows a growth of tyrannical pride. In the opening speech, Satan placed minor weight on his authority, restricting his observations on the subject to a subordinate clause ("Me though just right"), and, treating that authority, he placed only minor weight on his desert, "merit" being merely one of three offered justifications for his rank. Now, however, Satan places the major emphasis of his speech on his authority and on his merit as justifying that authority. In this way he reveals the tyrant's desire for domination.

The same desire marks his exercise of rule. By ordering his troops to palliate the pains of hell, Satan refers to his previous remarks on pain, and by ordering them to guard hell while he explores the "coasts of dark destruction," he refers to his previous remarks on the dangers of leadership; thus he keeps a façade of support for his previous position, that self-interested consent produces obedience. But whereas before, Satan appealed for consent, now he orders; and his final pronouncement, "this enterprise / None shall partake with me," indicates that the purpose behind his command is to assure his dominance.

Satan's repetition of his fall in virtue appears in his relationship with Beelzebub. First of all, he repeats his failure of love, in a manner that recalls the pattern of insight and reversion present in Satan's relationship with God. Satan's opening speech to Beelzebub (1. 84–91) begins with his realization of what he has done to his friend. Beelzebub's loss of beauty shocks Satan into a memory of that beauty before the fall, when love existed between them. Then Satan recalls the succeeding events, "United thoughts and counsels" referring to that conversation with Beelzebub during which Satan induced him to share his fall from virtue, and "glorious enterprise" referring to the war in heaven (as has been mentioned). The fact that Satan parallels these unions ("Joined . . . once") with the present union ("now . . . joined") suggests that Satan is aware that those alliances in sin have brought about the present union in misery—is aware, then, that he has brought ruin to his friend. But at this point, considering their state, Satan forgets his concern for his friend, turning to his relationship with God: "so much the stronger proved / He with his thunder" (1. 92–93) ; affection for Beelzebub vanishes, and it never returns. His decision not to repent his rebellion against God commits Satan to a sacrifice of friendship to political ends, and by this sacrifice, Satan repeats his initial abuse of friendship, on a lower level. When Beelzebub expresses his misgivings about their future (1. 128–55) , though Satan has like misgivings, being "racked with deep despair" (1. 126), he expresses these misgivings only in his first soliloquy (4. 86–92), when completely alone; he does not open his heart to his friend. At the time of the fall Satan wanted an improper intimacy with Beelzebub, wanted him as a partner in evil; now, consciously sacrificing all intimacy, he wants him only as a follower. Furthermore, when in his opening address to Beelzebub, Satan suggests a war by guile (1. 120–

21), and when he elaborates this suggestion in his address to his assembled forces (1. 645–59), Satan suggests to Beelzebub the proposal that he wishes him to make at the infernal council, and therefore involves him in a dangerous project, as he did before. But now Satan adds the evil of ulterior purpose, for by having Beelzebub make his proposal, Satan can hide his domination behind the appearance of popular opinion, and can dramatize his leaderly prowess in accepting the proposal. Thus in order to gain political power, Satan again sacrifices the intimacy of love.

Satan also repeats, on a lower level, that abuse of the power of shame which marked his fall. In falling, Satan reprimanded Beelzebub with "Both waking we were one"; now, when he replies to Beelzebub's expression of misgivings, he shames him with "Fallen Cherub" (1. 157), an address which is impersonal and which stresses Beelzebub's inferiority in rank; all affection, that concern for another's being which justifies reproach, has disappeared from the relationship. And whereas Satan previously coaxed Beelzebub into a neglect of God, he now shames him into a defiance whose evil he is fully conscious of (1. 158–62).

Thus the sexual deprivation of which Satan complains in his second speech about Adam and Eve (4. 509–11) is a physical symbol of the lovelessness that is the price of Satan's refusal to repent the harm done his friend, and of his rededication, for the sake of power, to the perversion of virtuous relationship.

The final stage of Satan's development resembles his deterioration in relation to God, for in it Satan repeats his rebellion on a lower level, and ends in a complete lack of insight. This final stage is interwoven with the last two scenes of Satan's religious decline, the scene of his temptation of Eve, and the scene of his return to hell.

In tempting Eve, Satan prepares for his attack on God by setting up a personal relationship with Eve. This relationship resembles to some extent Satan's relationship with his fellows during the war in heaven, but Satan is now conscious that the relationship he is establishing is false.

In order to separate Eve from Adam's governance, Satan in the second speech of the temptation scene tries to set up a relationship based on a false concept of authority. Opening the speech, Satan stresses Eve's rank and the serpent's duty to serve her:

> *Empress of this fair World, resplendent Eve,*
> *Easy to me it is to tell thee all*
> *What thou command'st, and right thou shouldst be obeyed.*
> 　　　　　　　　　　　　　　　　(*9. 568–70*)

Satan encourages Eve to accept the role of ruler and therefore to forget the obedience that she owes to the command (4. 432–33) which he in his first trip to Eden heard Adam give to her (4. 395–410). Ending the speech, Satan stresses the serpent's rationality and the value of Eve's beauty:

> *Thenceforth to speculations high or deep*
> *I turned my thoughts, and with capacious mind*
> *Considered all things visible in Heaven,*
> *Or Earth, or middle, all things fair and good;*
> *But all that fair and good in thy divine*
> *Semblance, and in thy beauty's heavenly ray*
> *United I beheld; no fair to thine*
> *Equivalent or second, which compelled*
> *Me thus, though importune perhaps, to come*
> *And gaze, and worship thee of right declared*
> *Sovran of creatures, universal Dame.*
> 　　　　　　　　　　　　　　　　(*9. 602–12*)

Satan's purpose is to undermine the acknowledgment of Adam's superiority which he heard Eve make on his first trip—her recognition that her own beauty is less valuable than Adam's "wisdom, which alone is truly fair" (4. 489–91). By claiming for himself Adam's attribute of wisdom while acknowledging Eve to be his superior, Satan encourages Eve to neglect the reverence that she owes to Adam's judgment. In addition to these direct encouragements, Satan, in his narrative of the serpent's supposed experience with the forbidden fruit, describes events in such a way as to stimulate violation of authority. Satan's tale is designed to contrast with Adam's opening speech to Eve about the fruit. Adam spoke of the fruit in connection with duty (4. 432–39) and in connection with the love of God (4. 411–32). Satan, relating the experience of an animal, can present an attitude toward the fruit completely uninfluenced by considerations of duty;

he stresses at the beginning of his story the animal character of the serpent:

> *I was at first as other beasts that graze*
> *The trodden herb, of abject thoughts and low,*
> *As was my food, nor aught but food discerned*
> *Or sex, and apprehended nothing high.*
>   *(9. 571–74)*

And instead of connecting the fruit with the love of God, Satan can describe it from the viewpoint of animal appetite; he describes the serpent's reaction to the sight (9. 575–78), the "savory odor" (9. 578–83), and the taste (9. 594–97) of the fruit. Satan's purpose in describing the serpent's outlook is to make Eve forget the importance that Adam has attached to the fruit, and to encourage her to disregard Adam's instructions. Satan also inserts into his tale an account of the envy of the beasts that could not reach the forbidden fruit (9. 591–93); by causing Eve to imagine what it would be like to be envied, Satan tries to undermine her acceptance of Adam's superiority.

In these tactics, Satan repeats his earlier position that obedience is not owed to superiors; he inverts the proper estimates of power and minimizes drawbacks, as he did before. And just as, in violating his rule, he ordered his followers to act in opposition to God's law, so he counsels Eve to reject her proper place, to violate, thus, her proper reverence for superiority. Now, however, Satan knows that what he proposes is wrong. Since, as he acknowledged before the temptation, he was glad to find Eve alone (9. 479–82), he knows that Eve needs Adam's guidance, contrary to his own proclamations of her sovereignty; and having heard Adam's speech, he knows that the taking of the apple would not be the insignificant action he suggests. Satan revealed in his thoughts before the temptation that he feared Adam, whose attributes are strength and wisdom, rather than Eve, "divinely fair" (9. 482–91); his real evaluation of the worth of Eve's beauty is the reverse of the stated one.

As Satan attempts to undermine Adam's governance by false argument, so he attempts in the first speech of the temptation scene (9. 532–48) to separate Eve from Adam's love by setting himself up as a lover. The opening address, "sovran mistress," is ambiguously the servant's and the lover's, but the play on the word "wonder" (9. 533) and the hyperbolic praise set the vein as Petrarchan, and show that the relationship that Satan proposes is an evil one based upon self-admiration in the recipient and upon ritualistically expressed sexuality in the lover. By calling attention to the fact that he is apart from his mate ("I thus single") and to the fact that she is apart from hers ("Thy awful brow, more awful thus retired"), Satan creates overtones of an adulterous encounter, and thus his pleas that she not repulse him suggest a perversion of shame, the fear not of failing in virtue before a lover, but of failing in sexual attractiveness before an object of desire. The relationship Satan attempts to set up is matched by his statements on the nature of love; he stresses the admiration paid to beauty rather than to worth, number of admirers rather than fidelity, receipt of service rather than service. The union on evil grounds which Satan offers to Eve here is analogous to his union with Beelzebub during the war in heaven, but here Satan is conscious that his suggestions are evil, having resolved in the speech before the temptation to feign love in order to destroy Eve (9. 492–93). Satan's degeneracy and dissoluteness show, then, in his promotion of relationships which are not only harmful, but which are intended to do harm.

Satan's preparation for his triumphant announcement in hell resembles the announcement itself in its revelation of Satan's loss of insight, here in relation to his authority among his followers. The scene which Satan prepares is an attempted analogy to God's relation to his angels in heaven. The list of dangers undergone (10. 469–80) which Satan inserts into his announcement reveals his belief that he has established the authority usurped from God, for by this list he reminds his followers that what he has performed are the deeds that he undertook in the speech ending the infernal council, deeds which were to demonstrate that authority. This same belief is revealed by the fact that before the announcement, Satan clothes himself in light (10. 447–52); he apes the radiance of the Son (3. 62–64), taking upon himself the symbol of divinity for having proved his denial of derived authority. The folly of his claim is shown by the contrast of God with his mimic. To the former, light is intrinsic, "Bright effluence of bright essence increate" (3. 6). To the latter, light is an assumed shape, equivalent to the shape of the "plebeian angel militant" which, shortly before, Satan donned to enter hell unnoticed (10. 441–43). And, since the angelic shape is the same shape that Satan assumed when asking directions from Uriel on his first trip to earth (3. 634–44), it is suggested that Satan is now fooling his followers as he fooled Uriel. God's authority, then, is intrinsic, while Satan's is an imitation and a fraud. Satan also shows a fatuous belief in his power of rule. Ascending his throne invisibly in order to observe (10. 443–48), Satan checks his followers for obedience to his commands, in imitation of the omniscient eye of God enthroned (3. 56–59). The folly of Satan's belief is shown by the fact that a multitude of his followers have failed to observe his orders to guard hell (10. 418–21), having acted in accord with Satan's own principle of self-interest by departing for earth (10. 422), presumed a place of lesser pain. Furthermore, the joy that Satan provides his obedient followers is only a parody of the bliss that the loyal angels receive from the sight of God (3. 60–62). The waiting followers desire to see Satan (10. 454–55), for according to Satan's theory of allegiance, their safety lies with his; but their suspense beforehand (10. 439–41) and their surprise at Satan's arrival (10. 452–54) are signs of their uncertainty, far removed from the angels' joy of acceptance by an all-powerful God. Having knowingly betrayed the truth about the relationships of creatures, Satan ends by losing all insight into that truth.

Satan's moral development, measured by his response to God's attributes, consists, then, of four stages correlative with the offices of God. Satan falls by breaking the laws of God the creator and lawgiver, then rebels against God the judge. Because God refuses to give him grace, Satan relapses, and in the absence of God's salvation, he deteriorates. This moral decline in relation to God is matched by a moral decline in relation to fellow creatures; for denial of the divine pattern for the relationship of creatures accompanies Satan's denial of God's authority and goodness, and there follow stages which correspond to his rebellion, relapse, and deterioration. This four-stage development makes up the secondary plot of *Paradise Lost*.

3

The Main Plot

IN *Paradise Lost,* the relationship of Adam and Eve to God, like that of Satan to God, is judged on the basis of God's two principal attributes. Like Satan, Adam and Eve are expected to be dutiful —to follow God's rule and to acknowledge his divine superiority —and they are expected to be virtuous—to return God's love and to fear his wrath.[1] During their state of innocence the pair are shown as fulfilling these requirements. When that state ends, the moral development of the pair corresponds with God's four offices; but whereas God refuses to exercise two of these offices with regard to Satan, he does exercise them with regard to Adam and Eve, thereby allowing the pair to return to God after their lapse. The four stages of the development of Adam and Eve are, first, their fall, during which the pair break the laws of God the creator and lawgiver; second, rebellion, during which they become dogmatic about their heresies, to be answered by God in his judgment; third, the repentance, during which they undo their fall; and fourth, the regeneration, whereby they reverse their condition during the rebellion. The pair begin their third stage in a state of relapse, doomed to repeat the fall, but when they exert mind and conscience against this relapse, God aids them with his gift of grace. In the last stage the pair accept the justification and salvation which God extends to them in his office of savior.

The state of innocence [2] of Adam and Eve comprises the opening scene on earth and the events on the day of Raphael's visit. The presentation of this stage in the pair's life serves two purposes. First, Adam and Eve are shown in their proper relationship to God, a relationship which helps to measure their later mistakes during their fall and rebellion. This proper relationship is demonstrated both in untroubled times and in the face of evil, the former condition being touched on throughout the section, but principally during the visit of Raphael, the latter being treated during the scene in which Eve wakes from her Satan-inspired dream. The second major purpose of the section is to reveal those limitations of Adam and Eve which, when acted upon, lead to their fall. This subject is treated during the parallel scenes in which Eve reveals her weaknesses in conversation with Adam, and Adam reveals his in conversation with Raphael.

Raphael's visit provides much of the demonstration of the proper relationship of Adam and Eve to God in untroubled times. Eve's role is little stressed, since Adam speaks for the two of them in the angel's presence. She does show her love for God, however; for when setting out to gather dinner for the angel, she plans her dinner as a demonstration of and a tribute to the generosity with which God has "dispensed his bounties" to man (5. 329–30). The task of voicing man's loyalty to God falls upon Adam, who, when he replies to Raphael's first warning, places major weight on the obedience of himself and Eve, pledging that they "never [will] forget" to "obey" God; and he shows his knowledge both of God's command and of the fact that man was "created free" (5. 548–53). In addition, when asking about the creation of the world, Adam demonstrates his awareness of the place of knowledge in man's life. He thanks Raphael for telling him the story of Satan's fall because the information will help him "to observe / . . . [God's] sovran will" (7. 70–80); Adam knows that knowledge is valuable insofar as it conduces to obedience. Furthermore, when Adam, prefacing his further inquiry, disclaims the intention of prying into "the secrets . . . / Of [God's] eternal empire" (7. 94–97), he shows his awareness of the limitations proper to human inquiry. Thus Adam submits to God's rule. Later, telling the story of his creation to Raphael, Adam acknowledges the divine superiority of God, recounting how he deduced from his own creation the existence of a creator

(8. 273–82). On the subject of love Adam again speaks for himself and Eve. In taking up the angel's first hint of his appointed subject, the need for fidelity, Adam places major weight on the love which he and Eve owe to a God so careful of their happiness; he expresses incredulity that they could "possibly his love desert / Who formed [them] from the dust" and gave them a life "Full to the utmost measure of what bliss / Human desires can seek or apprehend" (5. 514–18). Later, during his account of his creation, Adam completes his acknowledgment of God's goodness by displaying the fear owed to God's wrath. Repeating to Raphael God's threat, Adam adds that the pronouncement "resounds / Yet dreadful in [his] ear" (8. 334–35).

The responses of Adam and Eve to Eve's dream provide an example of the proper relationship to God in time of trouble.[3] Waking from her dream of disobedience, Eve instantly affirms her obedience by labeling the contents of the dream "offence and trouble" (5. 30–34). Eve shows her love of God in the prayer which she offers with Adam, a prayer whose thesis is that the universe reflects the goodness of its creator (5. 153–59) and whose application is a request for God to "give [her and Adam] only good" (5. 205–6) and for God to aid them against evil:

> *[I]f the night*
> *Have gathered aught of evil or concealed,*
> *Disperse it, as now light dispels the dark.*
> (*5. 206–8*)

Finally, Eve's awe is seen in the two tears she sheds after Adam's comforting, in fear of offending God (5. 129–35). This simple piety is complemented by Adam's subtlety. Adam explains the nature of moral choice to Eve, distinguishing the mental faculties and differentiating speculation from affirmation of evil in order to indicate what is to be avoided in choosing (5. 100–121). This abstract lesson he follows with an encouragement to duty, a reminder of the task of gardening: "[L]et us to our fresh employments rise" (5. 125). Having instructed Eve in obedience, Adam guides her toward a consideration of the love of God. Not giving way to her fright, Adam leads her to consider the beauty of the world, by citing examples, "the groves, the fountains, and the flowers" which, he says, "open now their choicest bosomed smells / Reserved from night, and kept for [her] in store" (5. 126–

28). Adam dwells longest on the flowers because, as he must know, they are Eve's special love (8. 44–47). By citing these examples, Adam prepares Eve's mind for the sentiments expressed in the prayer which he says with her.

The ideal relationship of God and man is epitomized in the evening prayer of Adam and Eve [4]:

> *Thou also mad'st the night,*
> *Maker Omnipotent, and thou the day,*
> *Which we in our appointed work employed*
> *Have finished happy in our mutual help*
> *And mutual love, the crown of all our bliss*
> *Ordained by thee, and this delicious place*
> *For us too large, where thy abundance wants*
> *Partakers, and uncropped falls to the ground.*
> *But thou hast promised from us two a race*
> *To fill the Earth, who shall with us extol*
> *Thy goodness infinite, both when we wake,*
> *And when we seek, as now, thy gift of sleep.*
> (4. 724–35)

The prayer's points of departure are the day and the night, and even these are viewed religiously, as evidences of God's divine superiority as creator. By the connection with man's "appointed work," day is linked with God's rule, and by its connection with God's material gift of Eden and with his gift of human companionship, day is linked with his love. Night is linked with two more evidences of this love. "Sleep," which entails lovemaking (the pair sleep "embracing" [4. 771]), is attributed to God's gift and is connected with offspring. Offspring (later explicitly linked with "wedded Love" [4. 750–51]) are also seen as a gift, since they are referred to in terms of God's promise; they are viewed, furthermore, as partakers in the other gifts of God—in his material gift of the world and also in his spiritual gift of love, since they are future sharers of family prayer. There are no tensions between the aspects of human life: human love is not isolated from love of God, nor in conflict with it; sex is not detached from love, from its product, or from holiness. This unity of life, it is suggested, is the object of the laws of God the lawgiver.

The limitations of Adam and Eve, which constitute the second main subject in the treatment of their state of innocence, are dealt with separately in the scenes that open and close this section of the story. The two discussions that reveal these limitations are parallel. First of all, Adam and Eve speak to their superiors, Eve to Adam, Adam to Raphael. Secondly, the pair reveal analogous limitations during the discussion of analogous subjects: when they are asking questions about the stars, they both reveal those limitations that relate to their duty to God, and when they are narrating their experiences just after their creation and telling the feelings they each have toward the other, they reveal limitations that relate to their love of God.

Eve reveals a tendency toward insufficient reasoning in her question to Adam about the stars: "[W]herefore all night long shine these? for whom / This glorious sight, when sleep hath shut all eyes?" (4. 657–58). Adam's reply suggests the nature of the limitation. Adam explains the physical use of starlight (4. 660–73) ; then, answering Eve's second question, he suggests that what is important about the stars is that God be praised for his works, not that man be delighted, and he stresses man's humble status by noting that angels would praise God even if man did not exist (4. 674–680). Eve's first question, then, reveals her tendency to be insufficiently logical (she fails to see the analogy which Adam sees between the functions of the stars and those of the sun), and her second question reveals a self-centeredness caused by a failure to view questions in a broad enough context. This limitation in reasoning is Eve's chief limitation, for Adam answers her at length. Her secondary limitation is her tendency to value lower before higher goods. In her reply to Adam's opening praise of God, Eve starts with a statement of her love for God ("For we to him indeed all praises owe, / And daily thanks" [4. 444–48]) ; then in her account of her creation and her love for her reflection in the lake,[5] Eve confesses her tendency to overvalue beauty; for what Eve loved in her image was its beauty (Adam she thought "less fair" [4. 478–80]), and for that beauty she rejected the human love of God's promising (4. 469–75).

In inquiring about stellar motions (8. 15–38), Adam reveals his rational limitation, a limitation whose nature is suggested by

Raphael's reply. Raphael suggests that Adam's guesses on the subject of stellar motion are absurd (8. 70–84), and refutes all his arguments on the subject (8. 85–118), then argues that Adam's question is irrelevant (8. 119–58) and counsels Adam to confine his thoughts to matters of duty (8. 159–78). Adam's limitation is a tendency to speculativeness, manifested in his inquiry into matters beyond human capacity and irrelevant to human conduct. In addition, Adam, like Eve, tends to value lower before higher goods. Completing his tale of his creation, Adam reveals his tendency to overvalue Eve (8. 521–59); in reply, Raphael cautions him against the sensuality (8. 561–94) implied in his statement of the power of passion (8. 528–37) and the effects of beauty (8. 537–59); and in relation to Adam's statement of delight in Eve's companionship (8. 596–606), Raphael adds a caution that man is to love God "first of all" (8. 633–35). Adam's principal limitation is this tendency to value Eve before God; for Raphael is "benevolent" in his rebuke of Adam's speculativeness (8. 64–65), but in rebuking Adam's improper love, Raphael replies sternly, "with contracted brow" (8. 560).

It is clear that these limitations are not meant to be seen as flaws. When Adam suggests that there is a deficiency in his makeup (8. 534–37), Raphael rebukes him (8. 561), and when Eve has her evil dream, Adam insists that it could not have sprung from any deficiency in her, who was "Created pure" (5. 97–100). The limitations are not absences in any of the powers appropriate for mankind, but are to be seen, rather, as defining traits—attributes appropriate for the fulfillment of the particular roles of Adam and Eve, or absences that distinguish one role from another. Since Adam is made for "contemplation" (4. 297), it is necessary that he have a curious mind, and since he is in authority over Eve (4. 300–301), it is necessary that she should need to defer to him in matters of judgment. Adam needs Eve both for companionship and for propagation, as he says to God (8. 419–33), and as God agrees (8. 444–45), and his feeling for her is necessary. Eve's wifely care requires the aesthetic ability which she demonstrates in her preparations of the food and accessories for dinner with the visiting angel (5. 331–49). These defining traits appear as limitations only when Adam and Eve forget that in addition to fulfilling their particular roles, they must live up to

their responsibilities as human beings, adhering to the rightful
relationship of man to God. Such forgetfulness is negligence on
their part, as Raphael's rebuke to Adam suggests:

> *Accuse not Nature, she hath done her part;*
> *Do thou but thine, and be not diffident*
> *Of Wisdom.*
>
> (*8. 561–63*)

The limitations, in turn, become sinful when negligence gives
way to deliberate violation of the rightful relationship of man
and God. When Adam explains to Eve after her dream that

> *Evil into the mind of god or man*
> *May come and go, so unapproved, and leave*
> *No spot or blame behind.*
>
> (*5. 117–19*)

he marks, in the words "so unapproved," the point at which sin
appears.

After the state of innocence, the first stage of the development
of Adam and Eve is that of the fall,[6] during which the pair violate
the laws of God the lawgiver. This stage comprises the scenes in
which first Eve and then Adam decide to eat the forbidden fruit;
in both cases, the decisions are contrasted with the previous piety
of Adam and Eve, and connected with their previously-demon-
strated limitations.

Eve's speech of decision[7] falls into three major sections. The
first (9. 745–60) is a direct defense of violating God's command;
the second (9. 760–75) is an indirect defense of violating God's
command, a proof that such violation will have no bad effects;
and the third (9. 776–79) is the conclusion. Eve begins and
ends her speech with doubts of God's rule. When, in the first sec-
tion, she argues that the fruit is good, she accepts Satan's premise
of its efficacy, and when she approves the serpent's attainment
of speech, she accepts Satan's argument that there is a creaturely
perfection attainable apart from obedience to God's law. By the
rhetorical question with which she ends her speech, Eve asserts
that she is free from external control.

Eve's acceptance of the notion that there might be an advantage
in disobeying contrasts with the simple horror she felt at the

dream of disobedience. Such unargued adherence to God's commands would have saved her here. Her conduct accords, however, with the limitation revealed in her question about the stars. Deficient logic allows Eve to credit the serpent's tale (comparison with the angels' treatment of Satan on his first visit reveals her lapses), and the failure to view her action in broad context accounts for her fallacious argument on freedom; for Eve does not see that the lack of divine hindrance is not a sign of her freedom from law, but rather God's means of allowing her a freely chosen obedience. An application of the lessons to be derived from Adam's rebuke could have saved her, in the absence of simple piety.

Eve's doubt of God's rule is her principal sin. Her acceptance of the argument that eating the apple could bring improvement provides the basis for Eve's doubt of her knowledge, for her doubt of God's motives, and for her argument against God's threat. Without such acceptance, Eve would be left with only her attraction to the fruit, insufficient motive for so serious an action.

In addition to disobeying, Eve doubts God's authority by doubting his divine superiority. In the second section of her speech, Eve argues that metaphysical ignorance keeps her from fearing the results of eating the forbidden fruit. The parallelism in her claim to "ignorance of good and evil, / Of God or death, of law or penalty" suggests that she means "ignorance of good and evil: of whether action would result in godhood or death, whether it would be lawful or punishable." From her premise about the character of the fruit, Eve derives an agnosticism in which, though she does not rule out the possibility that God is God, she finds it equally probable that God is not God, that her action is permissible and would lead to her deification. Thus she doubts God's assignment of his creatures' places, his control of their elevation, and, by implication, his divinity. Her argument here is contrary to what she has learned through Raphael's announcement of God's plan for mankind and through Raphael's description of the creation.

Eve doubts God's goodness as well as his authority. In the first section of her speech, she moves from the acceptance of Satan's premise that the fruit is good to arguments aspersing God's love for mankind. With increasing suspiciousness, she first deduces that God admits that the tree is good; then she deduces that God admits that man has a lack which the forbidden fruit can repair; then she draws the conclusion that God has the evil motive of depriving man of his proper knowledge, and she ends with an indignant rejection of what she takes to be divine oppression: "Such prohibitions bind not." Eve's suspicions are the antithesis of God's intention of rewarding man by elevating him for virtue, and of protecting man from the unhappy experience of learning good by suffering evil; and Eve should have seen the conflict of these suspected traits with the generosity she asserted when planning her dinner for the angel, and the protectiveness she acknowledged in her morning prayer.

Furthermore, there is an undercurrent of desire for the fruit itself in Eve's ingratitude. Before her meditation, Eve was attracted to the beauty of the fruit, "which to behold / Might tempt alone" (9. 735–36), as well as by its smell (9. 740–41), and in the conclusion of her argument, Eve alludes to these attractions when she describes the fruit as "Fair to the eye, inviting to the taste." The fact that Eve inserts into what should be a summary a factor not considered in her argument suggests that she is influenced by a motive to which she pays no conscious attention. Her attraction here recalls her earlier overvaluing of the beauty of her image and her concomitant rejection of Adam; she might have saved herself here had she acknowledged her reaction to the fruit and applied to her rejection of God the moral to be derived from her initial reaction to Adam.

Finally, Eve fails to fear God's wrath. In the second section of her speech, she again invokes the premise that the serpent's tale is true, and builds to the conclusion that God's threat is idle: she argues that though the serpent could not have been permitted the fruit, since he does not defend his property, yet as an unpermitted partaker, he has met with no ill effects. The elaborateness of this evasion contrasts with the simple piety that Eve displayed after her dream, with those two tears which she shed in innocent fear of having offended God.

When Adam first faces the fallen Eve, he reacts with unfallen piety (9. 900–905). He sees Eve's eating of the fruit as an act of disobedience, and he suspects the veracity of the serpent. He sees the moral ruin involved in Eve's failure to love God, as the words

"Defaced" and "deflowered" testify; and he fears the wrath of God, believing that Eve is "to death devote." But, though Eve does not persuade Adam with her arguments, she does move him with her seduction speech. Eve ends that speech with a picture of the separation that would result if only she were elevated (9. 881–85), a picture which causes Adam to picture the separation to result from her certain death:

> *How can I live without thee, how forgo*
> *Thy sweet converse and love so dearly joined,*
> *To live again in these wild woods forlorn?*
>   (*9. 908–10*)

Adam therefore decides to join Eve (9. 906–8), and this decision involves him in rationalizations whereby he shares Eve's heresies.[8] Adam's speech before his eating of the forbidden fruit (9. 921–59) is full of these heresies. First of all, Adam doubts God's rule in this speech. Arguing that God's omniscience would not permit him to create a world only to destroy it, and that his omnipotence would not allow him to give Satan the satisfaction of seeing mankind destroyed, Adam concludes that man's position as head of the world and as God's favorite protects man from destruction, even if he disobeys. Adam's heresy here is the opposite of the rational obedience that he displayed during God's test of him. In rejecting God's seeming command to be content with the company of inferiors, Adam rejected the temptation to consider himself analogous to God (8. 412–19) and demonstrated that the command was incompatible with man's nature as contrasted with God's (8. 419–33). Now Adam presumes to guess God's mind, crediting himself with superhuman knowledge, and he rejects a proper command by inappropriately attributing to man God's indispensability.

The protestations of faith which Adam made to Raphael contrast with his present disobedience. The hesitation about prying which he showed earlier would have prevented his present attempt to read God's mind. The awareness that the end of knowledge is duty would have kept him from applying to a justification of disobedience the information given him by Raphael, the information about God's actions as creator and about Satan's rebellion which he utilizes in this argument. The resolve to obey freely what he acknowledged to be God's command would have kept him from such an evasion of duty. Adam's argument also contrasts with his guidance of Eve after her dream, wherein he analyzed human faculties and encouraged duty, rather than speculating on God's mind in order to justify disobedience. Adam's argument does, however, recall the speculation and the deviation from strict attention to duty which were present in Adam's question about the stars, and it is suggested that by attending to Raphael's warning, Adam could have avoided this lapse.

Adam also doubts God's divine superiority. Accepting Eve's premise about the forbidden fruit, he argues that the serpent's ascent suggests that the fruit would make men gods; thus he accepts Satan's argument that the difference between man and God is a matter of diet. His argument is contrary not only to what he has learned of God from Raphael, but to the acknowledgment of divine preeminence which he made with his first words after creation.

Adam fails in his love for God. First of all, when he acquiesces in Eve's yielding to her longings of eye and taste, terming her action irreversible, Adam is excusing her undervaluation of God. Furthermore, Adam follows Eve's example, for when he returns to his earlier resolve to join Eve ("However, I with thee have fixed my lot") , Adam is overvaluing Eve in comparison with God. He does not remember that, as he told Raphael, God is the source of everything that he values. Nor does he act in accord with his behavior at the time of Eve's dream. Then he did not yield to empathy for Eve's fright, as he now puts himself into Eve's place, but instead guided her feelings toward a proper trust; and he did not pronounce her dream past, as he now resigns himself to her action, but instead led her to a corrective consideration of God's love. Similar action here would have saved Adam from neglect of God, and it is the only thing that could possibly have restored Eve to the virtue which made her worth loving, and that could have retained that unity of human and divine love which gave the state of innocence its happiness. Adam's failure clearly relates to the feelings about Eve which he revealed to Raphael, and both of Raphael's warnings are appropriate to Adam's present case: not only does Adam neglect to give primary love to God, contrary to Raphael's warning, but too great a degree of sensuality must be included in his love for Eve to account for his over-valuation and decision; for Adam does not consider what horrible changes in Eve's character her fall has wrought, or what can be done to reverse these.

The structure of Adam's speech before his eating of the apple indicates that insufficient love of God is his principal sin. The speech begins with a series of rationalizations, one suggested by the other, increasing in fallaciousness. The series opens with Adam's recognition of Eve's sin in yielding and his acquiescence in it, a position which has the merit of recognizing that sin has been committed. Then the idea that guilt cannot be removed afterwards, suggests the possibility that it can be removed before-hand, and Adam considers that the serpent may have caused the penalty attached to the fruit to be rescinded, and he adds the evidence that the serpent is not dead; this argument retracts the admission of sin, but it is at least an indirect argument, a denial of harm rather than a proof of advantage. Then the safety of the serpent recalls the serpent's supposed elevation, and Adam considers that man may be elevated by eating the fruit, an argument which attributes positive benefit to the deed, but which at least has the advantage of evidence (false though it be). Then the coming elevation of man suggests man's present elevation, and Adam ends by arguing that man is too great to destroy, an argument which, though returning to indirect proof, advances in the flimsiness of its support, being based upon presumptuous speculation. At this point Adam's defense collapses, and he reverts to the thought of death. The reversal shows that Adam is not convinced by his arguments, aware of their increasing tenuousness. Thus none of his heresies would have been sufficient to cause Adam's fall, and in the final section of his speech, he returns to his starting point, the love for Eve. The insufficient love of God is the lapse that is decisive in determining his action.

Finally, Adam fails to fear God's wrath, in his argument about the rescission of the penalty—a reinvention, with a new twist, of the argument first made by Satan and afterwards modified by Eve, that since God did not punish the serpent, he would not punish man. In this argument, Adam counters the fear which he acknowledged in his description to Raphael of God's threat.

The point at which the fall becomes final, at which the pair pass from consideration to affirmation of evil is, of course, the point at which first Eve (9. 780–81) and then Adam (9. 994–99) eat the forbidden fruit.

The second stage of the development of Adam and Eve after their state of innocence is their stage of rebellion, during which the pair become dogmatic about their heresies. This stage extends from the point at which each of the pair eats the forbidden fruit through the point in the narrative presenting the Son's judgment of the pair. The section falls into two parts, the first comprising the two instances of rebellion itself, the second the judgment scene.

Half of Eve's soliloquy after eating the fruit is devoted to the subject of God; here (9. 795–816), her certainty about her new beliefs is evident. She is now certain that the tree is efficacious in bringing wisdom. In addition, by her statement that the fruit would have been denied its purpose if not taken, she attributes a purpose to the fruit in defiance of God's purpose, that it serve as a token of obedience, and she makes a law regarding it in defiance of God's prohibition, thus asserting the right of the creature to determine his own laws in opposition to the laws of God. By her statement that the fruit is "offered free to all," she shows that, believing that the lack of physical hindrance to eating is the same as the permissibility of eating, she does not think of her freedom as the ability to obey or disobey God. These beliefs God dispels in his easy detection of Adam's evasion during his judgment of the pair and in his accusation of disobedience, though in his lack of anger he shows his mercy in judging what are beliefs induced by fraud. In connection with her beliefs, Eve openly violates God's laws; her resolution to make a daily practice of eating the fruit defies his prohibition, and her resolution to establish a morning ritual of tending the tree replaces the morning prayers which are part of the way of life ordained by God.

Eve's confidence in denying God's rule is matched by her confidence in denying his divinity. On the basis of her feeling that she is attaining godhood, Eve decides between the two alternatives posed in her earlier assertion of metaphysical ignorance; she decides that the denial of God's divinity is the correct alternative. Thus, when she claims that the tree cannot be God's gift, she impugns his creativity; when she argues that the tree's owner would not have made it available, she impugns God's omnipotence, accepting Satan's argument that God cannot be omnipotent if the tree gives wisdom without his permission; and in her accusation of envy, she denies God's divinity itself, repeating Satan's claim that God's envy proves that he is not God. This false lowering of God contrasts ironically with the true degradation of the incarnation, the reason that the Son has been elevated in his humanity to the office which he is sent to exercise here, that of judge.

Eve develops her previous doubt of God's motives into a doubt of his values. Convinced that the ignominy of ignorance is the state for man planned by the God she calls "Our great Forbidder," Eve claims that man can determine what is good by himself, through experience. Her moral debasement is indicated by the ironic contrast between the Experience she praises, which brings the suffering of evil, and the God she blames, who mitigates evil in his judgment. Finally, Eve shows her lack of awe when on the basis of her doubts of God's divinity, she argues that her action may go undetected and therefore unpunished. Her false security is answered in God's pronouncement on the necessity of punishing confident sinners.

These heresies Eve compounds in her two speeches to Adam before his fall. The first speech emphasizes the doubt of God's authority. Eve repeats her belief in the serpent's tale (9. 867–72), in the goodness of the apple (9. 863–67), in her right to disobey (9. 872–74) ; she repeats her belief in her attainment of godhood (9. 874–77). The fact that Eve is acting ("in her face excuse / Came prologue, and apology to prompt" [9. 853–55]) does not discredit her belief in these arguments, which tally with those in her soliloquy; the falsehood (as will be shown) lies in her relationship with Adam. Eve's second speech encourages Adam's disregard of God's goodness. She praises Adam for his overvaluation of human love (9. 965–72) and discourages his awe with declarations of safety (9. 983–89). Since Eve is "much won" by Adam's love (9. 991–93), these heresies are clearly offered sincerely.

After eating the fruit, Adam comes to share Eve's certainty (9. 1017–26). His former speculation on the results of disobeying becomes a desire for tenfold disobedience which resembles Eve's resolve of daily transgression. This disparagement of his rule God answers in calling Adam to judgment. Adam also progresses from his former acceptance of the possibility of advancement. Eve, in presenting her argument on the safety of disobeying, used as proof evidences of her "life / Augmented" (9. 984–85)

> *new hopes, new joys,*
> *Taste so divine, that what of sweet before*
> *Ha[d] touched [her] sense, flat seem[ed] to this*
> *   and harsh.*
>
> *(9. 985–87)*

Adam takes his hint from this declaration, and on the basis of his "True relish" in "tasting," he comes to believe that he has in fact been elevated. This false belief stands in ironic contrast to the true elevation of man to divinity in the person of the Son, wherein the Son receives that power of judgment with which the Father sends him to judge.

Adam aggravates his earlier neglect of God's love and his over-valuing of Eve. In praising Eve for her having "purveyed," he asserts that Eve showed superior foresight in first taking the fruit; thus he rejects his initial perception of her ruin, and turns his former acquiescence in her action to positive approval. By equating with wisdom Eve's yielding to eye and taste, he endorses her belief in the establishment of values through experience. There is an ironic contrast between this praise for Eve's excellence in discovering the means for Adam's moral ruin, and the love that is due and not given to the Son for that true love of man which he is sent to display. Finally, the fact that Adam fails to note the signs of nature in eating the forbidden fruit (9. 1000–1006) shows his lack of proper awe.

What Adam adds to Eve's certainty is a careless overconfidence and levity. Eve's evidences of "life / Augmented" are only a heightened form of the argument that since she has not died, death is not to be feared; furthermore, of these evidences, the heightening of taste is rationally the least strong. Adam expands Eve's unimportant argument against fear into the proof of his elevation, and he fails to examine the disparity between the divinity which he hoped (however unconfidently) to attain and the actually attained pleasure in eating. His insightful mind has been rendered oblivious. Furthermore, Adam's defense of Eve's values is only a witticism: tasting must be wisdom because the same terms, "savor" and "judicious," are predicated to both, and things equal to the same thing are equal to each other. The procedure is far from his former delicate moral guidance of Eve.

The sexual intercourse of Adam and Eve contrasts with their evening prayer before the fall, and proves the rebellion to be the antithesis of the way of life established for man by God. The fact that the intercourse takes place by day, ordained for work, rather than at night indicates that God's rule has been forgotten. Furthermore, Adam's statement that Eve is "fairer now / Than ever, bounty of this virtuous tree" (9. 1032–33) shows that instead of thanking God for his gifts of love and nature, Adam thinks of love in terms of nature, and pays to nature the thanks owed God—this last being especially evident in the fact that his statement is a revision of the tribute paid at the time of Eve's creation, that God was "Giver of all things fair" and Eve the "fairest . . . / Of all [his] gifts" (8. 493–94). The removal of the relationship from the context of divine blessing is also indicated by the fact that here there is sex on a "shady bank" (9. 1037–41), rather than love in a nuptial bower. Finally, the fact that Adam simply "seize[s]" Eve's hand (9. 1037) contrasts with the gentleness of his wedding day, when, as Eve says, his "gentle hand / Seized" hers (4. 488–89), and the fact that Eve is "nothing loth" (9. 1039) contrasts with the modesty of her wedding day, when, as Adam describes, she was "blushing like the Morn" (8. 511). Here sex is valued for itself, and is not connected with God's gift, or with its product, offspring. The order in man's life, the sense of sanctity in all its aspects, and the harmony between these aspects are all destroyed.

Adam and Eve show their rebelliousness during the judgment scene which ends this stage of their development; they reveal in their excuses to the Son the primary sins which caused their fall. Though Eve is cowed by Adam's ill success in outwitting God (10. 159–61) and implies in her confession that she was mistaken in her belief in the wisdom-giving properties of the fruit, nevertheless her answer demonstrates her disobedience. For by placing emphasis on the serpent's deceit ("The Serpent me beguiled and I did eat" [10. 162]), Eve avoids blaming herself for her defects in not detecting or rejecting the lies, and she admits that she was mistaken about the fruit rather than that she was blameworthy for having disobeyed, whatever the properties of the fruit. Her excuse demonstrates a disobedience attributable to insufficient thought. Adam's insufficient love of God is revealed in his confession (10. 137–43). He reminds God that Eve was supposed to be, according to God himself, Adam's "fit help" and his "wish exactly to [his] heart's desire" (8. 450–51). He suggests that Eve's power over him caused his fall, and that her power derives from the attributes which God gave her: her helpfulness is so great that he thinks of her as beyond suspicion, and her love-worthiness so great that he excuses her actions. Thus Adam neatly avoids blaming both himself and Eve, attributing his actions to Eve's qualities and Eve's qualities to God the creator. In so doing, he undervalues God and self-indulgently overvalues Eve, revealing the tendency rebuked before by Raphael, and now rebuked by God.[9]

The third stage of the development of Adam and Eve after their loss of innocence is the stage of repentance, which begins with Adam's laments over the miseries brought into the world by the fall, and ends with the penitential prayer of Adam and Eve. This stage falls into three phases. In the first, Adam and Eve are each seen to be in a state of relapse, doomed to repeat their fall. In the second, the pair turn from evil; step by step they reverse their fall, and in the end they are aided by God, whose grace gives them strength enough to enable them to repent and reform, undoing their fall. In the third phase, the pair ratify their decision to repent.

Eve's tendency to repeat her fall can be seen in the advice she gives to Adam on the remedy for their plight. The prologue of her speech reveals her relationship to God's authority (10. 967–70, 974–78). She begins with a partial recognition of the mistake in her previous beliefs. By calling her earlier words "erroneous," she acknowledges that she was mistaken about the properties of the forbidden fruit, and by calling her words "unfortunate" in their "just" consequences, she admits that her argument about her freedom was false, that she was free only to disobey, as the punishment for that disobedience proved. But after this admission, Eve returns to the heresies broached in her fall. When suggesting actions to cope with their sufferings, Eve uses the principle of self-determined rights; and when suggesting that ending sufferings would be "of easier choice" than bearing them, she views choice as a matter of what man can do, not of what man ought to do. As in her fall, she fails to think first of her duty and to see the implications of her actions, and in those lapses she neglects the service of God.

In the main section of Eve's speech, the first suggestion which she offers, that of barrenness, reveals her relationship to God's love (10. 979–91). She at least sees the harm done to Adam by her encouragement of his weakness, since she is now concerned for the welfare of others rather than for her own satisfaction. Even in this concern, however, there are traces of her former attitudes. Her concern for her children's pleasure in living relates to her sensory proclivities, and her abrupt "Childless thou art, childless remain" recalls the defiant tone of her rejection of what she took to be God's oppression: "Such prohibitions bind not." Furthermore, the suggestion itself shows an insufficient love of God and lack of trust in his love for man; by it, Eve repeats the distrust of God which figured in her fall. In her second suggestion, that of suicide, Eve shows herself to be aware of her folly in having expected to evade God's penalty; describing herself and Adam as "shivering under fears / That show no end but death" (10. 1003–4), she acknowledges the promised woes and expects the death decreed. But Eve repeats her folly by planning suicide to evade God's punishment (10. 999–1002).

Though Adam's lament is more complex than Eve's speech, it reveals the same basic moral characteristic, the tendency to relapse in the face of evidence of past folly and evil.[10] The lament has as its subject death; it contains an introduction, an examination of the suitability of Adam's own punishment, an examination of the question of the nature of death, and an examination of the suitability of the punishment inherited by mankind.

Adam's ruminations of the nature of death (10. 782–816) reveal his relationship to God's rule. He shows awareness here of his folly in supposing that God would not destroy man and the world created for man: his questions now are whether the death of man is a physical ending or an eternal state of misery of the kind seen in Adam's own life and in nature about him. But in arguing these questions, Adam speculates on the laws of non-contradiction and on the laws of nature as they affect God's conduct; and after proving that man's physical end is just and that it is reasonable—after proving, therefore, that death must be finite, Adam finds that a new definition of death can prove death eternal. The speculation on God's thoughts and the futility of the argument both recall Adam's thoughts during his fall, his speculation on how God would treat man's disobedience. What is suggested is that Adam is repeating the fall by speculating on matters beyond his knowing and neglecting to ask himself the nature of his present duty to God, though now Adam's sin is one of omission rather than commission.

In the introductory section of his lament (10. 720–42), Adam reveals his attitude to God's divine superiority. Because of the changes wrought in the world by the fall—the advent of inclement weather (10. 651–706) and of warfare among animals (10. 706–14) —and because of his own seclusion in "gloomiest shade" (10. 716), Adam, aware of his degradation, assesses his misery, noting both the separation from God implied by his hiding from God and his blame for the destruction of the world both presently and to come. The contrasts of past glory with present misery which begin and end this section reveal Adam's awareness that his former hopes of seizing godhood were folly, but Adam's consciousness of degradation does not bring him to an awareness that if God can lower, he can also raise. Thus, by neglecting to consider God's power to strengthen him, Adam repeats the denial of divine superiority made during the fall, though, as with the failure to submit to God's rule, his sin is now one of omission.

The section of the lament dealing with hereditary punishment (10. 817–41) is a struggle between Adam's love for God and his doubt of divine goodness. The section begins with an expression of Adam's love for his children: he wishes not to pass on misery to his descendants. Affection quickly leads, as it led in his fall, to a doubt of God's goodness, for Adam next questions God's punishment of all mankind for the guilt of a single man. At this point, however, Adam turns back toward God; he considers the moral changes wrought by the fall, the factor which he failed to consider when evaluating fallen Eve, and he therefore absolves God from blame. After this climb, Adam again falls; like Eve in her speech of advice, he wishes for the death which would save his children by preventing their birth. From this wish he is saved by his awe, his fear of God's wrath, but the rejection of evil leads to no acceptance of good. Instead, concluding that he can find no comfort in life or in death, Adam ends in a despair which precludes any love for God and trust in his love. Thus after a zigzag course in which moral insight conflicts with fallen weakness, Adam ends in a failure of love, like the failure that marked his fall.

Struggle and failure also appear in the section of the lament that deals with Adam's own penalty, and which reveals his attitude to the wrath of God (10. 743–82). He begins by rejecting God's penalty as excessive, arguing that a physical end would have been sufficient without the added punishment of misery. This rebelliousness he represses, arguing that he accepted God's bargain at his creation and that God as creator can punish his creatures as he chooses. From acceptance of God's punishment, however, Adam moves to a wish for death which resembles Eve's suggestion of suicide, and in the end he voices the desire to evade through death the misery allotted him—the desire which underlies Eve's suggested action. Though Adam does not doubt God's punishment, as he did in his fall, nevertheless, in spite of all his moral exertions, he repeats the sin of that fall by seeking to evade his punishment.

After this initial phase of relapse, Adam and Eve slowly work toward repentance, undoing their fall. The turning point (as will be shown later) comes in the personal realm, with Eve's plea that Adam forgive her sins against him. Her next speech, the advice on the remedy of their plight, provides the transition from the personal sphere to the religious, but the first stage of repentance in this sphere comes from Adam, in the refutation with which he opens his reply to Eve. This refutation serves to reverse Adam's yielding to Eve's seduction during his fall. The conditions of Eve's advice resemble those of her seduction speech, in that Eve appeals to grounds on which Adam is vulnerable; as her former mention of separation appealed to Adam's dread of losing her, so her present recommendations appeal to Adam's own despair. But now Adam keeps himself from sharing Eve's feelings, and instead of rationalizing, he corrects her reasoning: he suggests that the idea of evading punishment is not heroic (it "implies," he says, "Not [her] contempt" of life and pleasure, but her "anguish and regret / For loss of life and pleasure over-loved" [10. 1016–19]) and he argues that the idea is not practical (it would, he suggests, "provoke the Highest / To make death in [them] live" [10. 1020–29]) , and by these arguments Adam dissuades Eve from her proposed course. In this rationality and firmness, Adam avoids the error of his fall. He is, incidentally, reinstating a proper concern for Eve's virtue, rather than repudiating her, for he begins his speech with a tribute to Eve's moral potentialities:

> Eve, thy contempt of life and pleasure seems
> To argue in thee something more sublime
> And excellent than what thy mind contemns.
> *(10. 1013–15)*

The next step in the repentance is Adam's advice to Eve on the remedy of their plight. The speech is important first in that it undoes the heresies of Adam's fall and corrects the deficiencies of his lament, and second in that it demonstrates God's gift of grace, for it is here that God aids man and enables him to repent and to reform.[11]

The third resolution in Adam's speech (10. 1086–92) shows his return to dutifulness. His suggestion to go back to the place of judgment is a sign of obedience, a voluntary submission to divine governance; his suggestion to confess and seek pardon corresponds to God's requirements of repentance and prayer. Adam's submission to God's rule reverses his arguing away of duty at the time of the fall; his self-humiliation before God reverses the presumptuous speculations by which he tried to guess God's mind, and his sorrow for past faults the claim of human indispensability which he made during his fall. Furthermore, by his resolution, Adam is turned away from the useless speculation on the nature of his fate with which his lament is concerned, and is turned toward the essential question of his duty to God. There is evidence of God's grace in Adam's mention of the "hearts contrite" of himself and Eve, for the acts of duty proposed result from God's grace in softening the hearts of his fallen creatures, as the Son later affirms.

The confidence in God which ends Adam's speech (10. 1093–

96) serves as an acknowledgment of divine superiority. In falling, Adam counted upon the fruit to elevate him; in his lament, he mourned the degradation which exposed his error; now, relying on God's relentment, Adam believes in God's ability to restore the creature he degraded, and by his belief, he recants the folly of his fall and overcomes the negativity of his lament. There is evidence of grace in the memory of God's judgment which confirms Adam in this belief in God. When Adam speaks of the time when the Son seemed "angry most" and "most severe," he refers specifically to the Son's opening accusations in the judgment scene, and when he speaks of the Son's "look serene" he refers to the fact that the Son did not berate him in those accusations. What this memory does is make Adam aware of God's former mercy, for the absence of berating was a sign of God's power of lightening blame in judgment; and by this awareness, Adam is confirmed in his belief in God's ability to restore him. The presence of this strengthening memory is evidence of God's action upon Adam; for God clears Adam's mind by enlivening a crucial memory which reveals the divine nature. Furthermore, Adam's apprehending of God's favor is itself a partial awareness of God's present action upon him.

Adam's second resolution shows his return to love. Adam acknowledges God's love for mankind in his office of judge, the love seen in the Son's postponement of death and his alleviation of the physical evils leading to death (10. 1046–59). This acknowledgment leads Adam to trust that God will provide for him and Eve during their lifetime, helping to remedy their plight (10. 1060–85). His reliance on God's remedial aid reverses his former acceptance of the irrevocability of Eve's deed, and his love for God reverses his overvaluation of Eve during his fall; and by pointing out to Eve the ease of her punishment and by encouraging her with his own example of contentment, Adam leads Eve toward a love for God, guiding her as he did after her dream, and as he should have done after her fall. Adam's belief in God's provision here undoes the loveless acceptance of misery present in Adam's lament. There is evidence of God's grace in the fact that Adam, who previously thought of God the judge as man's condemner, is now moved by God's gentleness and mercy; God acts upon Adam by strengthening his conscience and thereby increasing his response to good. The perception of God's goodness which Adam is given constitutes a partial awareness of the concern for human happiness which God manifests in his gift of conscience.

Finally, Adam's first resolution (10. 1028–46) shows his return to proper awe. From the memory of the Son's oracular curse upon the serpent, Adam understands the secondary meaning of the threatened bruising of the serpent's head, the meaning concerned with Satan's final punishment, and through this knowledge, he comes to see the consequences of Eve's suggested remedies, and is strengthened in his rejection of them. Adam's acceptance of punishment from God and his rejection of the serpent reverses his acceptance of the serpent's tale and his disbelief in God's threats during his fall. Furthermore, the rejection of Eve's suggestions serves as a recantation of the desire of escape present in Adam's own lament, and the acceptance of God's planned revenge allows Adam to see a reason besides misery for his existence. There is evidence of God's grace in Adam's response to the oracular curse (though this instance of grace is the first and least important). By increasing Adam's response to good and evil, God causes Adam to see the justice of which God's hatred of evil is a part; Adam comes to see the repercussions of his decisions, the plan whereby God links good outcomes to the virtue of his creatures and causes punishment to spring from their disvirtue, and thus Adam is encouraged in his acceptance of his punishment. In his fear of God's increased wrath, Adam is made aware of the penalty that God allots to those who reject his offered chance of repentance and reform.

The third step in the repentance is Eve's yielding to Adam's plan. The fact that Eve follows Adam's advice reverses her initiation of action during the fall, and Eve's "remorse" (10. 1098) reveals her participation in the recantation which undoes the fall.

The prayer which ends this stage of the development of Adam and Eve serves as a ratification of their repentance. As the eating of the forbidden fruit made the fall final, so the prayer of Adam and Eve (10. 1098–1104) signals the passing of their repentance from thought into action. The fact that the account of the prayer repeats verbatim (except for pronouns) the words of Adam's proposal indicates the seriousness of the pair's resolve: they have carried out their resolution.

The final stage of the development of Adam and Eve extends from their speeches after the prayer to their final departure from the Garden. In this stage, the stage of regeneration, Adam and Eve, through God's action in his office of savior, attain justification and salvation, reversing their condition during their rebellion. This section of the story of the pair divides into three parts. The first, which consists of the speeches preceding Michael's prophecy, serves as a preliminary exposition of character. The second part, which consists of Adam's reactions to Michael's prophecy, shows Adam's growth to doctrinal and moral maturity. The third part, the final speeches of Adam and Eve, serves to reveal the pair's regenerate state.

The speeches which precede Michael's prophecy look both ways; they measure the present status of Adam and Eve by reference to the past, but they also provide a standard for measuring their final regenerate state. The speeches reveal three things about Adam and Eve: first, that having accepted grace, they are ready for regeneration; second, that Adam and Eve have the proselyte's ignorance of doctrine, needing the instruction which God later sends; and third, that they have traces of sin requiring purification.

Eve's reply to Adam's speech of encouragement reveals her readiness for regeneration and her ignorance (11. 163–73, 178–80). One sign here of readiness for regeneration is Eve's persistence in the path chosen during the repentance. Her opening acceptance of the title of "transgressor" reaffirms the acknowledgment of fault made during the prayer; her thankfulness for her role as "source of life" shows her belief in Adam's penitent suggestion that the two of them trust God's provision for their life; and her suggestion that they begin their now laborious work implements Adam's proposal that they accept the punishment allotted them.

In addition, Eve's speech strongly suggests that by her conduct here, she is atoning for her rebellion earlier. First of all, her reference to Adam's ideas constitutes a reversal of the spread of heresy from her to Adam during her rebellion. Her speech contain in each of its main divisions allusions to her own earlier words.

The fact that Eve mentions her snaring of Adam indicates that she is disavowing her seduction speech, in which she encouraged Adam to disobey. The parallel tributes to God and Adam suggest that Eve is remembering her soliloquy after eating the apple, in which she violated her relationship first with God, then with Adam; now she shows, in proper order, the love which she withheld before. The offer of work is Eve's penance for her speech before Adam's eating of the fruit; for whereas earlier she praised Adam for sharing her guilt and minimized the consequences, now she willingly shares Adam's penalty and willingly accepts punishment.

Eve's doctrinal ignorance is less prominent than her reversal of past harm. One suggestion of such ignorance is made through the irony of Eve's terming herself the "source of life"; for Eve is not only, as she knows, the mother of mankind, but the mother of the Vanquisher of Death, and therefore the source of life in a way unknown to her. Eve's ignorance of the punishment to befall her is, of course, made obvious in her final resolution to "live . . . content" in Eden.

Adam's speech of encouragement (ll. 141–58) reveals the same qualities as Eve's reply. Like Eve, he shows persistence in the chosen course, though his confirmations are more striking than Eve's, since he has the keener mind. Adam's opening wonder at God's responsiveness to human prayer is a confirmation of the policy that Adam enunciated during his repentance. His vision of God's listening and his belief in divine favor are equivalent to his earlier memory of God's "look serene" and his confidence in God's relentment, but the awareness of God's action upon him is stronger now. Finally, Adam's sense of peace, his memory of the Son's prediction, and his belief that "the bitterness of death / Is past" are equivalent to his earlier acceptance of sentence, his memory of the Son's judgment, and his confidence in God's provision for the lives of himself and Eve. Now, however, his love is stronger, and he has advanced in insight; for, whereas before he saw only the secondary meaning of the Son's oracular curse, now he has partial insight into the primary meaning, the meaning which pertains to man's salvation. Not only is Adam confirmed in his chosen course, however; he is also given intimations into God's role as savior, for the "favor" that Adam senses is God's revelation of the justification which the Son has given to him and

Eve, and the memory of the Son's prophecy is God's renewal of
his pledge of salvation.

There is little emphasis, in this speech, on Adam's reversal of
his rebellion, aside from the general parallel of situation: as the
rebellion entailed a confirmation in the views of the fall, so his
speech is a confirmation in the views of the repentance. But in
Adam's reading (11. 201–3) of the signs which God sends to fore-
warn the pair of their expulsion from the Garden (11. 181–92),
there is a reversal of Adam's action during the rebellion. Whereas
earlier, Adam missed the signs of nature that followed his eating
of the fruit, now Adam shows awe by suspecting that God is fore-
casting the imposition of some penalty (11. 193–200).

Lack of doctrinal knowledge is much emphasized in Adam's
speech; for despite his acuity, Adam is unable to understand fully
what has been revealed to him. He does not understand the ex-
tent of God's power, the fact that in favoring man, the Son is
crediting his own merit to mankind. And he does not understand
the extent of God's love; for though he deduces from the mention
of Eve's descendants that the death of himself and Eve has been
postponed, he does not guess that the faithful are destined for
eternal life, and though he remembers God's prediction, he can-
not guess its implementation through the Son's incarnation and
sacrifice. Thus, though ready for redemption, Adam has need for
the instruction that Michael later provides.

The reactions of Adam and Eve to Michael's announcement of
their banishment reveal the traces of sin remaining in them; for
in resisting their punishment, they reveal the principal limita-
tions that figured in their fall, and which could, God suggests,
lead them to another apostasy (11. 93–98). Eve's complaint of
surprisal ("O unexpected stroke" [11. 268]) shows a failure to
connect the penalty with the signs sent by God and with God's
original threat of expulsion into an unhappy world. Her ex-
clamation that the penalty is "worse than [the stroke] of Death"
(11. 268), that, in other words, she would rather die than leave
Eden, reveals her narrowness of vision. Michael in replying re-
minds her of the reasonableness of her expulsion (11. 287–88),
and by his rebuke, "set [not] thy heart . . . on that which is not
thine" (11. 288–89), he draws an analogy between her exclama-
tion and her attitude during the fall, reminding her that Eden,
like the forbidden fruit, must be viewed within the context of

God's interdiction. Adam is more careful in stating his resistance. Heeding the angel's rebuke of Eve, he acknowledges the justice of the expulsion, admitting that if he loses the mementos of divine presence (11. 316), he hid from God during his rebellion, when God called him to judgment (11. 330), and therefore deserves his loss; and he honors the absoluteness of the prohibition (11. 314), carefully noting that he would pray to remain if prayer could succeed (11. 307–13), and thus expressing his wish without suggesting that he would remain in defiance of God's prohibition. Nevertheless, in expressing his concern lest his sons lack memorials of God's appearance (11. 315–33), Adam, from affection for his children, distrusts God's love for mankind. In reply Michael points out that though Adam has lost the relation with his children which was part of God's intention for mankind (11. 335–48), God will not fail in his love (11. 349–54). These weaknesses revealed in Adam and Eve justify the trials decreed for them by God.

After this preliminary exposition of character, the growth of Adam and Eve is treated. Adam's growth is demonstrated in his reactions to Michael's prophecy. Through this prophecy, Adam learns what he did not know about man's salvation, and in addition, he demonstrates fidelity in the face of trial, and learns to accept the mitigated penalty placed upon him. With regard to Eve's growth, there is a compromise of thematic, philosophical, and dramatic considerations. For dramatic and for thematic reasons, the poem should end with the regeneration of Eve as well as of Adam. If the angel is to instruct Adam and Adam Eve, in accordance with the principle of supervision by superiors which was followed before the fall, then a dramatically awkward situation results, for Adam must repeat to Eve what he has learned, in an extension of an episode which no one has ever wished longer. If the angel is to instruct Eve simultaneously, however, by means of a dream, then there is the problem of how Eve is to receive moral trial; for if Eve is not corrupted by her Satan-inspired dream, she cannot be regenerated morally by a divinely-inspired one. The compromise works thus: in the ending Eve is presented in a regenerate state. In order to bring about this state, a dream is used, parallel to the instruction of Adam in its intellectual and moral functions (12. 595–97), but containing the philosophically questionable element of a morally redemptive dream. Finally,

Adam is told of his duty to instruct Eve in the future (12. 597–605). This suggestion presents an alternative to the means of regeneration actually shown, but it serves to present a philosophically acceptable solution to the problem of Eve's trial while avoiding the undesirable dramatization of it.

The structure of Michael's prophecy will be dealt with later; here it is necessary to note only that the prophecy has two main sections, one concerned with evil, the other with good, and that the section on evil has two subsections, one on death, the other on sin. What Adam is to accomplish in viewing evil is expressed by his resolve before the start of the vision; he is to learn to view death as "rest from labor" (11. 375) and, in the face of evil, to "overcome / By suffering" (11. 374–75). Viewing the unnatural deaths, Adam reacts with deepening resistance: his first reaction is puzzled dismay ("some great mischief hath befallen / To that meek man" [11. 450–52]), his second reaction horror ("But have I now seen Death? . . . O sight / Of terror . . . !" [11. 461–65]), his third reaction protest ("Why is life given / To be thus wrested from us?" [11. 500–514]). But the angel's assurance of God's justice in what seems unjust, both in the case of violent death (11. 457–60) and of disease (11. 515–25), leads Adam to inquire into natural death (11. 526–29), and, learning its nature from Michael (11. 530–46), he becomes resigned to death, discarding fear (11. 547–52).

Having attained resignation, Adam is next tried by the sight of evil. Suitably repelled by the evils represented by the giants (11. 675–82) and by the contemporaries of Noah (11. 779–84), and finding the evil of Nimrod irrational as well as repellent (12. 64–78), Adam reveals weakness only in the case of the marriage of the sons of Seth with the daughters of Cain; "Here Nature seems fulfilled in all her ends," he says, approving the presence of human love (11. 598–602). By his reaction, Adam reveals his tendency to overvalue man and to neglect the love of God, and for his failure to consider the relation of man to God he is rebuked by Michael:

> *Judge not what is best*
> *By pleasure, though to Nature seeming meet,*
> *Created, as thou art, to nobler end*
> *Holy and pure, conformity divine.*
>
> *(11. 603–6)*

In Adam's responses to the section of the prophecy dealing with good, emphasis is placed on Adam's progress from ignorance to knowledge. Adam is in the beginning grateful for God's favor to man (12. 270–79), but his questions about law and man's sinfulness (12. 280–84) show him to be aware of the necessity for salvation without knowing its plan or agent. In his next speech, Adam rejoices in his knowledge of the agent of salvation (12. 375–82), but when he asks "where and when" Satan will receive his "capital bruise" (12. 383–85), he shows himself ignorant of the nature of salvation. In his third speech, Adam rejoices in the goodness of salvation (12. 469–78), but his doctrinal knowledge is still incomplete; as his question shows (12. 479–84), he is ignorant of God's means of guiding and defending humanity. Only in the opening section of Adam's last speech to Michael is the subject of learning concluded, with Adam's expression of intellectual satisfaction:

> Greatly instructed I shall hence depart,
> Greatly in peace of thought, and have my fill
> Of knowledge, what this vessel can contain.
> (12. 557–59)

That this satisfaction is justified is indicated by the obvious connection between such knowledge as the doctrines concerned with salvation and those points which Adam only dimly or partially understood before.

In the final part of this final stage in the development of Adam and Eve, Milton demonstrates the regeneration of the pair; he contrasts their state at the end with the flaws and inadequacies revealed in the opening scene.

Though, as during the state of innocence, the task of theological expression is largely Adam's, Eve's last speech does demonstrate the remedy of her past ignorance. Eve's final statement that the "Promised Seed" will "restore" all that she has lost (12. 620–23) is a revision of her words before the instructional dream, that she, the bringer of death, was destined to be the "source of life." Through the dream, Eve has learned the means and nature of salvation, and her statement proclaims her saving love for the Son as savior. Eve's expressed willingness to leave Eden (12. 614–15) is clearly a reversal of her earlier protest; and her opening announcement of her dream (12. 610–14) suggests the overcoming of her limitations. By referring to her sorrow as something in the past, she implies that she has given up protest, as Michael advised, and by her responsiveness to God's dream, she acknowledges the divine guidance which she neglected in her complaint.

The second section of Adam's final speech is in fact a summary of the moral doctrines of *Paradise Lost,* a statement of the creature's proper relationship to God in all his offices:

> *Henceforth I learn, that to obey is best,*
> *And love with fear the only God, to walk*
> *As in his presence, ever to observe*
> *His providence, and on him sole depend,*
> *Merciful over all his works, with good*
> *Still overcoming evil, and by small*
> *Accomplishing great things, by things deemed weak*
> *Subverting worldly strong, and worldly wise*
> *By simply meek; that suffering for truth's sake*
> *Is fortitude to highest victory,*
> *And to the faithful death the gate of life;*
> *Taught this by his example whom I now*
> *Acknowledge my Redeemer ever blest.*
>
> (*12. 561–73*)

The first phrase relates to God the lawgiver. "To obey is best" refers to the obedience due to God's laws, and "[to] love with fear the only God" includes statements of the love and awe owed to God, as well as an acknowledgment of his divinity. The second phrase, "to walk / As in his presence," refers to God the judge, who sees and punishes transgression. The third phrase relates to God the giver of grace. The words "Merciful over all his works" refer to the grace whereby God shows his mercy to corrupted mankind, and the nature of this grace is explained in the succeeding lines. The first component of grace is the strengthening power referred to in the words "by small / Accomplishing great things"; the manifestations of this power are explained in the succeeding chiasmus—"[subverting] worldly wise / By simply meek" referring to the intellectual strengthening which permits the recipients to follow God's guidance in defiance of sophisticated error, and the words "by things deemed weak /

Subverting worldly strong" referring to the strengthening of will which permits the recipients to obey God in the face of oppression. The second main component of God's grace, his gift of the conscience which permits men to love good, is referred to in the words "with good / Still overcoming evil." Man's relation to these two facets of God's grace is contained in the opening statement, the first words of which ("ever to observe / His providence") refer to man's obedience to God's governance, and the remainder of which ("and on him sole depend") refers to the trust which conscience prompts and makes possible. The clause that is the fourth element in the series relates to the fourth office of God, that of savior. The first clause, "suffering for truth's sake / Is fortitude to highest victory," refers to God's trial by tribulation of those who accept justification from him. The second clause, "to the faithful death [is] the gate of life," refers to God's salvation of those who love him. The final phrase, "Taught this by his example whom I now / Acknowledge my Redeemer ever blest," serves as a pronouncement of faith in the Son in his two actions of obeying God's law, despite man's hate, in order to justify man, and of dying to be resurrected, in order to save man from death.

Adam's past flaw is recalled in Michael's reply to this last speech of Adam's. After commending Adam's summary of doctrine (12. 575–81), Michael reminds Adam of his earlier complaint at leaving Eden (he says that if virtuous, Adam will "not be loth / To leave . . . Paradise" [12. 585–86]), and he exerts corrective influences on the flaw revealed by the complaint, stressing the love of God (12. 582–85) and the deeds resulting from it (12. 581–83) which are needed to remedy the flaw. Thus, when Adam departs without protest, he demonstrates that he has overcome his previous weakness.

This final scene, then, shows Adam and Eve in a state of regeneration, reconciled with God and destined for salvation.

The relationship of Adam and Eve to God—the fall, rebellion, repentance, and regeneration which follow their state of innocence—is clearly the central concern of the main plot of *Paradise Lost*. Though the personal relationship of Adam and Eve is treated carefully and completely, it nevertheless depends on the divine relationship for its meaning, and has for its function the reinforcement of the plot's central concerns.

The bases for judging the development of Adam and Eve in the personal realm are the requirements governing the relationship of creatures. As a superior, Adam is expected to show a leader's authority: his authority being delegated from God, he must frame his commands in accordance with divine law, but he is also expected to rule, to exact obedience to his commands. Adam is also supposed to display a leader's virtue: he is to show a protective love for Eve, and to exert his power to shame in such a way as to encourage her in virtue. Eve, on the other hand, being an inferior, owes to Adam the sort of reverence she owes to God. She is supposed to honor his authority by obeying his commands and acknowledging his superiority, and to acknowledge his goodness with love and awe.

The original relationship of Adam and Eve to one another resembles their state of innocence before God, in that the pair are here shown in their proper relationship, a relationship which is used to judge their later deviations—and a relationship which is, incidentally, the pattern ordained for society at large, as well as for the household. For Michael in telling of Nimrod notes the "fraternal state" intended for man (12. 25–26), and Adam in his comment adds that the rule of man is the prerogative of God, not man (12. 64–71). Mankind is intended to be one family, and Michael notes that had Adam not fallen, he would have been the grand patriarch of that family (11. 342–46). At any rate, this initial relationship is treated principally in the opening conversations of Adam and Eve, though the departure of Eve which precedes the private conversation of Adam and Raphael provides additional information.

During the state of innocence, Eve demonstrates a proper respect for Adam's authority. When Adam at nightfall suggests that it is time to rest, Eve begins her reply with a statement of her obedience:

> [W]hat thou bidd'st
> Unargued I obey; so God ordains.
> God is thy law, thou mine; to know no more
> Is woman's happiest knowledge and her praise.
> (4. 635–38)

Eve's later action in leaving Adam while he is talking with Raphael accords with this obedience. By her preference for Adam's instruction (8. 52–54), Eve proves that, as she said, she believes that it is her place to follow Adam and Adam's place to consider God's law. In addition to obeying, Eve acknowledges Adam's superiority. In her answer to the exhortation to obedience with which Adam ends his opening speech, Eve acknowledges that she is Adam's aid, saying that she was created "for [him]" and that she is "to no end" without him, and she acknowledges her need for Adam's superior wisdom, saying that he is her "guide / And head" (4. 440–43). Eve's departure in "lowliness majestic" when Adam and Raphael turn to "thoughts abstruse" (8. 39–42) is an expression of Eve's awareness that she is not an equal participant with Adam in intellectual inquiry.

Eve also demonstrates her love for Adam. Explaining to Adam why she failed to notice that night had come, Eve expresses her love, saying that in Adam's company, she "forget[s] all time, / All seasons and their change," and declaring that without Adam, the natural beauty of no time of day would please her (4. 639–56). Her departure for her favorite flowers during the conversation of Adam and Raphael (8. 44–47) is not a violation of this declaration, for Eve is not neglecting love for natural beauty, but is rather passing time until her love is called for, and she is preferring the more loving activity of hearing Adam's explanations, accompanied with "conjugal caresses" (8. 54–57), to the purely intellectual experience of listening to the angel with Adam.

Adam, meanwhile, exercises his authority properly. He acknowledges the derivation of his rule when recommending rest. For he connects his suggestion with God's ordering of man's life ("God," he says, "hath set / Labor and rest, as day and night to men / Successive" [4. 610–14]), and he connects that ordering with its purpose in signifying God's supervision of man (man's work, he says, "declares his dignity, / And the regard of Heaven on all his ways" [4. 615–22]). Furthermore, taking advantage of dinnertime (4. 331) to raise the subject of God's bounty (4. 411–32), Adam ends by exacting obedience to divine laws, encouraging Eve to share his submission: "Then let us not think hard / One easy prohibition" (4. 432–39). Proper love Adam defines in answering Raphael's stern reproof of sensuality, explaining that he responds essentially to Eve's moral worth,

"Those thousand decencies that daily flow / From all her words and actions," rather than to her sexual attractiveness, "her outside formed so fair" (8. 596–606). The truth of his assertion is demonstrated by that display of affection which earlier provoked Satan's envy of the pair's happiness. In the speech preceding that display, Eve, agreeing with Adam's statement that love is owed to God, says that she is grateful for the reverential love for Adam which God has ordained for her (4. 444–48), and in the following account of her creation, she attests her folly in having at first preferred beauty to this love (4. 449–91). Thus it is Eve's due reverence, and not merely her own attraction to him (4. 492–93), to which Adam affectionately responds (4. 497–502).

The fall from this perfect relationship is analogous to the pair's fall in their relationship with God; in it, the pair first break the laws governing the relationship of creatures. Furthermore, the pattern of action in this personal realm resembles that in the religious sphere, in that Eve initiates the fall, and in that Adam at first responds virtuously, but in the end capitulates. The fall in the personal relationship occurs during the quarrel of Adam and Eve which precedes the serpent's temptation of Eve.[12]

Eve initiates the fall by insisting upon her plan to garden separately from Adam. The fourth speech in her quarrel with Adam violates the obedience that she owes to his rule:

> *With thy permission then, and thus forewarned,*
> *Chiefly by what thy own last reasoning words*
> *Touched only, that our trial, when least sought,*
> *May find us both perhaps far less prepared,*
> *The willinger I go, nor much expect*
> *A foe so proud will first the weaker seek;*
> *So bent, the more shall shame him his repulse.*
> (*9. 378–84*)

The fact that in professing to follow Adam's decision Eve disobeys him is made obvious by the relation between her arguments and the arguments they answer. Adam argued that error is likely enough to be made through lack of caution without seeking occasions for erring (9. 359–63). When Eve argues that one who seeks occasions is cautious, being consciously on guard, she is using Adam's premise about the danger of deception to deny his conclusion. This reversal she covers with the claim that she is "forewarned" by what Adam's "last . . . words / Touched only." Referring to Adam's grudging permission, "But if thou think trial unsought may find / Us both securer than thus warned thou seem'st, / Go" (9. 370–72), Eve claims to be agreeing with Adam, to be merely elaborating his words. Adam argued that unity would prevent attack upon Eve (9. 364–66). When Eve argues that an attack upon her would be prevented by her separation from Adam, in that no "foe so proud" as Satan would seek "first the weaker," Eve is using Adam's conclusion about the desirability of preventing attack to deny Adam's premise about the inadvisability of separation. In this second argument, Eve makes no specific announcement of her agreement with Adam, and in her final argument, Eve flatly disregards Adam's statements. Her final assurance of her ability to defeat Satan by herself is a flat rejection of Adam's statement of the mutual help needed by Eve and himself (9. 351–58), a rejection which exposes the entire falsity of Eve's claim of obedience. Eve's behavior here contrasts with her earlier conduct. By pretending agreement she repudiates her earlier proclamation of unargued submission to Adam's commands; and her earlier desire to listen to Adam's instruction contrasts with her present disregard of his reasoning.

Eve's neglect of duty also appears in her third speech (9. 322–41), in which she revokes the acknowledgment due to Adam's superiority. She begins and ends with the argument that the happiness that God intends for men would be impossible if she and Adam were not safe when separated. Her argument is true in the respect that the ability to resist sin has been given both to Adam and to Eve, but false insofar as it fails to consider that the inequality of Adam and Eve makes Eve less safe when separated from the guidance of her superior. The central portion of Eve's speech consists of two counterarguments. The first, that repulsed temptation reflects upon the tempter alone, giving honor to the tempted, is a rebuttal of Adam's statement that he wishes to save Eve from the insult of temptation (9. 293–305). Eve's desire for a superiority all her own, revealed in this wish to venture forth alone in search of glory, contradicts the recognition of inferiority which led Eve to her previous separation from Adam. The second

argument, that unaided trial is the only proof of virtue, is a re-
buttal of Adam's explanation of the value of witnesses in en-
couraging virtue (9. 309–17). In this argument, Eve forgets what
she knew before, that she was created not to be alone, but to aid
Adam and to rely upon his guidance.

Eve's initial sin against Adam, the one which begins her fall,
is her breach of love. Eve's wish to tend her flowers unaccom-
panied constitutes an overvaluation of beauty and undervaluation
of Adam, and the neglect of her husband permeates her arguments
(9. 205–25). Eve's definiteness about her own task shows her to
have thought about her own pleasure in advance, while the fact
that she is vague about how and where Adam should spend his
time reveals her failure to consider his happiness. Furthermore,
Eve's prologue plays upon Adam's love. Her request for advice
pays tribute to Adam's governance. Her description of their
gardening, with its references to the pleasantness of the work, to
their need of children to aid them, and to the growth of plants
which "derides" their ordering, repeats the contents of Adam's
words in recommending sleep (4. 623–33) and therefore pays
tribute to Adam's explanation of God's law. By this submission
Eve recalls her earlier assertion of her thankfulness for the rever-
ential love allotted her, and hopes for the response which Adam
made to her earlier statement. But Eve is belied here by the
quick presentation of her own suggestion for action, which vitiates
her request for advice, and by the familiarity of her opening
address, "Adam" (the address used by a superior, like Raphael
[5. 372]), which counters her assertion of respect. Sincerity has
given way to mere tact. Finally, there is an open derogation of
love in Eve's concluding argument, that loving interruptions in-
terfere with efficient gardening. Eve's conduct here contrasts
with her earlier statement that no natural beauty pleased her in
Adam's absence, with the sincere reverence which won Adam's
affection, and with the desire for Adam's words and endearments
which figured in her departure from the company of Raphael.

Finally, Eve's second speech constitutes a violation of proper
awe. By accusing Adam of disparaging her love for him and God
(9. 279–89), Eve tries to shame him instead of fearing his
displeasure, and tries to shame him into accepting her plan
rather than into doing what is virtuous.

Adam's initial responses to Eve are stubbornly virtuous—just as after her eating of the fruit, Adam sees Eve's action correctly. In his second speech, Adam both corrects Eve's lack of awe, and exhibits properly his power to shame. Refuting her accusation of disparagement, he defends his protective wish to keep her from being insulted (9. 291–305). Then, after explaining to her the moral utility of shame in aiding the resistance to evil (9. 306–14), he reproaches Eve for neglecting the encouragement to virtue provided by witnesses (9. 315–17). In his first speech, Adam both corrects Eve and demonstrates proper love. His central argument is that love and talk are fitting interruptions, as necessary as the refreshment of eating (9. 235–41); by this argument Adam counters Eve's derogation of love. In addition, when he praises Eve for "study[ing] household good" (9. 229–34) and when he addresses her, with his usual affection, as "Sole Eve, associate sole, to me beyond / Compare above all living creatures dear" (9. 227–28), Adam shows a sincere appreciation of Eve which contrasts with the mere tact that Eve displays in order to gain approval for her plan; and when Adam considers seriously Eve's possible desire to be alone for a while ("solitude sometimes is best society, / And short retirement urges sweet return" [9. 247–50]) and when he demonstrates his protective concern for her security from insult or harm (9. 251–69), Adam shows the interest in Eve's welfare that she fails to show toward him.

In Adam's third speech, the first section (9. 343–69) is a correction of Eve's failure to honor his authority. His first argument, that God did not leave man liable to external harm, but left him liable to inward failure, rebukes Eve for failing to question the extent of her powers when asserting God's provision for her safety. His second argument, that he and Eve should watch one another's judgment in order to prevent error, rebukes Eve for failing to aid him and to follow his guidance, as befits her station. His third argument, that avoiding temptation is better than searching for occasions in which error is possible, rebukes Eve for seeking a way to gain distinction for herself. Having thus countered Eve's failure to acknowledge his superiority, Adam ends the section of his speech with a reminder to Eve of her duty to obey him.

After this initial reaction, Adam collapses, just as he collapses after his initial proper response to Eve's eating of the forbidden fruit. The collapse comes in the final section of Adam's third speech in the quarrel:

> *But if thou think trial unsought may find*
> *Us both securer than thus warned thou seem'st,*
> *Go; for thy stay, not free, absents thee more;*
> *Go in thy native innocence, rely*
> *On what thou hast of virtue, summon all,*
> *For God towards thee hath done his part, do thine.*
>
> *(9. 370–75)*

Adam shows here, first of all, a failure in relaying God's commands. His remarks on freedom misinterpret God's law; for Adam would be forcing Eve to comply only if he prevented her going, not if he commanded compliance; and by obeying an unwelcome command, Eve would be properly recognizing Adam's rule, she being unfree only if physically hindered from carrying out her choice. His error here contrasts with his earlier correct exposition of God's rules for man. Secondly, Adam fails to command obedience; he leaves Eve to her own judgment, rather than commanding her to follow his, as he did earlier when encouraging her to obey God's command. Finally, Adam fails to exercise his protective love, trusting in Eve's purity and virtue to assure the constancy which he should guard and foster. Previously Adam responded to Eve's attraction, and to her virtuous self-correction and virtuous perception of the hierarchy of worth; now when Eve wishes to part from him, and when she not only misvalues but stubbornly persists in her misvaluation, Adam ought to have great misgivings about what would happen to her love for him and God should she be tempted.

Adam's chief sin here is his failure of rule. Eve's resistance is unchanging; her reproach is delivered with "sweet austere composure" (9. 270–72), her rebuttal with "accent sweet" (9. 321) (even after Adam has given in, she is "submiss" while taking her leave [9. 377]). Adam at first is patient, giving "mild answer" (9. 226), then conciliatory, replying with "healing words" (9. 290), and finally infuriated, retorting "fervently" (9. 342). What happens in the middle of the third speech is that faced with such imperturbable obstinacy, Adam gives up trying, convinced by

Eve's expression of sweet endurance that she cannot be turned. This surrender is a breach of duty; for Adam, not Eve, is the establisher of household law.

The seriousness of this personal fall is indicated by its connection with the fall of man in his relations with God. Adam's initial virtuous responses to Eve's arguments contain correct guesses of Satan's tactics. Adam's guess that Satan is "somewhere nigh at hand" (9. 256–57) and that he might use "Some specious object . . . suborned" by him (9. 361) fits Satan's inhabiting of the serpent. Adam's guess that Satan has a "greedy hope" of finding him and Eve "asunder" (9. 257–60) is corroborated by Satan's happiness at finding Eve alone. Adam's guess that Satan would like "to withdraw / [Their] feälty from God, or to disturb / Conjugal love" (9. 261–64) foretells the two steps in Satan's seduction of Eve, and Adam's warning of the danger of surprise by a "fair appearing good" (9. 354–55) and his warning that the seducer of angels must be "Subtle" (9. 307–8) foretell Satan's stratagem in praising the powers of the apple, and the strength of the arguments that he builds upon his premise. On the other hand, Eve's confident last arguments contrast ironically with the truth; for her boasted awareness does not prepare her for the surprise of a speaking serpent (9. 551–52) ; her assurance that Satan's pride will prevent his tempting her first, contrasts ironically with Satan's joy in finding an easy victim; and her confidence in her powers contrasts with her later susceptibility to heresy. Adam's failure to insist upon his insights prevents the frustration of Satan, and Eve's personal sins play into his hands.

There is a suggestion of a connection between the personal failure of Adam and Eve and their susceptibility to failure in the religious sphere. When Satan makes his personal seduction, Eve's reactions are inadequate to the occasion. In response to the serpent's encouragement to usurp Adam's authority, Eve only mildly protests, saying that the serpent's rationality is rendered suspect by his overestimation of her place, his "overpraising" (9. 615–16) ; and in response to his attempt to separate her from Adam's love, she remarks only that he is more "friendly" than the other beasts (9. 563–65) . The inadequacy of these replies to the improprieties in the speeches must be due to the fact that Satan's immoralities appeal to the insubordination and selfish neglect to which Eve has already yielded. Eve's main responses to the serpent's assault are the responses that lead to her religious fall: she is surprised at the serpent's power of speech ("What may this mean? Language of man pronounced / By tongue of brute, and human sense expressed?" [9. 553–61]) and she is curious about the magic tree ("But say, where grows the tree, from hence how far?" [9. 617–24]). Had Eve been properly reverent toward her husband, she would have been repelled by the serpent's attitude toward her, and therefore more wary of the talking beast and his tale. As to Adam, there is more than pathos in the description of his wait for Eve. While Eve, in conformity with her fault, is carefree (9. 431–33) and absorbed with her flowers (9. 424–31), Adam is anxious about Eve, full of misgivings (9. 845–46), and, as his making of a garland reveals (9. 838–42), he is lonely for her. These feelings contribute to the passionate overvaluation of Eve whereby Adam falls in his relationship to God; the feelings are the product of an absence which Adam should never have permitted.

The second stage after the pair's state of perfection resembles their rebellion against God in three respects: first, in that the violations of the law initiated during the fall become dogma; second, in that the new dogma leads to disharmony; and third, in that the validity of the dogma is disproved. The personal relationship of Adam and Eve is examined here under two conditions, prosperity and adversity. The first is treated during the period of intoxication which follows the pair's eating of the fruit; the second is treated in the quarrel which follows the onset of shame.

In the second section of her soliloquy after eating the forbidden fruit, Eve, debating whether or not to give the apple to Adam, becomes confirmed in the attitudes initiated earlier: [13]

> *But to Adam in what sort*
> *Shall I appear? Shall I to him make known*
> *As yet my change, and give him to partake*
> *Full happiness with me, or rather not,*
> *But keep the odds of knowledge in my power*
> *Without copartner? so to add what wants*
> *In female sex, the more to draw his love,*

And render me more equal, and perhaps,
A thing not undesirable, sometime
Superior; for inferior who is free?
This may be well. But what if God have seen
And death ensue? then I shall be no more,
And Adam wedded to another Eve,
Shall live with her enjoying, I extinct;
A death to think. Confirmed then I resolve
Adam shall share with me in bliss or woe.
So dear I love him, that with him all deaths
I could endure, without him live no life.

(*9. 816–33*)

As the third step in this internal debate, Eve discards obedience. Whereas before the fall she falsely professed obedience, now she desires superior knowledge in order to be free of Adam's commands. The second step in the debate is a revolt against Adam's superiority. In accord with her previous desire for a superiority all her own, Eve considers rivaling Adam in his own sphere of wisdom.

Love, however, is the aspect of Eve's life most thoroughly perverted. Though Eve begins her debate with the thought of revealing her discovery to Adam, when she uses the words "make known" for her disclosure, she shows that she considers herself superior by virtue of her hidden knowledge ("tell" would carry no such implication), and when she uses the words "give him to partake" to describe her act of dividing the apple with Adam, she shows that she considers herself superior by virtue of her possession ("share" would carry no such suggestion). Thus even in the most selfless thought which occurs to her, Eve reveals less a loving concern for Adam's welfare than an egotistical enjoyment of her own bounty. Previously Eve imitated love to win approval from Adam; now she imitates it to congratulate herself. After the two intervening arguments against sharing the apple, Eve returns to her initial position in her fourth argument, where, horrified to think that Adam will enjoy a second wife if she alone dies, she decides that he must "share with [her] in bliss or woe." Earlier, Eve pursued her own pleasure without considering Adam. Now she first of all begrudges Adam a pleasure which she cannot share, with a jealousy which is uncommon, since many dying wives begrudge a husband's remarriage, but few poison him to prevent that remarriage. And secondly, she is now willing to sacrifice Adam for her own benefit, since she thinks of Adam's company as a means for making her own death tolerable. In the close of her internal debate, Eve praises herself for her love of Adam. When she says that she could bear "all deaths" with him, however, she is misrepresenting her situation, for she is not joining Adam in danger, as the words imply, but causing Adam to share her danger; and when she says that she could "live no life" without him, she is misrepresenting both her situation and the reasons for her decision regarding him. Here Eve is deceiving herself into believing that her sacrifice of Adam is an act of love, adding self-deception to the self-congratulation with which she opened the debate.

The self-concern which permeates this section of Eve's speech is summed up in the question which opens it: "But to Adam in what sort / Shall I appear?" Eve is contemplating herself, rather than thinking of her husband.

This self-concern does not change when Eve confronts Adam himself. The apology which opens Eve's seduction speech is a response to what Eve surmises to be Adam's feelings (she has his expression and his gift as clues) :

> Hast thou not wondered, Adam, at my stay?
> Thee I have missed, and thought it long, deprived
> Thy presence, agony of love till now
> Not felt, nor shall be twice, for never more
> Mean I to try what rash untried I sought,
> The pain of absence from thy sight.
>
> (9. 856–61)

When Eve apologizes for her disobedience by promising not to repeat her absence, she reveals that she is aware of Adam's worry and disapproval, and she shows her failure to repent by the conflict of the obedience she expresses with her actual desire for freedom from command. When she tells how much she has missed Adam, she reveals by her description her awareness of Adam's feelings of loneliness, and shows her failure to care about her neglect of her husband by the contrast between the "agony" she professes and her actual absorption with the ordering of her flowers before the arrival of the serpent. By the pretense of repudiating her conduct at the time of the fall, Eve reiterates and aggravates her offenses, feigning obedience and neglecting love with what are now conscious lies designed to win Adam over.

Eve returns to personal appeals at the end of her speech (9. 877–85). When she claims that she has taken the apple for Adam's sake and wants no happiness unshared, she restates the question in her soliloquy as to whether she should tell Adam of her discovery and should let him share her happiness. When she asks Adam to share her "lot" and "joy," she restates her earlier claim that her love makes her wish to share death and life with him. When she warns Adam that they may be separated by her ascent, she restates her fear of losing Adam by her death. Comparison of the restatements with their originals reveals the extent to which Eve exaggerates her concern for Adam and conceals her fear of dying alone; she puts into action the sacrifice of Adam which she contemplated before, and she conceals this activity with a simulation of love which is now a conscious lie. Eve's awareness of the duplicity in her personal appeals accounts for the blush which accompanies her speech (9. 887).

Eve's speech before Adam's eating of the apple is not, like her seduction speech, insincere, since she is moved by Adam's decision, but it is no less self-concerned. In the center of her speech, after encouraging Adam to neglect God's love, and before encouraging him to disregard God's wrath, Eve inserts references to the personal relationships of herself and Adam. She praises the fruit for providing a test of Adam's love, "which else / So eminently never had been known" (9. 973–76), and she claims that if she believed in the deadliness of the fruit, she would rather die alone than ask Adam to share her danger (9. 977–83). The first statement reveals a self-congratulation like that in Eve's thoughts of her beneficence in sharing her discovery with Adam: she plays the Petrarchan mistress giving her servant an opportunity to prove his worth. The second statement is not a lie, even though it is belied by Eve's earlier thoughts on the intolerableness of dying alone, for in this speech Eve is emotional rather than calculating. Nevertheless, the statement reveals the same combination of self-congratulation and self-deception that was present at the end of her soliloquy, when she boasted the depth of her love for Adam.

In the second section of his speech after eating the apple, Adam joins Eve in the dedication to the principles of the fall:

> *But come; so well refreshed, now let us play,*
> *As meet is, after such delicious fare;*
> *For never did thy beauty since the day*
> *I saw thee first and wedded thee, adorned*
> *With all perfections, so inflame my sense*
> *With ardor to enjoy thee, fairer now*
> *Than ever, bounty of this virtuous tree.*
>
> (9. 1027–33)

Adam violates the rules whereby he is supposed to govern. During the fall, Adam misrepresented the nature of freedom; now, with his suggestion of "play[ing]," he upsets the ordered life of work, intermission, and sleep which he interpreted for Eve in ending their earlier day's labor. Adam also violates the requirements of love. In falling, Adam failed to show sufficient concern for Eve's moral status. Now, by the emphasis that he places on her beauty, Adam disregards her moral nature altogether; and in his reference to the effects which that beauty has upon him, he denies Eve even an objective admiration of her external qualities, thinking instead of his own sensory pleasure.

The union that results from fallen principles under comfortable conditions is a union based upon mutually compatible vice. The shared lust of Adam and Eve which figures in the epitomizing of their rebellious state is the symbol for this kind of unity.

The shame which is the foretaste of divine judgment serves to test the relationship. Adam defends his conduct in two ways. First, he tries to evade God's warning by external means, by covering himself and Eve to forestall shame (10. 1091–98) ; and second, he seeks to prove his own uprightness by blaming Eve (9. 1134–42) . When he says here that insistence on proving loyalty is a sign of failure, Adam restates the argument that loyalty should be proved by obedience, the argument which climaxed his third speech in the morning quarrel. When he condemns the search for trials of faith, he recalls an argument from his third speech, the argument against seeking temptation by which he rebuked Eve's failure to acknowledge his superiority. He repeats, in addition, the rejection of Eve's presented plan which he made in the first speech; and in blaming Eve for having brought ruin with her plan, he recalls his contention that unity would avert trouble and encourage resistance to evil, the burden of his second speech. In short, Adam recalls the virtuous parts of his speeches during the morning quarrel —all his virtuous exhortations to obedience, humility, love, and awe—in order to prove that all adversity must be attributed to Eve. He omits, however, the part of the argument in which he demonstrated his blameworthy neglect, and he increases his guilt by his present lack of guidance and love.

Eve thereupon follows Adam's lead. Finding Adam neither guide nor lover, she justifies herself (9. 1144–61) by shifting blame to Adam, as he has shifted blame to her. When she condemns Adam for not commanding her to stay, Eve points out the element of his conduct that Adam failed to mention. When she says that the serpent's argument and the situation would have fooled Adam, she doubts his superiority, and she uses against Adam the premises of his own arguments against seeking temptation, his references to the danger of surprisal by "some fair appearing good" and to deception through "Some specious object by the foe suborned." By claiming that staying by Adam would be as bad as remaining a "lifeless rib," Eve accuses Adam of a selfishness in refusing her plan like hers when she decided that it would be better for Adam to die than for him to have a happiness apart from her. And in arguing that the serpent might have approached them both or approached Adam first with like ruinous results, Eve refuses to be shamed, using against Adam two points in his own argument, that an attack on the two of them would fall on Adam first, and that a repulse of Satan's subtlety would require the encouragement provided by a witness. What Eve does is cast doubt on Adam's worth through citation of the arguments by which he was claiming merit, in order to prove that all adversity is Adam's fault, and that the plight is due not to her plan but to chance, the serpent's accidental meeting with her rather than with Adam. Eve's charge of neglected rule is as just as Adam's claim of virtue, but her doubts of Adam's superiority, of his love, and of his justice in shaming her are as blameworthy as Adam's failure to mention his irresponsibility; and by these aspersions, Eve aggravates the faults of her fall.

At this point Adam has to face an open challenge to his superiority, and all he can do (9. 1163–82) is to insist more loudly and more invalidly upon his worth. He claims to have performed his duty to explain God's law, and in so claiming he repeats the heretical explanation of freedom from his third speech in the morning quarrel. He cites Eve's confident parting speech in order to prove her disobedience to command, but fails to acknowledge that his own surrender preceded her speech. He admits overvaluing Eve, but his admission is not a way of taking responsibility for his insufficient concern for her, but rather a means of disparaging her—as is clear from the fact that he immediately condemns Eve for having questioned his conduct. Adam begins his speech by trying to shame Eve, pointing to the contradiction between her present reproach and the earlier tribute in which she swore that she would rather die than cause the death of one so devoted to her. But by claiming that he could have lived happily without her, Adam contradicts his own equivalent to her tribute, the declaration with which he concluded his speech before eating the apple, his statement that he could not live without her. The fact that Adam commits the same fault for which he blames Eve indicates that his motive in speaking is not to correct her, but to win the fight; thus he misuses his power to awe in the same way that Eve misused shame during her fall.

Having in this way weakened both his case and his relationship with Eve, Adam proceeds to a moralizing summary:

> *Thus it shall befall*
> *Him who to worth in women overtrusting*
> *Lets her will rule; restraint she will not*
> *brook,*
> *And left to herself, if evil thence ensue,*
> *She first his weak indulgence will accuse.*
> *(9. 1182–86)*

In the generalizations of this summary, Adam refers to the specific conduct of himself and Eve. The words "restraint she will not brook" generalize Adam's claim that Eve persisted despite all his explanations. His reference to the man who "Lets [woman's] will rule" generalizes his complaint that Eve disobeyed his command. His reference to the man who is "overtrusting" generalizes Adam's disparaging confession with regard to Eve. And the words

"She . . . his weak indulgence will accuse" generalize the pro-
tests against Eve's reproaches with which Adam tried to shame
her. By the process of generalization, Adam blows up his experi-
ence into the experience of all his descendants, and turns himself
into the type of the mistreated husband. His self-contemplation
balances Eve's consideration of the "sort" in which she should
appear to Adam, this stage of the pair's development closing as it
opened, on a note of self-concern.

When Adam and Eve in their new relationship are confronted
by adversity, then, incurable disharmony results. What this dis-
harmony proves is that only the God-given pattern for human
relationships can produce a lasting harmony between people; the
attitudes which Adam and Eve adopt in their rebellion against
God's pattern are invalidated by the results.

The third stage after the pair's state of perfection resembles
their repentance in relation to God. First of all, as in the religious
sphere, Adam and Eve undo their fall by repenting. Secondly, the
general pattern used in the religious repentance recurs here: the
pair begin in a state of relapse, but thereafter exert their minds
and consciences in a repudiation of their fallen condition.
Thirdly, the tyranny that marks Adam's state of relapse is related
to the lack of reason and conscience which characterizes man in
his ungraced state. This stage of the pair's development begins
with Adam's rejection of penitent Eve, and ends with his accept-
ance of her.

The initial state of relapse is seen in the denunciation of Eve
that follows Adam's lament. There Adam reveals his tendency to
become a tyrant, repeating his fall on a lower level.

The kind of tyranny that is displayed by Adam fits the negative
nature of his sins against Eve. Instead of claiming divine power
over her, Adam asserts his domination by denying Eve's human-
ity; he achieves the tyrant's elevation over his followers not by
claiming to be God in relation to a human, but by being a human
in relation to what he claims is an animal. In his diatribe, Adam
begins with a dismissal of Eve which stresses her lack of humanity
(10. 867–73). By calling Eve a serpent "leagued" with the ser-
pent, Adam denies her claim to his authority, asserting that her
fealty has been pledged elsewhere. By arguing that Eve deserves
"shape" and "color serpentine" as a sign of "inward fraud," Adam

denies her claim to human love, since love is responsive to beauty
and to worth; and he emphasizes this denial when he calls Eve's
body "too heavenly": he suggests that Eve's true status is belied by
a form resembling the form of angels. This degradation of Eve
Adam continues in the third section of his speech (10. 888–95).
By his suggestions for a human race without women, Adam gen-
eralizes his disavowal of Eve's relationship to himself, and by his
characterization of woman as a "fair defect," he generalizes his
charge that Eve is not worthy of love. And Adam now adds a
corollary; his thesis, that God should have made mankind entirely
masculine, generalizes what is implied in his denunciation of Eve,
that he alone is the representative of humankind. By unwarrant-
edly debasing Eve, Adam can claim superiority without having
to assume the responsibility that goes with rightful superiority in
human relationships; for a man does not owe guidance and love
to an animal. Thus when Adam, sending Eve away, repeats and
worsens the sin he committed when he allowed her to set out
alone, he does so with an assumption of righteousness.

The fact that Adam is unrepentant in the face of evidence of
failure is made obvious in the second section of his speech, in
which he resumes his afternoon's attack on Eve:

> But for thee
> I had persisted happy, had not thy pride
> And wandering vanity, when least was safe,
> Rejected my forewarning, and disdained
> Not to be trusted, longing to be seen
> Though by the Devil himself, him overweening
> To overreach, but with the Serpent meeting
> Fooled and beguiled, by him thou, I by thee,
> To trust thee from my side, imagined wise,
> Constant, mature, proof against all assaults,
> And understood not all was but a show
> Rather than solid virtue, all but a rib
> Crooked by nature, bent, as now appears,
> More to the part sinister from me drawn;
> Well if thrown out, as supernumerary
> To my just number found.
> (10. 873–88)

In parts of this denunciation, Adam makes direct attacks upon the speeches that Eve made in falling, instead of, as before, dwelling on his own correctness. When he speaks of Eve's rejecting of his "forewarning," he condemns her parting speech in the morning quarrel; when he speaks of her desire "to be seen / . . . by the Devil," he condemns her third speech, in which, aspiring beyond her place, she spoke of the honor to be gained by trial. Eve's neglect of love he touches upon in his reference to her "pride / And wandering vanity"—he refers to the proposal which she made in her first speech and insisted upon thereafter; and when he says that Eve "disdained / Not to be trusted," he recalls her improper attempt to shame him during her second speech. In parts of the denunciation, on the other hand, Adam merely repeats ideas from his speeches of the afternoon. "But for thee / I had persisted happy" recalls Adam's claim, in his second condemnatory speech, that he could "have lived and joyed immortal bliss" without Eve; and the phrase "wandering vanity" recalls the earlier phrase "Desire of wandering," which Adam applied to Eve's plan in his first condemnatory speech. Finally, when Adam tells how he was "Fooled" by Eve, he makes revisions upon his earlier admission of having "erred." He omits what partial confession of blame was present in that confession, and greatly expands the element of deprecation, even going so far as to deny his marriage vow in order to deny that Eve is worth loving. For when Adam says that Eve was extracted from the "sinister" side, he negates the allegory by which he claimed her love: he told her then that she had been extracted from the side "nearest [his] heart" (4. 483–85). All this vituperation—new, old, and revised—constitutes a reaffirmation of Adam's policy of shifting blame from himself to Eve, a policy whose earlier pursuit accomplished nothing but an unending discord.

The increasing absurdity into which Adam is plunged by his failure to repent is evident in the arguments and the likely consequences of his speech. Adam's denial of Eve's humanity is contrary to reason. Adam in the despair of his lament says that he is "To Satan only like"; he also admits the moral changes which have accompanied his fall. Thus he cannot impugn Eve's humanity for her league with the serpent nor deny her right to human form because of her lack of virtue; both have sinned, and neither can claim superiority from the other's fault. Adam's wish for a masculine human race like, he says, the race of angels is foolish in that the angels are no more masculine than feminine, as Adam knows from Raphael's description of angelic love (8. 622–29), and in that, even if the angels were masculine, the masculinity of Satan and Beelzebub did not prevent their corruption. Furthermore, Adam's extended deprecation of Eve on the basis of her origin is foolish. Adam cannot infer a wrong woman from a "bent" rib, a "sinister" woman from a rib on the left, a despicable woman from a "supernumerary" rib without deducing a vile man from one made (as Raphael has told him) of the "Dust of the ground" (7. 524–25).

The domestic evils which Adam attributes to women in the final section of his diatribe convict him of irrationality. If women had not been created, he says,

> *This mischief had not then befallen,*
> *And more that shall befall, innumerable*
> *Disturbances on Earth through female snares,*
> *And strait conjunction with this sex. For*
> *   either*
> *He never shall find out fit mate, but such*
> *As some misfortune brings him, or mistake,*
> *Or whom he wishes most shall seldom gain,*
> *Through her perverseness, but shall see her*
> *   gained*
> *By a far worse, or if she love, withheld*
> *By parents, or his happiest choice too late*
> *Shall meet, already linked and wedlock-bound*
> *To a fell adversary, his hate or shame;*
> *Which infinite calamity shall cause*
> *To human life, and household peace confound.*
>
> (*10. 895–908*)

In the first place, all the troubles that Adam envisions as befalling men because of women are troubles totally inapplicable to his relationship with Eve: with Eve Adam has had no problem of choosing a wife, of winning a wife, of meeting rivalry, of gaining permission to marry, of loving a married woman. In the end of his second speech in the afternoon's altercation, Adam generalized

Eve's action and pitied himself for like suffering in his descend-
ants. Now he goes one step further and banishes Eve for crimes
which are not generalized from her actions, but which he only
imagines, and he pities himself for sufferings which are not only
not his, but which are not even within the range of his possible
experience. In the second place, Adam judges these imagined
problems by inconsistent standards. Women are blamed if a man
marries through "misfortune" or "mistake," but men are not
blamed if a woman has the misfortune to marry before she meets
her most fit mate or if she mistakenly marries the lesser of two
men. Finally, Adam is so busy denouncing Eve for the imagined
faults of other women in the future that he does not stop to
check his accusations by the real and present Eve, who had ap-
proached him (10. 864), offering her service, and has tried to
comfort him (10. 865), offering her love.

Not only are Adam's arguments at fault, however, but his rejec-
tion of Eve is absurd from the standpoint of its likely conse-
quences. If Eve before her defection from God made sorry use of
her solitariness, she would not be likely in her fallen state to make
better use of the absence which Adam here tries to force upon her.
What she would be likely to do is to kill herself, as Adam should
be able to guess from the despairing moments of his own lament,
and as Eve's suggestion for remedying their plight later confirms.
Such an action would (as Adam later says) bring catastrophic
results.

After this initial state of relapse, Adam and Eve work toward
repentance, undoing their fall. Eve makes the first step (10. 914–
36), correcting her relationship with Adam by her suit for peace.
First of all, by his speech Eve meets Adam's allegations against
her. In answer to Adam's charge that she disregarded his counsel,
she asks how she can live apart from that counsel. In reply to his
accusation that she wished to exhibit herself before Satan, Eve
seeks unity with Adam against the serpent. She pleads her humble
love and unintentional sin in reply to Adam's condemnation of
her "wandering vanity" and his supplementary proclamations of
her worthlessness. Finally, by admitting that she has sinned, Eve
counters Adam's denunciation of her lack of awe in "disdain[ing] /
Not to be trusted."

More importantly, however, Eve by her plea recants the errors
in her fall, and submits herself to the authority and care which

she earlier denied. Her reluctance to leave recants the willingness to leave voiced in her final speech in the morning quarrel, and returns her to the rule which Adam urged in that quarrel. Her desire for union against the serpent reverses her proclamation of the advantages to be obtained from an unaccompanied confrontation with evil, and constitutes a request for Adam's aid, in conformity with Adam's advice on the advantages of shared judgment in preventing error. By her denial of intention to harm, Eve proclaims an interest in Adam's welfare contrary to the neglect evident in her first speech in the quarrel, during which she presented her plan; her proclamation of love for Adam recants the denigration of love with which she ended that speech, and her humble and sincere plea for aid recants the merely tactful request for advice with which she opened the speech. By this behavior, Eve conforms to the example set by Adam in his first speech—the concern he demonstrated, the love he defended, the appreciation he expressed for her accomplishments. Finally, by mentioning her sin against both God and Adam, Eve recants her reproach to Adam for suspecting her fidelity to God and him, and by her offer to ask God to place blame upon her alone, Eve confesses her blame in having rejected both Adam's expressed desire to keep her from attack and his reproach for neglecting the encouragement to virtue provided by witness in a time of trial.

The first section of Adam's reply, his refutation, serves to undo the surrender to Eve's persistence which marked his participation in the fall of their personal relationship:

> *Unwary, and too desirous, as before,*
> *So now, of what thou knowst not, who desirest*
> *The punishment all on thyself; alas,*
> *Bear thine own first, ill able to sustain*
> *His full wrath whose thou feel'st as yet least*
>   *part,*
> *And my displeasure bear'st so ill. If prayers*
> *Could alter high decrees, I to that place*
> *Would speed before thee, and be louder heard,*
> *That on my head all might be visited,*
> *Thy frailty and infirmer sex forgiven,*
> *To me committed and by me exposed.*
>
>   *(10. 947–57)*

By explaining the presumption in Eve's plan, and likening it to the presumption in her desire for trial, Adam takes over his responsibility to explain God's laws to Eve, undoing the heresy whereby he abnegated this task during the fall. And by encouraging restraint, Adam governs Eve's conduct, instead of, as in his fall, letting her do what she chooses. Adam's statement of his guilt in exposing his wife to danger serves as valid confession of error in his overtrusting of Eve, a confession which acknowledges his insufficient concern for her welfare. (Incidentally, this rebuttal of Eve's argument is intended to contrast with Adam's unjust repulse of Eve: here Adam takes charge of Eve, rather than disposing of her; corrects her for her own good, rather than disparaging her in order to exonerate himself; and makes a just assessment of her present conduct, rather than totally damning her on the basis of prediction and with oblivion to her present state.)

Though the second section of Adam's speech (10. 958–65) does not relate to his speeches during the fall, it does serve to repudiate his tyrannical dismissal of Eve, and seals the peace lost during the fall. In place of the contemptuous rejection which opened his diatribe, Adam now asks for an end of fighting. Instead of resuming an endless series of accusations, he asks for a cessation of blame, and by noting the guilt of himself and Eve before God, he ends their attempts to exonerate themselves by blaming one another. By his final proposal of mutual love in the face of the sorrows ordained for them and their children, Adam replaces the predicted mishaps of his diatribe with suggestions for a loving household, and replaces the imagined and misattributed problems with an appraisal of present and deserved distress.

The seriousness of the personal fall was indicated by its connection with the fall in relation to God; the repentance of Adam and Eve in their personal relationship is important for its connection with their repentance in regard to God. For this second turning point in the development of Adam and Eve, the reversal of the progressive decline which began with their fall, comes with Eve's penitent speech to Adam; and Eve's humility and renewal of affection set the pattern for the pair's return to God.

The final stage in the development of the personal relationship of Adam and Eve resembles their regeneration in relation to God, in that the pair reverse their condition during their rebellion,

and end in a state of restoration. This stage of the pair's develop-
ment is interwoven with the three scenes of their religious regen-
eration—the first of these serving as a preliminary exposition of
character, the second showing Adam's growth, the third revealing
the pair's final state.

The speeches that precede Michael's prophecy serve both to
mark the advances that Adam and Eve have made and to suggest
the possibility of further improvement.

In their opening speeches, Adam and Eve repudiate their treat-
ment of one another during their rebellion. Adam ends his speech
with a personal address to his wife:

> [*H*]*ail to thee,*
> *Eve rightly called, Mother of all Mankind,*
> *Mother of all things living, since by thee*
> *Man is to live, and all things live for Man.*
> (*11. 158–61*)

In this address Adam restores Eve to the status of lawful wife,
mother of his children, and thereby reverses his attitude during
the rebellion, when by thinking of Eve's beauty in isolation from
all other qualities, he reduced her to his whore. Eve makes a cor-
responding return to domestic propriety at the end of her reply to
Adam. Having retracted the principal speeches of her rebellion,
touching, in her tribute to Adam's mercy (11. 169–71), upon her
betrayal of him in the soliloquy which followed her eating of the
fruit, Eve at the end of her speech inserts a personal pledge to
Adam:

> [*L*]*et us forth,*
> *I never from thy side henceforth to stray,*
> *Where'er our day's work lies, though now*
> *enjoined*
> *Laborious, till day droop.*
> (*11. 175–78*)

Eve's promise to stay beside Adam reverses her earlier assertion
that staying beside him would be worse than remaining a "lifeless
rib"; and by suggesting that they set out together, Eve reverses the

plan of divided labor which she defended with her assertion.

The tendency to sin which remains in Adam and Eve and which requires purification is suggested in Eve's response to Michael's announcement that the pair have been banished from Eden. After her initial reproach to God, Eve laments her loss, and in so doing, she neglects Adam because of her attraction to beauty, as in her fall:

> [*T*]*hus* [*must I*]
> *leave*
> *Thee native soil, these happy walks and shades,*
> *Fit haunt of Gods? where I had hope to spend,*
> *Quiet though sad, the respite of that day*
> *That must be mortal to us both. O flowers,*
> *That never will in other climate grow,*
> *My early visitation, and my last*
> *At even, which I bred up with tender hand*
> *From the first opening bud, and gave ye names,*
> *Who now shall rear ye to the sun, or rank*
> *Your tribes, and water from the ambrosial fount?*
> *Thee lastly nupital bower, by me adorned*
> *With what to sight or smell was sweet; from thee*
> *How shall I part, and whither wander down*
> *Into a lower world, to this obscure*
> *And wild, how shall we breathe in other air*
> *Less pure, accustomed to immortal fruits?*
>   (*11. 269–85*)

After pledging her love to Adam, Eve added a consoling reminder of the pleasantness of life in Eden:

> [*W*]*hile here we dwell,*
> *What can be toilsome in these pleasant walks?*
> *Here let us live, though in fallen state,*
>   *content.*
>   (*11. 178–80*)

Now, in her reference to "happy walks and shades," Eve recalls her earlier statement, and she laments her loss without considering Adam's company as a mitigating circumstance. Furthermore, when Eve laments her flowers, she shows them the favor which suggested to her the plan of gardening apart from Adam. Finally, when Eve laments her bridal bower, she values for its own sake her activity in decking it, instead of thinking of her aesthetic activity as a means of serving Adam; for the bower ought to be important as an expression of Eve's love for her husband. This misvaluation is evident in the final reasons which Eve gives for her reluctance to leave Eden. When she calls the outside world "obscure / And wild," she is thinking of its color and composition in comparison with the bower, decorated with everything beautiful "to sight." When she protests that she will not be able to "breathe in other air / Less pure," she is again thinking of the bower, decorated with everything sweet "to . . . smell." Thus she uses her bower as a standard of beauty, ignoring its significance. When Michael reminds Eve that her home is wherever Adam dwells (11. 290–92), his remarks are directed at the domestic fault revealed in her complaint.

During the scene in which Adam is tested and educated through Michael's prophecy, his tendency to lapse is revealed and corrected. After his praise for the marriage of the descendants of Seth and Cain, praise which reveals his primary weakness in regard to God, Adam reveals his weakness in regard to Eve; in response to Michael's explanations regarding the marriage, Adam remarks, "But still I see the tenor of Man's woe / Holds on the same, from Woman to begin" (11. 632–33). He reverts here to his altercation with Eve, blaming her in order to exonerate himself. Michael's rebuke, that the fault lies in "Man's effeminate slackness" (11. 634), points out the connection between Adam's central domestic fault, his failure to exert his duty of command, and his later irresponsibility in blaming Eve for his own weakness.

During the final passages of the poem, in which the regeneration of Adam and Eve is demonstrated, the restoration of the pair's personal relationship is also shown. Adam, prominent in theological matters, is only touched on in this regard; but the bitterness toward women which he expressed to Michael is shown to be absent from his final feelings toward Eve: Adam is "Well pleased" with the speech (12. 624–25) by which Eve reveals her final religious and personal state.

Eve's final words, on the other hand, are primarily devoted to

her relationship with her husband. Her tribute to Adam shows
that she has overcome the last weaknesses revealed in her lament:

> [W]*ith thee to go,*
> *Is to stay here; without thee here to stay,*
> *Is to go hence unwilling; thou to me*
> *Art all things under Heaven, all places thou,*
> *Who for my wilful crime art banished hence.*
>   (*12. 615–19*)

Eve's expressed desire to stay with Adam corrects her earlier error
in overvaluing the Garden and forgetting the consolation pro-
vided by Adam's company. When Eve says that Adam is "all
things" to her, she alludes to her former regrets for her flowers,
and when she says that he is "all places," she alludes to her re-
grets for her bower; here Eve ranks aesthetic feelings below hu-
man love. Finally, when she recalls her blame for the expulsion,
Eve recants the expressions of reluctance which ended her lament.
She replaces protests with acknowledgment of her sins against
her husband, and she thinks not of her own loss of aesthetic
pleasure, but of her husband's loss of his home.

In the end, then, Adam and Eve are sent forth not only recon-
ciled to God and saved, but restored in their relation to one
another.

The moral development of Adam and Eve, measured by their
response to God's attributes of authority and goodness, consists,
then, of a preliminary state and four subsequent stages which cor-
relate with the four offices of God. During the preliminary state,
the state of innocence, Adam and Eve demonstrate their duty and
virtue. Thereafter they fall by breaking the laws of God the cre-
ator and lawgiver, then rebel against God the judge. But, with the
help of God's grace, they repent, and then are regenerated through
the Savior's gifts of reconciliation and salvation. This moral de-
cline and reascension in relation to God is matched by a decline
and reascension in personal relationships. Adam and Eve begin in
a relationship whose perfection matches the perfection of their
initial relation to God, but a personal fall accompanies their reli-
gious fall, and there follow stages analogous to their rebellion,
repentance, and regeneration. Furthermore, the two realms are
shown to be interconnected; whatever affects the creature's rela-

tions with other creatures for better or worse, affects the crea-
ture's relations with God for better or worse, and the creature's
relations with God affect his relations with other creatures. This
development, with its initial state and its four subsequent stages,
makes up the main plot of *Paradise Lost*.

4

The Minor Elements

IN ADDITION to the major elements of *Paradise Lost*—the secondary plot and the main plot—there are two minor elements which require examination, the minor characters and the expository episode, Michael's prophecy.

The first group of minor characters, the loyal angels, demonstrate the moral virtue intended for God's creatures: whereas all other creatures change in their relationship to God, the loyal angels remain in a constant state of innocence; and whereas all other creatures lapse from the duty and virtue expected as responses to God's authority and goodness, the loyal angels triumph in the trials of their resistance to evil. From these two qualities come their two general functions in *Paradise Lost*—to contrast in their unchangeableness with the change of other characters, and to provide examples of the sort of conduct necessary for the preservation of innocence.

The contrast of the unchanging angels with other characters is accomplished by their appearance at each stage of those characters' development. The angels praise God for his creation of the earth (7. 602–32) in contrast to Adam and Eve in their later ingratitude. (Abdiel similarly contrasts with the fallen angels, but his conduct at the time of their fall has a further and more important meaning.) After the fall of man, the angels guarding Eden plead their innocence before God (10. 17–31) and are pronounced guiltless (10. 34–37) in contrast to the guilty resistance of the rebellious Adam and Eve. Likewise, after the fall of the angels, Abdiel, pronounced guiltless by God (6. 29–37), contrasts with the defiant angels in that trial by combat that constitutes their judgment by the Son. During the opening assembly in heaven, the angels hymn God for the "pity" with which he has extended his grace to man (3. 400–402); they contrast here both with man and with the fallen angels—with man in that they retain the state of innocence which requires no grace; with the fallen angels in that they possess that state which, it is shown, the fallen angels have lost, and, lacking grace, are unable to regain. Finally, the loyal angels are summoned from their "blissful bowers" to hear the fate decreed for man regenerated (11. 72–125), and so are contrasted in their happy state with Adam and Eve, upon whom falls the mitigated penalty of expulsion from the Garden. And when God reveals that the angels have watched the transformation of the fallen angels and have thus been "confirmed" in their "state" (11. 68–71), he contrasts their unchanging loyalty with the fatuousness of the degenerated angels, blamed earlier for their false belief that they had defeated him (10. 616–40). By their appearance at every stage in the stories of the fallen creatures, the loyal angels recall that unchanging state of innocence which God intended for all his creatures.

Three incidents involving the loyal angels stand apart from the others as tests of the angels' ability to resist evil. These incidents are the confrontation of Abdiel and Michael with Satan during the war in heaven, the encounter of the angels guarding earth with Satan during his first visit to earth, and the confrontation of Abdiel with Satan during the angels' fall. Each of these tests focuses on a different aspect of resistance, the first dealing with the refutation of heresy, the second with the controversion of guile, and the third with the conduct expected of a creature in a time of conflicting loyalties.

Abdiel and Michael successfully combat Satan's heresy. Abdiel in his two speeches answers Satan's arguments about God's authority, his first speech containing the proper denial of Satan's argument on monarchy. In contrast to Satan's claim that angels can establish their own laws by vote, Abdiel asserts that it is God's pronouncements, not majority opinion, that determine what is law; when he says that "few sometimes may know," he refers to those who obey God's laws, while the "thousands" who "err" (6. 148) are those, however many, who disobey. Abdiel also extolls those who "faith / Prefer, and piety to God" (6. 143–44), offsetting Satan's argument that angels owe obedience not to God but to fellow creatures. In his second speech, Abdiel refutes Satan's arguments on freedom:

> *Unjustly thou depravest it with the name*
> *Of servitude to serve whom God ordains,*
> *Or Nature; God and Nature bid the same,*
> *When he who rules is worthiest, and excels*
> *Them whom he governs. This is servitude,*
> *To serve the unwise, or him who hath rebelled*
> *Against his worthier, as thine now serve thee,*
> *Thyself not free, but to thyself enthralled;*
> *Yet lewdly darest our ministering upbraid.*
>
> *(6. 174–82)*

By arguing that it is not servility to obey a superior, Abdiel replies to one of Satan's arguments, that it is servile to choose to obey, and in so doing he denies, by implication, that angelic freedom is freedom from external control. By calling angelic service "ministering," Abdiel implies, furthermore, that angels choose obedience, and therefore suggests that freedom means the freedom to choose whether or not to obey. In addition, by calling Satan self-enslaved, Abdiel replies to the second of Satan's arguments, that angels can uphold their laws by force. Abdiel suggests that what Satan demonstrates is not strength, but rather the weakness of a creature who, having once chosen to disobey, is no longer free to reverse himself. And by defining servitude as the service of the "unwise" or of a rebel, he asserts that the defecting angels are also weak, in that they have failed to choose obedience in defiance either of the foolishly or the willfully disobedient. Abdiel defends God's divine superiority as well as his rule. In his first speech (6. 131–42), he asserts the folly of Satan's deprecations of God's powers, and defends God's attributes of omnipotence ("vain," he says, to oppose), of creativity (God could, he says, have "raised incessant armies to defeat" Satan), and of control (God could have degraded Satan and his armies "at one blow," he says).

Michael properly answers Satan's denial of God's goodness. In the first part of his speech he defends God's love:

Author of evil, unknown till thy revolt,
Unnamed in Heaven, now plenteous as thou seest
These acts of hateful strife, hateful to all,
Though heaviest by just measure on thyself
And thy adherents: how hast thou disturbed
Heaven's blessëd peace, and into Nature brought
Misery, uncreated till the crime
Of thy rebellion! how hast thou instilled
Thy malice into thousands, once upright
And faithful, now proved false!

(*6. 262–71*)

In blaming Satan for creating evil, Michael asserts the contrary of Satan's denial of divine values; Michael argues that God is the source of good, and that deviations from his standards constitute evil. In claiming that the defecting angels have discovered only what is "hateful," Michael asserts the opposite of Satan's claim that experience teaches what is good; he argues that experience teaches nothing new, that it teaches only the truth of God's values, and teaches this by a hard method. Finally, Michael asserts the opposite of Satan's idea that glory is a value; he rejects the aggressive war which "glory" denotes, and defends God's values of "peace" and of love (the opposite of "malice") . In the second part of his speech, Michael reminds Satan of the awe which is due God's wrath. He recalls God's threat of expulsion ("Heaven casts thee out," he says) and God's threat of exile "to the place of evil, Hell" (6. 271–80) .

Michael and Abdiel in their confrontation with Satan show that appeal to God's authority and goodness can combat Satan's heresy. When the angels guarding earth encounter Satan during his first visit to earth, they show how Satan's disguises can be combatted. Satan uses two kinds of disguise during his visit, physical disguises, and the verbal disguise whereby, once discovered, he tries to conceal the nature of his mission to earth.

Satan's physical disguise is defeated by angelic vigilance and logic. Uriel succeeds by his vigilance. When Satan takes the form (3. 634–44) , the deferential manner (3. 736–38) , and the pious words (3. 654–80) of a cherub, he is undetectable; Uriel does not suspect him, nor, as the commentary indicates, has he reason to be suspicious:

[N]either man nor angel can discern
Hypocrisy, the only evil that walks
Invisible, except to God alone,
By his permissive will, through Heaven and
*   Earth.*

(3. 682–85)

But Uriel keeps watch even when he has no cause for suspicion, and it is by this vigilance that he detects Satan when, alone on Niphates, Satan forgets to maintain a cherub's manner (4. 114–30). Ithuriel and Zephon, the guardians of Eden, defeat Satan through reasoning. Informed by Uriel of Satan's interest in mankind (4. 564–67), Gabriel tells Ithuriel and Zephon to pay special attention to the bower of Adam and Eve when searching the Garden (4. 788–91). In their search, the two angels are quick to find Satan, even though, crouching at Eve's ear, he is disguised as a toad (4. 797–800). They deduce that the toad is Satan in disguise by connecting the toad's attentiveness to Eve with Satan's known interest in mankind.

After his capture, Satan ratifies his decision not to repent by concealing his plan to destroy mankind. In so doing, he tests the angels' ability to detect evil, and is defeated by their application of principles and their use of logic. In interrogating Satan, Gabriel interprets Satan's answers according to divine standards, and as a result suspects him of deceit. First of all, he is made suspicious by Satan's attacks on God's rule. To Satan's boast of leaderly prowess, Gabriel replies with an indignant appeal to that obedience which a leader owes to God:

Was this your discipline and faith engaged,
Your military obedience, to dissolve
Allegiance to the acknowledged Power Supreme?
(4. 954–56)

And to Satan's accusation that the loyal angels are servile minstrels, Gabriel replies:

[W]ho more than thou
Once fawned, and cringed, and servilely adored
Heaven's awful Monarch? wherefore but in hope
To dispossess him, and thyself to reign?
(4. 958–61)

His argument is that servility is the pretense of obedience without the substance, and thus that Satan, having the highest aims of disobedience and the greatest pretense of obedience, is of all the defecting angels the most servile. Therefore, instead of viewing Satan as a warrior, as Satan wishes, Gabriel views him as a traitor (4. 950–51) and a "sly hypocrite" (4. 957), and distrusts him on the basis of his oath-breaking and pretense. Again, when Satan scorns the loyal angels for needing divine aid, Gabriel counters with a warning for Satan to stay away from the "hallowed limits" of earth (4. 962–66); Satan's taunt causes Gabriel to view him not as a warrior, but as a reprobate, unresponsive to holiness and law. Gabriel is also made suspicious by Satan's attacks on God's love. In reply to Satan's defense of the credibility of his stated reasons for being on earth, his argument that his reasons seem cogent to him because of the knowledge he has gained through the experience of evil, Gabriel replies with scorn ("O loss of one in Heaven to judge of wise") and notes that Satan has not learned much from experience if he tempts God's anger having once experienced it (4. 904–16). Instead of being lulled by Satan's argument, Gabriel views Satan as an unreformed evildoer, and so distrusts him. When, thus, Satan speaks as a warrior and empiricist in order to conceal his new plans to tempt and destroy mankind, Gabriel, testing his words by divine standards, finds in them evidences of duplicity and ill intent.

Gabriel also uses logic against Satan. When Satan claims to have come to earth to escape pain, Gabriel employs a reductio ad absurdum to refute him: he argues that those grounds would have led "all Hell" to accompany Satan, and that they conflict, furthermore, with Satan's boasts of courage (4. 917–23). And when, driven by this argument, Satan replies that he has come to earth as a spy, Gabriel, noting the discrepancy between the two explanations, quickly concludes that Satan is "no leader but a liar" (4. 947–49). Thus, instead of being deceived by Satan's arguments, Gabriel, examining them logically, is made suspicious of Satan.

God's intervention marks the success of the angels in this test of their resistance to evil. God allows Satan to test the angels with guile, but when the test is over and the angels have controverted Satan's guile, God hangs his scales in the heavens to keep Satan from proceeding to violence.

The third test of the angels' resistance to evil is Abdiel's con-

frontation with Satan during his fall, in which Abdiel shows the
conduct expected of a creature in a time of conflicting loyalties.
Abdiel tries first to reconcile these loyalties, to defend God and to
return his fellows to their proper religious state, but when rec-
onciliation proves impossible, he chooses the higher allegiance.

In his first speech at Satan's council (5. 809–48), Abdiel, reply-
ing to Satan's argument, attempts to maintain his connections
both with God and with his fellows. In loyalty to God, Abdiel
answers Satan's heresies. He condemns Satan's disobedience to
God's "just decree," and continues with a parallel defense of the
Father and the Son in regard to their divine superiority and love.
He asserts the right of the Father to assign the roles of the crea-
tures whose natures he has determined, and defends the Father's
loving intention to exalt the angels; then, in parallel, he asserts
the Son's divine superiority as agent of creation, and defends the
Son's loving union with the angels. Finally, his closing references
to the "incensëd Father and the incensëd Son" (5. 847) constitute
a reminder of what awe is due God's wrath.

But Abdiel also tries to save his fellows. He does not only an-
swer Satan's arguments, but tries to guide Satan back to a proper
relationship with God—tries first of all to correct those feelings
whose indulgence has caused Satan's defection. While denouncing
Satan's rejection of duty, Abdiel adds to the words condemning
the doctrine ("blasphemous" and "false") a word which con-
demns the holder of the doctrine, "proud." Abdiel guesses the
sense of slight present in Satan's meditations (that overestimation
of his place which Raphael describes to Adam), and he tries to
correct Satan by labeling these feelings with their moral name.
When Abdiel calls Satan an "ingrate" for refusing to love a God
who has so favored him, he again guesses Satan's thoughts, for in
the Niphates soliloquy, Satan recalls that at the time of the fall, he
resented the debt of gratitude owed to God. Here too Abdiel tries
to correct Satan by pointing out to him the moral significance of
his feelings. In addition, in the exhortative close with which he
ends his speech, Abdiel tries to guide Satan by showing him the
moral results of his defection. In the words "Cease then this impi-
ous rage, / And tempt not these," Abdiel tells Satan what changes
his defection has made in him—that a leader who should encour-
age obedience is attempting to corrupt those dependent upon

him, and that a creature made for a tranquil and harmonious existence has fallen into chaotic discontent. By referring to the causes and effects of Satan's lapse, Abdiel hopes to shock Satan into self-awareness and so into a reversal of his course. Not only does Abdiel attempt to influence Satan, he also tries to influence Satan's followers. The descriptions of the circumstances of Abdiel's speech suggests that he interrupts Satan:

> *Thus far [Satan's] bold discourse without control*
> *Had audience, when . . .*
> *[Abdiel] Stood up, and in a flame of zeal severe*
> *The current of his fury thus opposed.*
>
> (5. 803–4, 807–8)

Abdiel not only attempts to prevent Satan's further influence upon his followers, but also, by his breach of deference, he encourages the angels to withhold that respect due to superior status when that status is being abused (the fact that Abdiel speaks for all the angels—"Words which no ear ever to hear in Heaven / Expected"—shows that he intends to encourage his fellows in resistance to heresy) .

In his second speech, Abdiel, forced to decide between allegiances, chooses to follow God. From Satan's reply, his doubt of the divine superiority of the Father and the Son and his challenge to God's wrath, Abdiel learns that Satan will not change his course, and from the fact that the other angels do not second his own position (5. 849–51) and that they do approve of Satan's (5. 872–74), Abdiel learns that they are unwilling to resist evil. Thus, unable to reconcile his two loyalties, Abdiel chooses between them, announcing his choice in his second speech. He affirms his loyalty to God by answering Satan's new aspersions on God's superiority (5. 894–95) and on his wrath (5. 888–93). He blames Satan and his followers for their persistence (5. 877–81), and makes clear to his former companions what ruin awaits them (5. 881–88) —a ruin which he earlier tried to avert.

The loyal angels, then, serve first to recall that unchanging state of innocence which God intended for his creatures and which the fallen creatures have lost, and they demonstrate, secondly, the ways in which evil may be repelled and the state of innocence preserved. They show that heresy can be combatted by unwavering belief in God's authority and goodness, and that disguise can be pierced by vigilance, by logical analysis, and by moral analysis according to God's standards; and in addition they show that, faced with a conflict of loyalty to God and loyalty to fellow creatures, a creature should try first to reconcile these loyalties by saving his fellows, but that forced to choose, he should choose the higher allegiance.

The second group of minor characters, the fallen angels, follow in their development the course of Satan's decline. Their importance varies from episode to episode; though at times they are merely figures in the background, at times they broaden the significance of the stages of Satan's decline.

The angels add no new meanings to the analysis of Satan's rebellion against God or Satan's deterioration. During Satan's rebellion they appear only as fellow-warriors, and during his deterioration they merely duplicate Satan's moral state (they approve Satan's last fatuous and depraved speech [10. 545]) and are thus subjected to the same transformation by which God exposes Satan's loss of insight and virtue. They contribute somewhat more in the personal realm. As has been shown, Nisroch's questioning of Satan's rule and superiority proves that rebelliousness results from Satan's rejection of the divine pattern for the relationship of creatures. And during the final episode in Satan's story, the fallen angels prove the decadence of Satan's monarchical principles. As has been mentioned, when some of the fallen angels desert their appointed posts in hell to fly to earth, they follow Satan's principle that self-interest is the ground of obedience. And as has also been mentioned, when some of the angels obey Satan's commands and await his return with anxiety, they too act on the basis of self-interest, since according to Satan, their interests are bound up with his. By their conduct, then, the fallen angels prove that Satan's principles produce at best a gang, and at worst anarchy.

The angels are more important in the analysis of the fall. Their apostasy serves to supplement Satan's, for whereas Satan falls from an overestimation of his own worth, the angels fall not from their own defiant pride, but from intellectual conformity. When Abdiel objects to Satan's arguments against God, the angels judge his opposition "out of season" or "singular and rash" (5. 849–

51). To the independent analysis of arguments displayed by Abdiel, they prefer habitual responses to the recommendations of a superior. This same conformity accounts for their fall in the personal realm. Beelzebub is described as being "unwary" in his acceptance of Satan's order (5. 694–96), and when Beelzebub repeats Satan's ambiguities to the captains, they are described as obeying the "wonted signal" and the "superior voice / Of their great Potentate" (5. 696–706). Despite the fact that Satans' command is not a legitimate command framed in accordance with divine law, both Beelzebub and the captains obey it because of their reliance on habit and their lack of intellectual independence.

The fallen angels contribute most, of course, to the analysis of the state of relapse, exposing, in their debate in the infernal council, the range of relationships to God open to a creature lacking grace. The two basic positions offered in the debate, those of war and peace, represent the two basic alternatives of opposition to God and separation from him, and these positions are offered both in simple and in subtle form. Each proposal, furthermore, centers around a different element in the relationship of the creature to God's attributes; the speakers, according to their characters, focus on God's rule or his superiority, his love or his wrath. All the proposals, however, have in common that they repeat the fall, for all are evidences of the relapse which is inevitable in the absence of God's gift of grace.

Moloch's speech to the council divides into two parts. The first (2. 51–70) contains his proposal, and the second (2. 70–105) is a confutation of possible objections. Moloch proposes the alternative of opposition to God in its simplest form; by proposing to war against God, he comes the closest of all the speakers to urging a literal repetition of the fall. Described as "the strongest and the fiercest spirit / That fought in Heaven" (2. 43–45), Moloch reveals by his ferocity his desire for domination, and in accord with this desire, he centers his argument around the defiance of God's rule. During the first battle in heaven, Moloch boasted his ability to subdue Gabriel and even God, speaking in terms of the classical warfare then in use: he threatened to "drag" Gabriel "at his chariot wheels" (6. 354–60). Now, as the second, positive, argument in his statement of policy, Moloch repeats his defiance of the angels and of God, but modifies his threats to include the latest weaponry, the "thunder" and "lightning" which God introduced in the third battle in heaven. Thus Moloch redevotes himself, without a change in tactic, to the defiance of God's rule, but now he acts in the face of evidence, for after his threats to Gabriel during the war in heaven, Gabriel sent him fleeing "Down cloven to the waist" (5. 360–62).

Moloch supports his defiance of God's rule by denying all the other elements of a creature's relationship to God. He refuses to acknowledge God's divine superiority. When, in the second section of his speech, he describes the angels' descent from heaven, he recognizes the angels' forced degradation, but instead of acknowledging the divine control proved by this degradation, Moloch only deduces that it is the nature of angels to ascend. By this argument, Moloch supports the first point in his statement of policy, his negative argument that the angels should reject the degradation which God has imposed upon them—an argument which is itself offered as support for Moloch's positive proposal of defiance. Moloch also rejects virtue. The second argument in Moloch's confutation is his reply to possible objections to his proposed war. As the second point in this reply, Moloch urges revenge as a motive for fighting, and thereby refuses to love God; and as a first point, he argues that God can inflict no worse punishment than that which he has already inflicted, and in so arguing, he refuses to hold God's wrath in awe.

Belial opens his speech (2. 119–86) by confuting Moloch's own confutation; then he makes his own proposal (2. 187–203) ; and in the third section of his speech (2. 204–15), he offers supporting argumentation. Belial proposes in its simplest form the second basic position with regard to God, that of separation from him; what he proposes is closer to repentance than any of the other proposals made in the council. (Belial does not, however, come as close to repentance as Satan does in the Niphates soliloquy, and he does not, like Satan, exert his mind and conscience against his tendencies to error and to evil.) The sophistication of speech and inner depravity attributed to Belial, as well as the cowardice imputed to him in the phrase "to nobler deeds / Timorous and slothful" (2. 108–17), all suggest that weakness is Belial's central characteristic. In accord with this weakness, Belial centers his speech around the fear of punishment. Formally, it is true, the matter of punishment is only a secondary issue— one of two questions treated in a preliminary section of the speech. But the argument takes up nearly half of Belial's speech, and it is filled with the emphatic description of torments, both those which have been and those which might be inflicted. The subject of punishment thus receives more weight in the speech than its formal place would suggest, and may fairly be considered as Belial's chief concern. Yet, though Belial in his fear comes close to the awe expected of God's creatures, he falls short of repentance, for he makes no positive acceptance of punishment, and does not see the place of punishment in God's scheme of justice. Furthermore, when, in the third section of his speech, he proposes some action with regard to God's punishment, he suggests acclimation to pain, seeking forgetfulness rather than an unprotesting awareness of God's just wrath. Thus Belial is impenitent, and he relapses in spite of his partial awareness of past error. For during the second battle in heaven, Belial shared Satan's overweening confidence, and, being sophisticated, traded puns with his leader (6. 620–27). His present fear shows that he had learned from the Son's judgment not to underestimate the wrath of God. Yet, by failing to repent, Belial repeats, through omission, his earlier sin.

Because of his fear of future punishment, Belial argues for an inaction which refrains from active sinning but which falls short of contrition and reform. With regard to God's rule, Belial sins by omission. He begins his proposal of policy with an argument that counters the opening proclamation of Moloch's speech: "My sentence is for open war." Alluding to Moloch's words in his opening statement, "War therefore, open or concealed, alike / My voice dissuades," Belial argues, in opposition to Moloch, that the defiance of God is futile. The third argument in his proposal of policy is the contrary of Moloch's defiance of God and the angels; in opposition to the proposed renewal of war, Belial argues that the fallen angels should abide by the decision of the war in heaven. In both cases Belial argues against a renewal of resistance, but he fails to show contrition for his fall from allegiance, and he does not recommend that the angels seek pardon from God, or that they repledge their loyalty to him.

He fails, thus, to support obedience to God's rule. Belial also sins by omission with regard to God's divine superiority. The second argument in his statement of policy counters Moloch's preparatory argument that the angels should reject the degradation imposed on them. He alludes to Moloch's argument in his rhetorical question, "Shall we then live thus vile, the race of Heaven / Thus trampled . . . ?" And he answers by building upon his central argument about punishment; he argues that the present degradation is better than a future greater degradation. In the final section of his speech, Belial adds two supporting arguments to this recommendation of inaction: as the third argument in the section he suggests that, since the angels' present state is not so bad as it might be, the angels should wait for future improvement; as the first argument he suggests that if the angels accept their state, God may lessen their torments. In this set of arguments Belial comes close to relying upon God's ability to restore those whom he has degraded, but he stops short of a full acknowledgment of God's superiority: Belial hopes to avoid a state worse than hell, but he does not seek a restoration of his former condition; he hopes that God will grant a change, but does not think of seeking change through contrite prayer; he thinks of a cessation of God's wrath, but does not think of God's ability to restore lost powers to his fallen creatures. Giving up his former status, he fails to acknowledge God's restorative power. Finally, Belial sins by omission with regard to the love of God. He opens his confutation with a rebuttal of the argument for revenge with which Moloch closed his own confutation. He argues that the idea of revenge is impractical, and for proof he alludes to and attacks Moloch's argument on the ease of reascension and his description of the new war which he wishes to see waged in heaven. Thus Belial refrains from active hatred of God (his opening proclamation of hatred—"I should be much for open war . . . / As not behind in hate"—is clearly a rhetorical device, a concession to forestall criticism), but Belial attains no love for God; he settles for a state of indifference. Belial is characterized as recommending "ignoble ease, and peaceful sloth" rather than "peace" (2. 226–28) ; the description points to the absence of positive dutifulness and virtue which distinguishes Belial's arguments from the attitudes of the penitent.

Mammon's speech to the council divides into three parts. The first is a confutation (2. 229–49); the second, Mammon's proposal (2. 249–62); and the third, the section in which Mammon counters Belial's supporting arguments with his own (2. 262–83). Mammon supports Belial's basic position with regard to God, that of separation rather than opposition, but his proposal, more subtle than Belial's, involves a more complete separation from God, and is further from repentance. Described as admiring before the fall "The riches of Heaven's pavement" more than "aught divine or holy" (1. 678–84), Mammon is struck by his loss of former glory. His central concern is to undo his degradation by his own efforts and to return to his former state of material splendor. In the first section of his speech, Mammon argues both the impossibility of returning to heaven and the impossibility of relying upon God's relentment; by his argument that heaven cannot be regained by war, he answers Moloch's rejection of the ignominy of exile in hell, and by his assumption that the angels can only win total forgiveness together with a return to heaven and can only offer total repentance, he answers Belial's proposal of a partial reliance upon God. His position coincides with Belial's in its abandonment of heaven, but Mammon modifies Belial's position of partial reliance into a suggestion for total indifference toward God. By this argument he prepares the way for the proposal that he makes in the second section of his speech, the proposal of self-elevation with which he counters the proposals both of Moloch and of Belial. By extolling the possibilities for "greatness" in hell, Mammon counters Moloch's rejection of what he saw to be degradation; and by stressing the angels' opportunities to better their condition, he counters Belial's grudging acceptance of their state as better only than some future more degrading one. His position resembles Belial's in its acceptance of life in hell, but Mammon views this acceptance as a good rather than as a necessity. Finally, in the third section of his speech, Mammon modifies Belial's two supporting arguments on the subject of accepting hell. In the last argument of his speech Mammon modifies Belial's final point, that the angels should wait for future improvement; Mammon proposes that the angels should spend their time planning remedies for their lot. In his first supporting argument Mammon modifies Belial's first supporting argument, that the angels should rely on God's relentment to lessen their torments; Mammon proposes that the angels should by their own efforts turn hell into heaven. Mammon turns Belial's passive waiting into a proposal for positive action—a proposal which defines the ends of angelic self-elevation as the re-creation of that material "Magnificence" lost with the exile from heaven.

All the aspects of this plan of Mammon's deny God's divine superiority. Because Mammon cannot see the nature of his loss, he proposes material restoration as a substitute for the spiritual restoration that comes with grace. Because Mammon, ignorant as to the nature of his loss, believes in his power to restore himself, he proposes self-advancement as a substitute for reliance on God's restorative power. Content with these substitutes, Mammon cannot see the need for accepting grace and for returning to his former state, and by his suggestion for indifference he turns his back on both. Mammon thus relapses, and he relapses in the face of evidence. For the loss which Mammon is aware of is evidence of God's ability to control his creatures' places, that power which Mammon here fails to comprehend.

Mammon's attitude to God's rule parallels his attitude to God's divine superiority. When, in his confutation, Mammon argues that to "unthrone" God is impossible, he rejects Moloch's plan of defying God, and when he argues that worshiping God in heaven would be intolerable, he rejects Belial's proposal that the angels should abide by the decision of the war in heaven. On the basis of this position, Mammon argues, in the beginning of his statement of policy, that the angels should live in isolation from God, "Free, and to none accountable," and that they should "seek / [Their] own good from [them]selves." Mammon thus rejects Belial's partial acceptance of divine law without embracing Moloch's defiance; and by calling for indifference to divine law and for freedom, he reinforces his central proposal, that the angels substitute self-elevation for divine aid. Mammon's attitude to divine goodness repeats Belial's position. On the subject of the love of God, Mammon is silent, tacitly accepting Belial's argument that revenge against God is impossible; as to the wrath of God, Mammon takes over for his own second supporting argument Belial's second supporting argument, that the angels will become acclimated to their punishment—though as befits his own more active position, Mammon places little stress on the avoidance of pain. In refining Belial's position, then, Mammon duplicates Belial's sins of omission in connection with God's goodness, while worsening Belial's sins of omission in connection with God's authority—for by proposing indifference to God, Mammon comes less close than Belial to acknowledging that authority.

Beelzebub begins his speech with a confutation (2. 310–44), proceeds to his proposal (2. 344–58), and concludes with supporting arguments (2. 358–78). He returns to the first basic position with regard to God, that of opposition, but his plan is subtler than Moloch's idea of resuming the war in heaven. As the comment on its "malice" and "spite" suggests (2. 380–85), Beelzebub's plan centers on the hatred of God, and it is upon this hatred that Beelzebub's speech climaxes. All the other speeches in the council climax near the center, and build toward and recede from their climax: Moloch's speech climaxes with the description of the war that Moloch wishes to promote. Belial's speech climaxes with its catalog of torments, and its proposal and supporting arguments are low-pitched, their tone emphasizing the relief to be gained by avoiding offense to God. Mammon's speech climaxes with its exhortation to self-elevation. Beelzebub's speech, however, though it follows the same formal pattern as the two speeches preceding it, builds to a climax at its end. For Beelzebub's proposal of policy, instead of arguing, is devoted to the presentation of background material; the suggestion of a course of action is touched on only at the end. Thus emphasis is shifted to the final section of the speech, and particularly to the only positive advantage which Beelzebub offers for his plan, that it "would surpass / Common revenge." The hatred of God receives central emphasis, then, and Beelzebub argues his intended revenge against God in such a way as to outdo Moloch in his opposition. Beelzebub begins the third section of his speech by defending the practicality of his plan. By admitting that heaven is unassailable, he conciliates Belial, conceding his opening objections to the kind of revenge proposed by Moloch; but at the same time, by suggesting earth as a place for encroachment, Beelzebub reinstates Moloch's central point, that God can be disturbed by attacks upon his territory.

With this preparation, Beelzebub then appeals for revenge, playing, in his arguments, upon all the central concerns of the earlier speakers. When he proposes the possibility of "wast[ing]" earth with "Hell fire," he alludes to Moloch's plan for attacking heaven, and appeals to those who share Moloch's desire for domination, suggesting that they convert their lust for power into a malicious enjoyment of destroying. When he offers the possibility that God may annihilate man, he alludes to Belial's argument that annihilation is a "sad cure" for pain, and appeals to those who share Belial's fear of future punishment, suggesting that they convert their fear into spite, inflicting upon others what they fear to have inflicted upon themselves. And when Beelzebub argues that the angels may "possess" earth and "drive as [they] were driven, / The puny habitants," he appeals to those who share Mammon's sense of loss concerning heaven and who share his desire for a reconstruction of their original home; he suggests that they can achieve their own ends more easily by attacking earth, and can at the same time gain spiteful pleasure in inflicting upon others that loss which they themselves feel. In this all-embracing appeal to malice, Beelzebub intensifies Moloch's suggestion of revenge.

Although the other speakers in the council are portrayed as relapsing in the face of evidence, only in the case of Beelzebub is there reference to the central pattern characteristic of Satan's relapse, the pattern of insight, choice, and descent. In response to Satan's opening speech on the burning lake, his expression first of dismay and then of defiance, Beelzebub voices his own dismay. He argues that God can compel the angels to do his "service as his thralls / By right of war" (1. 143–52), thus acknowledging God's rule, and he says that he "see[s] and rue[s]" the results of challenging God's "supremacy" (1. 128–42), thus acknowledging God's ability to degrade his creatures. In reply, Satan (as has been mentioned) attempts to shame Beelzebub into defying God, and in addition (as has also been mentioned) he voices his desire to disturb God by doing what he knows to be evil. By his second speech, Beelzebub shows that he responds to Satan's influence. By his address to Satan, "Leader of those armies bright, / Which but the Omnipotent none could have foiled" (1. 272–73), and by his parenthetical comment on the angels' stunned condition, "No

wonder, fallen such a pernicious height!" (1. 282), Beelzebub re-
veals that he remembers his earlier dismay, but by his emphasis on
Satan's leadership in battle (1. 274–78) and by his statement of
Satan's ability to rouse his followers (1. 278–81), he shows that
he recants his earlier admission of God's rulership and divine
superiority. Thus, under Satan's influence, he chooses not to re-
pent; and his speech to the infernal council measures his descent,
for in that speech he embellishes all of Satan's hints, deriving his
plan of revenge from Satan's earlier statement of his desire to
disturb God.

In connection with his plan for revenge, Beelzebub suggests
active defiance of God's authority. First of all, he revives Moloch's
notion of active disobedience. In his opening confutation he at-
tacks, first of all, the proposal of Mammon; in arguing that hell
is God's empire, Beelzebub counters Mammon's argument that the
angels can be free in hell. Beelzebub also attacks Belial's two
arguments on obedience. When he proclaims the inevitability of
war, Beelzebub counters Belial's argument that the angels should
abide by the decision of the war in heaven; and in arguing the
point, he reverses the procedure by which Belial urged the ac-
ceptance of hell. Belial aroused fear by describing the punishment
to result from a renewal of war; he then used this fear as an in-
ducement to accept existing conditions. Beelzebub arouses anger
by describing the punishment which the angels will receive even
if they accept hell; he then uses this anger as an inducement for
disobeying. In the words

> *what peace can we return,*
> *But to our power hostility and hate,*
> *Untamed reluctance, and revenge though slow,*
> *Yet ever plotting*

he connects the passive antagonism, "hostility," with passive re-
sistance, "Untamed reluctance," and the active antagonism,
"hate," with active plots to counter God's will. Thus Beelzebub,
denying Belial's acceptance of defeat, returns to Moloch's policy
of defiance, and in his final argument, that defiance of God need
not take the form of an assault on heaven, Beelzebub concedes
Belial's argument on the futility of Moloch's proposed plan for
war, while reinstating Moloch's aim of active disobedience. Be-

elzebub also revives Moloch's defiance of God's divinity. He attacks, first of all, Belial's proposed reliance on God's eventual relentment. In the words "terms of peace yet none / Vouchsafed or sought," Beelzebub alludes to Mammon's indirect answer to Belial's plan of partial reliance upon God—Mammon's assumption that the only possible terms would be total forgiveness for total repentance. Beelzebub argues as if defending Belial from the charge of treason, and by this tactic he rules out even the consideration of repentance. Then, by his description of endless tortures in hell, Beelzebub answers Belial's supporting argument, that if the angels accept their state, God will eventually lessen their torments; Beelzebub insists that the acceptance of hell means simply the continuation of their present degraded state, and thus he rules out even partial reliance upon God's aid. In addition, Beelzebub attacks Mammon's plans for self-elevation, beginning and ending his speech with scornful references to that proposal. Opening his confutation, Beelzebub sarcastically restates Mammon's argument that the angels should "Thrive" and achieve "greatness" in hell:

> *Thrones and imperial Powers, Offspring of Heaven,*
> *Ethereal Virtues; or these titles now*
> *Must we renounce, and changing style, be called*
> *Princes of Hell?*

In closing, Beelzebub attacks Mammon's supporting arguments. Asking if it is worthwhile "to sit in darkness," he refutes Mammon's first argument, that the angels should make a heaven of hell; alluding to Mammon's suggestion that the angels should "Imitate" God's "light," Beelzebub insists that hell is hell and that it cannot be turned into heaven. Asking if the angels should sit "Hatching vain empires," he refutes Mammon's last argument, that the angels should plan remedies for their lot; Beelzebub insists that any such planning would be mere daydreaming. Thus Beelzebub rejects all forms of the acceptance of hell, and returns to Moloch's position that the angels should reject the degradation imposed upon them, and thus should refuse to admit the divine superiority of which that degradation is evidence. In order to translate his hatred of God into action, then, Beelzebub modifies but reasserts Moloch's defiance of God's authority.

The fact that each of the four proposals offered in the infernal debate emphasizes a different aspect of the creature's relationship to God, and the fact that the four proposals cover differing versions of differing positions suggests that the debate embodies the full range of unrepentant responses to God. The course of the debate shows, further, that the unrepentant contribute to one another's corruption; for the opening simple proposals provide the basis for subtler proposals which are further from obedience and love, and the debate ends with the worst proposal offered—a proposal which urges opposition to God, worse than the alternative of separation, and which urges a subtle form of opposition, worse than the alternative of direct defiance.

With Beelzebub's second speech to the council, the focus shifts from the fallen angels' relationship with God to Satan's relationship with his followers; after Satan's departure, however, the focus returns to the fallen angels. At this point—the episode of the heroic games in hell—the activities of the fallen angels are contrasted with the activities of the loyal angels in heaven, the contrast revealing the fallen angels' loss of the unity of life intended for God's creatures.

The first aspect of that lost unity is the connection between creatures' personal lives and their religious lives. For mental recreation, the loyal angels spend "happy hours" in "hymning" (3. 416–17), and think about the doctrines which God has revealed to them. Their hymn at the end of the opening assembly in heaven shows their ability to comprehend their experience. In this hymn, after an opening exposition of the nature of the Father (3. 372–82) and of the Son (3. 383–89), the angels refer in turn to the offices of God—to God's office of creator (3. 390–91), of judge (demonstrated in his expulsion of the defecting angels [3. 391–99]), of giver of grace (3. 400–402), and finally of savior (3. 403–15). Thus they integrate what they have just learned about God's gift of grace and salvation with what they had learned in the past about his office as judge, and with what they had been told or had deduced still earlier about his creativity. The mental recreations of the fallen angels, however, lack religious orientation. When they sing, the fallen angels sing tragic accounts of their fall (2. 546–51), paying tributes to themselves rather than to God, and when they try to comprehend their experience, they are doomed to the "wandering mazes" of philosophic speculation (2. 557–69), being cut off from divine truth. Again, for physical recreation, the loyal angels on "solemn days" dance, and their dance has spiritual significance, is "Mystical" (5. 618–24). The fallen angels, however, at best engage in tourneys or races (2. 528–32) —they celebrate their own prowess— and at worst they uproot the hills (2. 539–41), reenacting the second battle in heaven. Love of self or hatred of God replaces the love of God in their lives. Finally, for physical refreshment, the loyal angels find everything they need at hand, both food and setting, and they see their refreshment as an evidence of God's love for them (5. 630–41). The fallen angels seek comfort in hell (2. 570–73) —seek refreshment apart from God's giving, in a place from which God has withheld his generosity, "A universe of death, which God by curse / Created evil" (2. 622–23); thus, though they search far and wide (2. 614–18) they find only barrenness, "many a frozen, many a fiery Alp, / Rocks, caves, lakes, fens, bogs, dens, and shades of death" (2. 618–21). Having lost the connection between their activities and God, the fallen angels, it is suggested, lose the essential characteristics of those activities, their truth, love, and joy.

The fallen angels have also lost a second element of unity, the unity within the self. The activities of the loyal angels involve a harmony of faculties: their hymns involve the sensory component of music as well as the rational component of doctrine (3. 365–69), and their dances involve the mental component of music as well as the physical component of action (5. 625–27). The activities of the fallen angels are more fragmented: the fallen angels who pursue physical recreation separate from those seeking mental recreation, and each group further divides, the poets separating from the philosophers, the sportsmen from the warriors (2. 528–69). What is suggested is that the fallen angels have become specialists, integration of qualities giving way to divergent and one-sided development.

The final element of that unity of life which the fallen angels have lost is the unity between creatures. The activities of the loyal angels are all shared activities: "No voice" is "exempt" in heavenly singing (3. 370–71); everyone dances, for the participants must be as numerous as the stars to which they are compared

(5. 620–24) ; and all the angels join in the banqueting, which is therefore called "communion sweet" (5. 636–38). The activities of the fallen angels lack this sharing. First of all, the fallen angels engage in individual activities: the singers are lone performers, listened to by a nonparticipating audience (2. 552–55) ; and the angels who uproot hills act in individual rage, and are thus compared to Hercules in his pain (2. 542–46) —to a single violent man, rather than to an enraged group. Secondly, even the organized groups, the angels who are exploring hell, lack cohesion: the members break ranks in their attempts to drink from Lethe (2. 604–9), and they make a "cónfused march" (2. 615), a disorderly journey. Finally, the angels compete with one another: the racers "contend," the jousters form "fronted brigades" (2. 528–32), and the philosophers "argue" (2. 562–65). Released to their separate devices by Satan's command that they seek whatever ease can be found in hell, the fallen angels place individual considerations above thoughts of their fellows, losing, it is suggested, social cohesion.

The fallen angels, then, elaborate Satan's decline, and particularly the two turning points in that decline, the fall and the relapse. In regard to the former, the account of the angels' intellectual passiveness serves to supplement the account of Satan's active pride. In regard to the latter, the angels' debate serves to demonstrate both the forms that impenitence can take, and the tendency of the unrepentant to corrupt one another; in addition, the episode of the heroic games reveals the impoverishment of the angels' lives, their loss of the kinds of harmony which God intended for his creatures: harmony between creatures, harmony within the creature himself, and harmony between the creature's personal and religious life.

Though the reactions of Adam to Michael's prophecy connect the prophecy with the story of Adam's moral development, the focus during the narration is certainly less upon Adam than upon the events narrated to him. Furthermore, this episode, unlike that of Raphael's history, is not a part of the narrative structure: Raphael's recital is concerned for two-thirds of its length with the presentation of the early stages in the secondary plot, and for one-third of its length with an account of the creation which is at least tenuously connected with the lives of Adam and Eve, while the events of Michael's prophecy are not part of the lives either of Adam and Eve or of Satan. Thus this episode stands apart from the rest of *Paradise Lost,* and requires an inquiry into its structure and its meaning.

There are several suggestions that, despite the prophetic framework, the structure of the prophecy is expository rather than simply chronological. In the first place, the chronological sequence is broken twice: the vision of a hospital of later times is presented between the vision of Cain and Abel and that of the descendants of Cain and Seth, and the second coming of Christ is mentioned after the narration of his life but before the description of the modern era. In both these cases, unity of subject takes precedence over chronology: in the first instance, materials related to death, and in the second, materials related to the Son's office of savior, are brought together. Furthermore, the opening dialogue of this part of the poem is clearly devoted to a subject—death—rather than to an event. What these facts suggest is that the prophecy is a vehicle for ideas, and that its structure is logical rather than chronological, the events being made to serve the purposes of moral and doctrinal exposition. Viewed in this way, the prophecy falls into two main sections, one dealing with good, God's influence upon mankind, the other with evil, Satan's influence—this latter being subdivided according to the two principal evils which Satan brings, sin and death.

The part of the prophecy dealing with death starts with the opening vision, and ends at the vision of the descendants of Cain and Seth (11. 423–555). Milton places emphasis upon death as Satan's doing. The vision of the murder of Abel (11. 429–47), and the vision of the "lazar-house" (11. 477–93), the two visions presented in this section, share between them the two kinds of death attributable to vice, death by crime and death by disease ("intemperance . . . shall bring / Diseases dire," Michael explains [11. 472–74]). Because these two particular kinds of death are shown while natural death is only talked about, the connection of death with Satan's corruption of mankind is emphasized. Furthermore, even natural death is described in a sober way, in terms of the loss of physical, sensory, and mental capacity (11. 538–46). Yet, as with other evils treated in this first section of the prophecy, there are reminders of God's power to counter Satan. Divine retribution is promised for crime (Michael says that the "bloody fact" of Abel's murder "Will be avenged" and that Abel's "faith approved" will "Lose no reward" [11. 457–59]) ; the justice of disease as a punishment for evil is defended at length (11. 515–25) , and is admitted by Adam (11. 526) ; and despite the rather grim description given to natural death, sufficient consoling images are attached to it to prove it a fitting end for a life rightfully led: Michael tells Adam that he may live

> *till like ripe fruit [he] drop*
> *Into [his] mother's lap, or be with ease*
> *Gathered, not harshly plucked, for death mature.*
> *(11. 535–37)*

Thus there are reminders that the evil of death cannot overcome God's power to redress wrong and to increase or lighten punishment.

The part of the prophecy dealing with sin starts with the vision of the descendants of Cain and Seth and ends with the discussion of Nimrod (11. 556–12.104) . The topic of sin is treated by reference to the stages of spiritual decline demonstrated in the secondary plot and in the opening stages of the main plot; for insofar as they are influenced by Satan, men follow in the footsteps of Satan and of Adam fallen. There are, then, four sections in this part of the prophecy, and they deal with apostasy, rebellion, relapse, and deterioration (though here the order of the last two stages is reversed) .

The first section consists of the vision of the descendants of Cain and Seth and the commentary appended to it (11. 556–637) ; the incident forms an analogy to the stage of the fall. The seduction of innocent men by already fallen women (so Michael explains it [11. 621–27]) clearly recalls the seduction of Adam by Eve—so clearly that, as has been noted, Adam is reminded of his fall; and the characteristics assigned to the participants reinforce the analogy. The daughters of Cain behave seductively (11. 580–84) , and they are described as lustful, and as "empty of all good wherein consists / Woman's domestic honor and chief praise" (11. 613–20) . They recall Eve in her speech of seduction, in her encouragement of Adam's overvaluation of her, and in the sacrifice of Adam which marks her soliloquy after eating the fruit—in the three speeches which characterize Eve during her seduction of Adam. The sons of Seth are shown to be pious men (11. 573–80) whose attraction to women causes them to lapse (11. 585–92), to "yield up all their virtue," as Michael says (11. 621–25). They clearly recall Adam in his initial righteousness, and in his yielding to the overvaluation of Eve. Even the sons of Cain, not directly involved in the seduction episode, aid in the analogy to the fall. They are shown to be ingenious inventors (11. 558–73) and are described as "Unmindful of their Maker" (11. 611–12); in their detachment of reason from duty they recall Adam in the secondary fault by which he fell.

The second section in the treatment of sin consists of the vision of the wars of the giants and the commentary that follows it (11. 638–711); this incident forms an analogy to the stage of rebellion. The fact that war is the subject of the vision (11. 638–59) of course recalls the war in heaven, and the character of the warriors as described by Michael reinforces the analogy. Michael's comment that "in those days might only shall be admired" (11. 689) recalls the Son's statement that the rebel angels "by strength . . . measure all"; and the desire of the giants "To overcome in battle, and subdue / Nations" in order to attain "glory" (11. 691–96) recalls Satan's desire to wage aggressive war, the war he calls "The strife of glory." In this episode there is a reminder of God's office of judge, the office whereby he counters rebellion. Enoch, seen in council with the warriors, defends divine truths and warns specifically of God's judgment (11. 660–68); thus not only does he serve as a denier of heresy, like Abdiel or Michael during the war in heaven, but also he predicts the last judgment. Furthermore, the fact that Enoch is carried off to heaven (11. 668–71) is said by Michael to demonstrate that the good will be saved from the judgment visited upon the evil (11. 700–710); the episode thus foretells the events of the last judgment.

The third section in the part of the prophecy dealing with sin contains the two visions pertaining to Noah and the flood, together with their commentary (11. 712–901); this section forms an analogy to the stage of deterioration. Degeneracy is clearly the attribute of those destroyed by the flood. Describing the "pleasure," "ease," "sloth," "Surfeit," "lust," "wantonness" and "pride" of the conquerors, and the "worldl[iness]" and "dissolute[ness]" of the conquered, Michael sums up humanity as "all . . . degenerate, all depraved" (11. 794–807), and Adam himself wonders at the power of peace "to corrupt" men (11. 779–84). Mankind's total lack of insight at this point recalls Satan in his final state, and there are several details that reinforce the analogy. The "jollity and game" which precede the flood (11. 714–18) recall Satan's final overconfidence, and the "civil broils" which erupt in time of peace (11. 718) recall the anarchy among part of Satan's followers. Furthermore, the destruction of corrupt men by flood (11. 738–53) is clearly a type of that death of eternal damnation which the Son predicts as punishment for Satan's degeneracy (and which is also assigned to those who follow Satan).

In this episode there are strong reminders of God's power as savior to deliver man from damnation. First of all, Noah clearly represents the regenerate man, his life and fate contrasting with the life and fate of the degenerate (11. 808–21). Secondly, the rainbow, "Betokening peace from God, and covenant new" (11. 863–67), prefigures the covenant whereby the Son pledges to save those who accept his justification and sacrifice. Finally, there are phrases applied to Noah which suggest that he is not only one of the regenerate, but also a type of Christ. Adam says that he rejoices

> For one man found so perfect and so just,
> That God vouchsafes to raise another world
> From him, and all his anger to forget;
> (11. 876–78)

and Michael repeats the phrases: "Such grace shall one just man find in [God's] sight / That he relents, not to blot out mankind" (11. 890–91). These phrases recall that were it not for the Son, "without redemption all mankind / Must have been lost" (3. 222–23), that the Son is the one just man whose "merit" absolves mankind (3. 290–94), and that in the Son "As from a second root shall be restored, / As many [of mankind] as are restored" (3. 287–8a).

The amount of emphasis placed upon this particular section of the prophecy has a dramatic justification. The section contains two visions instead of the one vision devoted to previous incidents; it is twice as long as the preceding sections; and, despite the fact that it does not end the part of the prophecy devoted to the subject of evil, this section contains the last of the incidents presented by means of vision. Thus the section receives particular emphasis, and as a consequence the prophecy is connected with the character of its hearer; for the subject of God's power as savior is relevant to the particular stage of development which Adam has reached, and the subject of deterioration is appropriate to Adam's present case, in that Adam would have fallen to such a degenerate state had he not accepted salvation. Thus at this point the expository prophecy is tied to the poem's narrative line.

The final section in this treatment of sin is Michael's account of history through the time of Nimrod (12. 1–104); this episode forms an analogy to the stage of relapse. The central characteristics of Nimrod's activities are the irrationality of his plan to build a tower to heaven and the tyranny of his rule over men; the former is commented upon by Adam, who asks how men could eat or breathe at the top of the tower (12. 74–78), and the latter is commented upon both by Adam, who calls Nimrod's kingship a usurpation of divine powers (12. 64–71), and by Michael, who connects tyranny with loss of reason (12. 79–96). Loss of reason and tyranny are the characteristics of Satan's stage of relapse, and there are several details that connect Nimrod with Satan. Adam blames Nimrod for attempting "Siege and defiance" against God (12. 72–74); the charge connects the outcome of Nimrod's irrationality with the outcome of Satan's ungraced decisions. Furthermore, when Michael says of Nimrod,

> *A mighty hunter . . . he shall be styled*
> *Before the Lord, as in despite of Heaven,*
> *Or from Heaven claiming second sovranty,*
> *(12. 33–35)*

the description links Nimrod's tyranny with Satan's, for Satan appeals for sanction to the "laws of Heaven" and at the same time claims for himself the authority which he earlier denied the Son. In this episode there is evidence of God's power to counter Satan by strengthening his creatures through grace. During the opening assembly in heaven, God proclaims his intention to withdraw grace from those who refuse it, and to leave them to progressive

enfeeblement. Nimrod's act of irrationality leads to a further
state of confusion, the multiplication of languages which gives his
Tower the name "Confusion" (12. 48–62). His story is thus a
parable of the enfeeblement that follows from the refusal of grace,
and through the negative example, God's power to give grace is
recalled.

Thus, in the part of the prophecy that treats of sin, the behav-
ior of mankind when under the influence of Satan is compared to
the behavior of Satan himself in the four stages of his decline (or
of Adam and Eve when they themselves follow Satan's example).
The second main division of the prophecy treats of good—specifi-
cally of God's plan for rescuing mankind. This portion of the
poem extends from the story of Abraham through the account of
the last judgment (12. 105–551); it is divided into four sections,
the stages of God's plan being correlated with God's four offices.

The first section consists of Michael's account of history from
the time of Abraham through the time of Moses (12. 105–269);
God's actions during this period are connected with his powers as
creator and lawgiver. God's delivery of the law (12. 223–44) and
his residence with "men / Obedient to his will" (12. 244–58) —
the culminating events of this episode—are reminiscent of his ac-
tions in interdicting the tree of knowledge and assigning duties to
Adam, and in visiting man before the fall. It is true, of course, that
the two cases are not identical; Mosaic law and the priesthood are
described as foretelling the Messiah (12. 231–44) and are there-
fore intended to be temporary, as is later stated (12. 300–302);
the laws given to Adam, on the other hand, were intended to be
permanent. The mode of procedure, however, is the same: in both
cases, God makes commands in order that men may demonstrate,
by their obedience, that they serve and love him. Other details in
the account reinforce this reference to God's first office. One of
these details is the repeated mention of the journey to Canaan
(12. 114–46, 151–72, 214–22, 258–69), the topic by which the sec-
tion is unified. Canaan is a type of heaven—Joshua in leading the
Jews there is said to be a type of Jesus leading men to heaven
(12. 307–14). Eden is another such type—the words "eternal
Paradise," applied to heaven (12. 314), compare it to the Garden.
Canaan and Eden are therefore analogous, and thus the journey
to Canaan reenacts God's initial placement of man in Eden.

Furthermore, God's office of creator and lawgiver is recalled in the account given of the covenant with Abraham and of the exodus from Egypt. Michael explains that God's covenant with Abraham constitutes a fresh start in his relations with man, a new beginning from "one faithful man" (12. 105–13) ; this beginning entails a release from enslavement to the godless, for Michael places great emphasis on the overcoming of Pharoah (12. 173–214) , "who denies / To know [the] God [of Israel], or message to regard" (12. 173–74) . These events are reversals of man's defections from allegiance: the release from bondage to evil counters such entrapments by evil as befell the sons of Seth, and the choice of a single man suggests that God is renewing his plan to create "out of one man" a world of creatures obedient to him (7. 150–61) , the plan which Adam's fall subverted. God, it is suggested, begins his rescue of mankind by opposing his power as lawgiver to man's tendency to sin.

God's office of savior is the subject of the second section in the part of the prophecy devoted to good; this section contains two speeches, the first covering history from the time of Joshua through the birth of Christ (12. 285–371), the second treating the life of Christ, including his second coming (12. 386–465) . The subject of the first speech is God's preparations for the coming of the Messiah. The core of this speech is its opening explanation of man's need for a savior, an explanation which repeats what God announces in the opening assembly in heaven, that man has no means of atoning for his fall, and therefore needs a redeemer to save him (3. 203–16) . The focus here, however, is upon God's revelation of this principle to mankind: Michael explains that God gives man law in order that men may find themselves unable to obey, and so may know their need for sacrificial atonement (12. 285–99) . The remainder of the speech deals with less philosophic matters: the foretelling through types of God's new covenant (12. 300–314), the announcement of the Messiah through divine promise and through prophecy (12. 315–30), the lineage of Christ (12. 331–60), the circumstances of Christ's birth (12. 360–71) . After this introductory speech, Michael in his second speech explains God's office itself, the exposition again adapting material from the opening assembly in heaven. When, in the beginning of the speech, Michael tells how the Son's obedience

and death save mankind by destroying Satan's "works" in man
(12. 386–401), he repeats the Father's explanation of the mission
which the Son has accepted (3. 287–302). Furthermore, Michael's
account of Christ's life follows in general the topics of the Son's
speech of acceptance: both speeches refer to the incarnation
(3. 238–40; 12. 402–10), the death (3. 240–41; 12. 411–19), the
resurrection (3. 242–53; 12. 420–35), the ascension (3. 254–56;
12. 451–58), and the second coming (3. 256–65; 12. 458–65).
Michael's speech, however, is oriented about the effects upon man-
kind of this office of God. Therefore in his account of Christ's life,
he focuses upon the significance of events rather than upon the
events themselves, continually returning to his initial point, that
the Redeemer brings justification and salvation to those who ac-
cept his gifts. Michael also supports his thesis in the segment of
the speech which departs from the Son's outline, the account of
the apostolic duties laid upon the disciples after the resurrection
(12. 436–50); in this section Michael explains how, in fulfillment
of the promise to Abraham that "in his seed / All nations shall be
blest" (12. 120–26), God through the apostles extends the pos-
sibility of salvation to all mankind. Finally, Michael's account of
the second coming, like the Son's, stresses the salvation of the
faithful, and so pertains to the subject of God's office of savior and
its consequences for man.

The third section of the part of the prophecy dealing with good
consists of the account of history from the time of the apostles to
the end of the world (12. 485–537); this section treats of God's
office as giver of grace. In the first part of the speech, Michael sup-
plements the account of grace given in the opening assembly in
heaven. There God stressed the extension of grace to all men, only
mentioning the special case of the "Elect," the men "of peculiar
grace" (3. 183–84). Here Michael, explaining the actions of the
Holy Ghost, tells the effects of grace upon the elect. First of all, he
explains, the elect are

> arm[ed]
> *With spiritual armor, able to resist*
> *Satan's assaults, and quench his fiery darts,*
> *What man can do against them, not afraid,*
> *Though to the death, against such cruelties*

> *With inward consolations recompensed,*
> *And oft supported so as shall amaze*
> *Their proudest persecutors.*
>
> (*12. 490–97*)

Whereas ordinary men are given sufficient vision and will to obey God, the elect are given extraordinary vision and will, enough to resist error and persecution. Furthermore, the elect, Michael says, have "the law of faith" written "upon their hearts . . . / To guide them in all truth" (12. 488–90). Whereas ordinary men are given sufficient conscience to love good, the elect are given extraordinary fervor. In the second part of the speech, Michael elaborates God's concluding statements on the ability of men to reject grace (3. 198–99). Michael contrasts the apostles and their converts (12. 497–507) with the false teachers of later times, who pervert religion first by human reasoning and worldly motives (12. 507–14), and secondly by the use of secular power to impose ritual in the place of divinely given insight and love (12. 515–24, 531–37). This contrast Michael interprets in terms of God's office as giver of grace. The apostles and their successors are treated as examples of those who accept grace, "endue[d]" with "wondrous gifts" by the "Spirit / Poured" on them (12. 500, 497–98); and the sins of the ritualists are treated in terms of their denial of "the Spirit of Grace itself" (12. 524–30). Thus Michael contrasts those who accept God's grace with those who reject it. The events narrated in this section of the prophecy also contribute to the topic. The decline of mankind after the age of the apostles recalls the decline of mankind after the period of piety that followed the flood (12. 13–24), and the tyranny of the religious persecutors recalls the tyranny of Nimrod; thus the subject of God's grace is connected with the contrary topic of the state of gracelessness, the state of relapse.

The fourth section in the part of the prophecy which deals with good consists of Michael's account of the end of the world (12. 537–51); the section treats God's office of judge. Once again Michael uses materials from the opening assembly in heaven, for his account follows the outline of the Father's closing speech: both speeches refer to the Son's reception of supreme power (3. 317–29; 12. 545–46), to the punishment of wicked men and angels (3. 330–33; 12. 546–47), and to the purging and rebirth of the world (3. 333–38; 12. 547–51). Michael's account, however, begins with an introduction which indicates the place of the last judgment in God's plan to rescue mankind:

> *So shall the world go on,*
> *To good malignant, to bad men benign,*
> *Under her own weight groaning till the day*
> *Appear of respiration to the just,*
> *And vengeance to the wicked.*
>
> *(12. 537–41)*

At the end of the world, God completes his plan by remedying earthly injustices and punishing those who have refused him.

Michael's prophecy, then, divides into two main sections. One deals with good and treats of God's influence upon mankind in terms of God's four offices. The other deals with evil and treats of Satan's influence in terms of the two main evils of his bringing, death and sin, the latter being examined by reference to the four stages of spiritual decline illustrated in his story. In both form and substance the prophecy is connected with the theological premises and with the secondary plot of *Paradise Lost*.

5

Interrelationships

THE END of *Paradise Lost* is explicitly stated: to "assert Eternal Providence" and "justify the ways of God" (1. 25–26). The assertion of God's "Providence," his guidance, is a defense of divine authority; the "justif[ication]" of God is a defense of divine goodness. If the poem accomplishes its end through its double plot, it accomplishes it obliquely—by showing what effects the affirmation or denial of God's attributes has upon the creature. Satan, then, becomes a negative example—a demonstration of what happens to the creature who denies God's authority and goodness. What is significant about Satan's development is first of all the progressive nature of denial; initial doubt turns into mistaken certainty, and perverse choice into total loss of insight. The second significant fact is Satan's impotence; despite the fact that during his relapse he sees his error and evil, he is unable without God's aid to act in accordance with his knowledge. Adam and Eve, on the other hand, are positive examples—demonstrations of the value of acknowledging God's authority and goodness. What is significant about their development is the fact that by accepting God's gifts, they are enabled to undo the harm wrought by their initial denial. By accepting God's gift of grace, they can repent and reform, reversing their fall and avoiding an otherwise inevitable relapse, and by accepting God's gifts of justification and salvation, they are regenerated, reversing their rebellion against God, and averting otherwise inevitable deterioration. Thus the two stories form complementary defenses of God, the good effects of acknowledging God's attributes being juxtaposed to the bad effects of denying them. Accounts of the central characters' relationships with creatures reinforce these two basic defenses of God; the parallels and causal connections between the personal and religious realms show that the relationship of a creature to God is not a separable aspect of his life, but is bound up with his life as a whole.

Both of the plots of *Paradise Lost* make thematic contributions, then, and those contributions are complementary. The complementariness is pointed up by structural parallels and antitheses between the stories. It is true, of course, that the secondary plot is causally connected with the main one (it is explicitly introduced as a cause [1. 27–49]), that the story is begun in medias res at that point relevant to Satan's effects upon Adam and Eve, and that the early portions of the story are narrated to Adam and Eve as factual information necessary to their defense (5. 238–41) —all of these procedures according, more or less, with epic conventions. But these external connections should not obscure the moral comparisons which are being made through the double plot—the parallels between the fall and rebellion of Satan and the fall and rebellion of Adam and Eve, and the antitheses (basically) between the former's relapse and deterioration, and the repentance and regeneration of the latter.[1]

Satan's fall in relation to God parallels the fall of Adam and Eve. The meanings of the events are the same: both Satan and the earthly pair violate the laws of God the lawgiver—Satan by refusing to obey the Son as head of angels, Adam and Eve by disobeying God's prohibition of the tree of knowledge; and the arguments by which they doubt God's attributes are the same. Satan refuses the first aspect of God's authority, his rule, by claiming an inherent perfection for angels, apart from their adherence to law; similarly, by praising the serpent's accomplishment, Eve accepts the notion that creaturely perfection can be attained by other means than obedience, while Adam argues that man has so high a rank that God cannot destroy him even if he disobeys. In addition, Satan rejects God's definition of freedom by arguing that angels are free from external control, not merely free to choose obedience; and Eve makes a parallel assertion about man when she claims the freedom to pluck the forbidden fruit. Satan denies the second aspect of divine authority, God's divine superiority, by denying God's creativity and his right to assign his creatures their roles, and by claiming independent strength in defiance of God's power to degrade his creatures; when Eve offers her expressions of metaphysical ignorance, she repeats both these denials, expressing an agnostic doubt about God's divinity, and (in her dreams of self-elevation) God's power to control his creatures' places, and Adam, in his acceptance of the idea that the fruit can elevate man to godhood, also doubts God's supremacy and control. In refusing to acknowledge the first aspect of God's goodness, his love, Satan begrudges God the gratitude owed him and asperses his motives, arguing that he intends to deprive the angels of proper honor; Eve repeats the second of these faults when she suspects God's motives in forbidding the tree of knowledge, and Adam repeats the first when by overvaluing Eve he fails to pay God the love due him. Finally, Satan defies the second aspect of God's goodness, his wrath, countering threat with threat, and displaying his fearlessness; Eve, when she argues herself into belief that God will not do as he threatens, resembles Satan in his show of fearlessness, and Adam, when he argues that God's threat may have been rescinded, pits legal loophole against legal penalty as Satan has matched threat with threat.

These parallels are reinforced by resemblances in the personal realm. In both cases, the fall in this realm precedes the fall in relation to God, and, while there is no external likeness in the incidents of Satan's seduction of Beelzebub and the quarrel of Adam and Eve, there is a moral similarity between the events. Insofar as Satan's fall is an active defection from the divine requirements governing the relationship of creatures, rather a neglect of those requirements, it resembles Eve's fall in her relationship with Adam. Satan's first abuse of authority, his failure to frame his commands in accordance with divine law (he calls a council in dispute of God's law) prefigures Eve's refusal to acknowledge her superior (she refuses to rely upon Adam's guidance), and Satan's second abuse of authority, the equivocations whereby he appears to ask obedience to God's law when he is in fact challenging that law, prefigures Eve's pretenses of obedience when she is in fact violating Adam's wishes. When he abuses Beelzebub's friendship by inducing him to share his own discontent and by introducing

him to dangerous ideas, Satan prefigures Eve in her neglect of love
for Adam, her use of tact in the attempt to persuade Adam to ap-
prove her plan, and her failure to consider his happiness when for-
mulating that plan. Finally, Satan's abuse of shame (he uses
shame to encourage Beelzebub to choose loyalty to a fellow crea-
ture in preference to loyalty to God) resembles Eve's abuse of awe
in attempting to shame Adam into accepting her plan. But inso-
far as Satan's fall entails a violation of a superior's responsibilities
to his inferiors, it resembles Adam's fall in his relationship with
Eve; both Adam and Satan fail to relay God's commands properly,
fail to command obedience properly, fail to exercise a superior's
protective love, and to exercise properly the power to use shame
for the encouragement of virtue.

The parallel between Satan and Adam and Eve is continued in
their respective rebellions against God. In both cases, there are
two main parts to this stage of the characters' development, the
rebellion proper and the judgment scene. During the rebellion
proper, both Satan and Adam and Eve show dogmatic belief in the
heresies broached during the fall. Satan's arguments to Abdiel and
Michael during the first battle in heaven parallel the arguments
of Eve's soliloquy after eating the forbidden fruit. Satan expands
his denial of God's law by arguing that angels can make their
own laws, and that obedience is owed to angels rather than to God,
and he expands his definition of freedom by asserting that obedi-
ence is servility and that angels can uphold their laws by force.
Eve too expands her neglect of divine law, assigning a purpose to
the fruit in defiance of God's prohibition, and pledging obedi-
ence to her own rituals rather than to God's rules; and she be-
comes confident that she is free to do whatever she is able to do.
Satan denies God's divine superiority by denying that God is the
source of angelic power and by denying his omnipotence; Eve be-
comes certain that she has been elevated without God's permission,
and she develops her agnostic doubt of God into an atheistic cer-
tainty that God is not divine. Both Satan and Eve develop their
doubt of God's motives into doubts of his values, and embrace
experience as the source of values; and both Satan and Eve feel
certain that they will evade God's threatened punishment. Dur-
ing the second battle in heaven, Satan adds to his former heresies
a certainty that he will succeed, and the tone of his joking is re-

peated by Adam when in his speech after eating the fruit he offers
flippant proofs and quips in the place of his earlier half-hearted
rationalizations. The central action of Satan's rebellion, the war
in heaven, and the central action in the rebellion of Adam and
Eve, their dalliance, are both treated as emblems of the rejection
of the way of life ordained by God. The action of Adam and Eve
is contrasted with their evening prayer before the fall, the epitome
of their state of innocence, and the war in heaven is clearly an in-
version of the way of life intended by God for his creatures—as
indeed Raphael says:

> [S]*trange to us it seemed*
> *At first, that angel should with angel war,*
> *And in fierce hosting meet, who wont to meet*
> *So oft in festivals of joy and love*
> *Unanimous, as sons of one great Sire,*
> *Hymning the Eternal Father.*
>
> (*6. 91–96*)

Love and war can be paired because they are the twin values of
the romantic epic—values here, of course, rejected. During the
second part of their respective rebellions, the judgment scenes,
the behavior of Satan and Adam and Eve is again parallel. Satan
and his followers show themselves to be rebellious by the way in
which they come to their trial by combat, the third battle in
heaven; by their refusal to be taught or softened, they show the
denial of God's superiority which was the central sin in their fall.
Similarly, by excusing themselves, Adam and Eve rebel against
God's judgment, and the particular excuse which each of the pair
offers reveals his own central sin; in her excuse Eve shows disobe-
dience due to insufficient thought, while in his, Adam shows an
undervaluing of God and overvaluing of Eve.

The parallel between rebellions is maintained in the personal
realm. In both cases, the relationship between creatures is treated
in prosperity and in adversity, and in both rebellions the behavior
in time of adversity shows the invalidity of that union which the
creatures establish in defiance of God's standards. In the case of
Satan, the union of him and Beelzebub during the war in heaven
(touched on briefly in Satan's opening speech) shows that in times
of prosperity, those who revolt against God's standards are united

by compatible vice. The same is shown by the union of Adam and Eve during that period of intoxication which follows their eating of the forbidden fruit. The dedication to vicious principles is evident in Eve's soliloquy after eating the fruit and in the references to her relationship with her husband which she inserts into her seduction speech and her speech of encouragement to not-yet-fallen Adam, and a like dedication is evident in Adam's speech after eating the forbidden fruit. The shared lust that ensues is symbolic of union through compatible evil. The foretaste of divine judgment—the pain that is visited upon the rebelling angels, and the shame that descends upon Adam and Eve—causes a dissolution of union in both instances; under the pressure of adversity, Satan's followers question his rule and force him to seek new grounds of leadership, while Adam and Eve become incurably divided, each trying to evade blame by shifting it to the other, and forcing the other to increasingly culpable defenses.

At the stage of relapse in Satan, and the stage of repentance in Adam and Eve, the two plots diverge, and parallels yield (in general) to antitheses. At the beginning of their repentance, however, Adam and Eve are in a state of relapse, and at this time they resemble Satan in his relapse. First, they, like Satan, have been made aware of God's attributes of authority and goodness, the attributes they have denied. Satan sees evidences of God's authority in hell, and he reveals his awareness in his opening address to Beelzebub, in his speech upon first glimpsing hell, and in his exhortation to his engulfed troops. Similarly, Eve sees her error in denying God's rule, admitting that her ideas on the utility of the fruit and her notions of freedom were mistaken, and Adam in his lament shows his awareness that his neglect of God's authority was foolish, for he recognizes that man is not too great to destroy, and that man cannot attain godhood. On earth, Satan sees God's goodness reflected in Adam and Eve, God's creatures; and in Zephon he sees the beauty of the virtuous love of God. In addition, in the first section of his soliloquy, Satan feels the fear that he owes to God's wrath. Similarly, Eve sees the harm that she did to Adam by encouraging him to disregard God's goodness and to overvalue her; and she sees her folly in expecting to evade God's penalty. Likewise, Adam admits God's blamelessness in his dealings with mankind, and he accepts God's punishment. But despite these insights,

Satan and Adam and Eve repeat the sins of their fall. After each of his admissions, Satan reaffirms his heretical denials of God's authority; despite her recognition of past error, Eve repeats her sins against God's rule by relying upon self-determined rights and freedoms; and despite his awareness of his mistakes, Adam repeats his sins against God's rule by speculating upon God's thoughts instead of attending to his duties, and he repeats his denial of God's divine superiority by failing to consider God's power to strengthen him—though now Adam's sins are sins of omission rather than of commission. Satan represses his responses to God's goodness and his fear of God's wrath. Eve's proposal of barrenness shows an insufficient love for God and an insufficient trust in God's love for man, and Adam's feeling that he can find no comfort in life or death is a similar failure to love and trust God. In her suggestion of suicide, finally, Eve attempts to evade God's punishment, as does Adam in his analogous desire for death. The parallel between the angelic and the human relapse is reinforced by the similarity of Adam's lament to the first section of Satan's soliloquy. The zigzag course which is characteristic of the argument in that section of the soliloquy is also characteristic of the last three sections of Adam's lament; in both cases the structural pattern represents the struggle of mind and conscience against the tendencies to error and evil brought by the fall.

But the state of relapse which constitutes the first part of the penitential stage of the development of Adam and Eve gives way to a reversal, and in this reversal Adam and Eve are contrasted with Satan in his relapse. In the first place, Satan's rejection and defiance of insight is contrasted with Adam's attainment of insight. Satan retracts the opening admissions of God's authority in his address to Beelzebub on the burning lake and in his speech upon first glimpsing hell, and he adopts his final position in the face of indubitable proof of its folly; similarly, in addressing his assembled troops, Satan rejects the awareness of God's authority revealed in his earlier exhortation to them as they lay on the burning lake. In addition, in his two speeches upon first viewing Adam and Eve, Satan inch by inch rejects his awareness of God's goodness. Adam, on the other hand, in his suggestions for the remedy of the plight of himself and Eve, returns to the recognition of God's authority and goodness lost at the time of the fall. By suggesting that he and Eve return to the place of judgment to pray, Adam suggests submission to divine rule; by his confidence in God's relentment, he recognizes God's restorative power; by his trust in God's aid during the lifetime of him and Eve, he acknowledges and returns God's love; and by his acceptance of punishment, he shows due awe for God's wrath. Secondly, whereas Satan in his relapse repeats his fall on a lower level, Adam and Eve undo their fall. Satan in his opening address to Beelzebub, his speech upon first glimpsing hell, and his address to his assembled troops announces his refusal to repent, and reaffirms the heretical rejections of God's authority broached at the time of the fall; on earth, he resumes his hatred of God by opposing God's plans even though he now admits that the plans are not evil. Adam and Eve, on the other hand, reverse their errors in falling, step by step. By countering Eve's suggestions for remedying their plight, Adam reverses his action in yielding to her seduction during his fall, and resumes the responsibilities which he neglected then. Adam's suggestions for action reverse the heresies of his fall (as well as correcting the deficiencies of his lament), and Eve's submission to his proposals reverses her initiation of action during the fall. The central pattern of Satan's state, the pattern of insight, choice, and descent by which he reenacts the fall, is contrasted, then, with the step-by-step reversal of the fall which is the central pattern of the repentance of Adam and Eve; the heart of the contrast is the opposition between Adam's penitent suggestions and the second section of Satan's Niphates soliloquy. During the second section of his soliloquy, Satan seriously considers repentance and reform, yields to pride and weakness of conscience, and senses that God has denied him the grace which would give him sufficient strength to enable him to change his course. During Adam's speech, on the other hand, Adam, having exerted his powers toward repentance and reform, is aided by ideas and memories that strengthen his resolution, and which are signs of God's action in restoring the mind, will, and conscience of his fallen creatures. At this point the powerlessness of the fallen creature to restore himself is juxtaposed to the ability of the creature to change his life if he accepts God's gift of grace.

Finally, the closing episodes of the two sections of the double plot are antithetical. Satan's stage of relapse ends with his attempt to conceal from the guardian angels of Eden his new plan for opposing God; the repentance of Adam and Eve ends with their performing, to the letter, their plan of penitence. The deceit which ratifies defiance is juxtaposed to the sincerity of repentance.

The comparison is continued in the personal realm. At the beginning of the stage of repentance, Adam is in a state of relapse which, like Satan's, is equated with tyranny. Both Adam and Satan seek unwarranted elevation over their subordinates. Satan appropriates for himself the undelegated authority that belongs to God alone, while Adam (whose sins against Eve have been sins of neglect rather than of aggression) attains his improper elevation not by self-aggrandizement but by the degradation of Eve—he claims that she is an animal rather than a human being. Furthermore, in both cases tyranny is connected with the lack of reason that is characteristic of the state of relapse. Satan's claims of authority are contrary to evidence and logically unjustified, while in his diatribe against Eve Adam shows himself to be unrepentant in the face of evidence, and absurd both with regard to the logical substance and the likely practical consequences of his speech.

Adam's tyranny, however, is transitory, unlike the tyranny of Satan, and the succeeding relationship of Adam and Eve is contrasted to Satan's relationship with his followers. First of all, Satan's isolation from his fellows is contrasted with the reunion of Adam and Eve. In the two speeches which he addresses to the council in hell, Satan shows a growth in monarchical pride; he increases the gap between himself and his followers. In his relationship with Beelzebub, Satan consciously sacrifices all intimacy with his friend, and when shaming Beelzebub, he rebukes him in a manner devoid of all affection. In contrast, Eve, suing for peace, insists that she is Adam's wife and that she needs and loves him, and Adam, replying, returns to his proper role of husband; thus they restore the unity between them. In the second place, Satan's repetition of his fall is contrasted with the reversal of the fall which is characteristic of the repentance of Adam and Eve. In his speeches to the council in hell, Satan repeats his abuses of authority. By proclaiming his monarchy, he worsens his earlier failure to frame his commands in accordance with divine law, and by his appeals to selfishness as a grounds of obedience, he worsens his earlier violation of the fealty which he is supposed to command. In his relationship with Beelzebub, Satan repeats his abuses of virtue. Rejecting his insight into the misery which he has brought to his friend, Satan worsens his earlier sacrifice of Beelzebub's welfare, for he degrades him into a mere tool here and makes use of him for an ulterior purpose; and he worsens his earlier abuse of shame, exercising a new impersonality in the interest of a more evil cause. In contrast to this repetition of the fall is the step-by-step reversal of Adam and Eve. After the diatribe against Eve in which Adam repeats and worsens his neglect of her, Eve makes the first step toward repentance by suing for peace; in her speech she recants the sins of her fall and resubmits herself to Adam's authority and care. In rejecting Eve's plan to take all blame upon herself, Adam corrects his earlier negligence in failing to guide Eve, and recants his failure to protect her, and in his counterplan, he restores the domestic harmony lost at the time of the fall. Thus in the personal realm, the central pattern of Satan's relapse, the tyrannical isolation whereby Satan repeats his fall, is contrasted with the reversal of the fall which Adam and Eve achieve in their penitence.

The final stage in the development of Adam and Eve, their regeneration, contrasts with the final stage of Satan's development, his deterioration. In both cases, the stages are divided into three sections, the first of these being a preliminary exposition of character. The expositions of the two stages contrast. First of all, Satan has already deteriorated as a result of his relapse, and his basic evil is contrasted with the basic good of Adam and Eve, who, having repented, are now ready for regeneration. Satan's second soliloquy reveals his deterioration. In this speech, when Satan defies God's rule and superiority, he shows a self-contradiction, an absence of struggle, and a weakness of insight which contrast with his responses during the Niphates soliloquy. When he shows his hatred for God by choosing evil, he reveals a lack of response to good, an incoherence in his charges against God, and an easy resignation to evil which contrast with his earlier responses; and he shows a deadened response and a lack of struggle in relation to God's wrath. In contrast to this weakness is the growth in strength of Adam and Eve. After praying, Eve atones for her rebellion by recanting all the speeches that she made to Adam after eating the apple; furthermore, after their prayer, both Adam and Eve show persistence in their chosen penitent course. By admitting the guilt of her disobedience, Eve shows her submission to divine rule; and Adam, strengthened in his acceptance of divine authority, is certain that God responds to prayer and that he restores man to acceptability. Furthermore, Eve accepts Adam's suggestion that they trust in God's provision for them and their offspring, and Adam is so much convinced of God's goodness that he almost guesses God's role of savior; finally, Eve willingly takes on God's punishment, and Adam shows his awe by guessing from God's signs that a further penalty is at hand.

The good of Adam and Eve is balanced against the evil of Satan, then, and in addition, the last trace of sin in Adam and Eve is balanced against the last trace of good in Satan. When Satan encounters Eve before the temptation, he responds with a final instance of love—a vestige of his earlier love for God's goodness as reflected in God's creatures—though even this last trace is attenuated by comparison with Satan's responses upon first viewing Adam and Eve. This remnant of good appears in that aspect of Satan's moral life which was not the principal element in his fall; it is balanced against that remnant of their central sins which remains in Adam and Eve. When, after Michael's announcement, Eve laments the loss of Eden, she shows the insufficient thought which figured in her initial disobedience, and in his complaint, Adam shows his tendency to let concern for man overweigh his trust in God—the tendency which was central in his fall. The final contrast between the expositions in the two stages lies in the preparations for the coming action; Satan's preparations for the evil act which seals his fate are balanced against the suggestions of the coming enlightenment by which Adam and Eve are redeemed. Satan's imbrutement and his formulation of strategy prepare for his temptation of Eve, while the revelations of doctrinal ignorance in the speeches of Adam and Eve show their need for the enlightenment presented by Michael in his prophecy (and in the dream which he sends to Eve).

The middle section in the account of the regeneration of Adam and Eve consists of Adam's responses to Michael's prophecy; this section is balanced against the corresponding episode in Satan's deterioration, his temptation of Eve. In the first place, Adam's strengthened adherence to God is contrasted with Satan's renewal of war against him. In order to defeat God, Satan encourages sin in man and brings death to him, while Adam, showing fidelity to

God and overcoming mistrust of him, learns to resist sin and to respond piously to death. Furthermore, Adam's acquisition of doctrine is the contrary of Satan's promulgation of heresy. Satan teaches falsehoods about God to Eve, and falsehoods which he does not himself believe, while Adam learns the truth about God from Michael, and shows a sincere belief in that truth. In the two sections, then, the means by which Satan dooms himself to total unawareness are juxtaposed to the means by which Adam attains his final regenerate state.

The final scenes in the two stories are also opposites. In both cases, the final states of the central characters are compared with their condition during the opening exposition of character, and by the comparisons, the growth of Adam and Eve is contrasted with the degeneration of Satan. In his second soliloquy, Satan showed some feeble recognition of God's rule and superiority, his love and wrath; but in his final assembly in hell, Satan shows his loss of all insight by his final boasts of his rule and triumph over God, of his own divinity, of his success in spiting God, and of his freedom from significant punishment. In contrast to this loss is the success of Adam and Eve in ridding themselves of what faults remained to them before Michael's visit. By her show of willingness to leave Eden and by her reliance on God's guidance, Eve demonstrates that she has overcome the faults revealed in her earlier lament. Adam's faults are recalled by Michael in his final speech; and by his readiness to leave Eden Adam shows that he too has overcome his earlier misgivings. Thus complete restoration is juxtaposed to complete decadence; furthermore, the two closing scenes serve to contrast the two actions of the sections in their concluding phases. God's transformation of the fallen angels, his revelation of their state of total unawareness, recalls Satan's imbrutement and his temptation of Eve; thus it serves to conclude the action by which Satan attains his final state. Eve's concluding proclamation of faith in the Son as savior and Adam's concluding summary of moral doctrine recall the doctrinal ignorance which the pair displayed before Michael's visit; Adam's speech, furthermore, summarizes the lessons learned from Michael. Thus the pair's final speeches complete the action of their enlightenment, and by the two endings, the action of ascent is contrasted with that of a descent.

Though in the sphere of the creature's relationships with other creatures, the contrast of Adam and Eve with Satan is not so systematically developed as it is in the religious realm, nevertheless the general antithesis of decline and ascent is maintained. Satan's decline is treated in connection with the last two scenes of the religious action. In the personal temptation with which he prefaces his attack on Eve's piety, Satan attempts to undermine Eve's obedience to Adam and her reverence for his superiority, and to destroy her proper love; when urging this rejection of God's standards for creaturely relationships, Satan is conscious that what he proposes is harmful. After this act, Satan loses all insight into such relationships. Claiming an improper status with regard to his followers (he desires divine rule and fealty), Satan in the last assembly in hell deceives himself into believing that he has attained this status. In contrast to this loss of insight is the restoration of Adam and Eve, a restoration traced in the three scenes of the religious action. During the opening exposition, both Adam and Eve reveal the soundness of the relationship that has developed from their reunion, for each of them retracts the denunciations of the other made during their rebellion. Eve's lament shows a remaining tendency to sin, however; mourning the loss of Eden, she shows that disregard of her husband which was the primary sin in her fall. While Adam is receiving religious instruction, his personal regeneration is touched on. During Michael's prophecy, Adam shows his irresponsibility by blaming women for men's corruption, and Michael rebukes him in such a way as to recall Adam's initial sin against Eve. In the final section of the poem, both Adam and Eve reveal their personal perfection. In her final speech, Eve displays her love for Adam and abjures the weaknesses revealed in her lament; and Adam by his final approval of Eve rejects his weakness. Thus in the personal realm as well as in the religious, restoration is contrasted with deterioration.

The structural parallels and the antitheses between the two plots of *Paradise Lost* serve to intensify the points made by the plots separately. The analogy between the fall and rebellion of Satan and the fall and rebellion of Adam and Eve indicates that all sinners follow the same course and that, thus, they are doomed to the same end unless they accept God's gifts; the analogy shows, therefore, the seriousness of rejecting God. The contrast between the relapse and deterioration of Satan and the repentance and regeneration of Adam and Eve indicates that the fate of those who accept God is not simply to some extent different from the fate of those who reject him, but is, rather, diametrically opposite; thus the contrast shows how great the advantage is of accepting God.

The minor characters of *Paradise Lost* contribute directly to the defense of God offered in the poem. The fallen angels are negative examples, like Satan; in elaborating Satan's decline, they expand the demonstration that the denial of God brings pernicious results. The loyal angels are positive examples; by their exemption from change—from the progressive deterioration of the deniers and the arduous restoration of the penitent—they show how much better it would have been for all creatures had they not doubted God's authority and goodness; and by their ability to resist evil, they prove that other creatures could have averted their fall. In addition to these direct functions, however, the minor characters bear on the theme indirectly; they contribute to the positive defense of God by contributing to the moral analysis of Adam and Eve.

At the points at which the fallen angels have the greatest importance, the turning points of the fall and of the relapse, they not only expand the meaning of Satan's development, but complete the analogies and antitheses between the story of the angels and that of mankind. First, the contrast between the fall of Satan and that of his followers resembles the contrast between Adam and Eve in their fall. In both the personal and the religious fall, Eve initiates the action, while Adam at first reacts properly, but later follows Eve into sin. Eve thus shares the guilt of Satan, who initiates the angels' personal and religious fall, while Adam shares the guilt of Satan's followers, who yield to Satan's example. Secondly, the contrast between the two basic positions offered in the infernal council resembles the contrast between Adam and Eve at the beginning of their stage of repentance. Eve's suggestions to remedy her plight and Adam's constitute a defiance of God, while Adam in his lament separates himself from God: Adam plans no resistance (he only speculates on God's intentions and laments his own degradation) but he sins by failing to consider his duty and God's power to elevate him, while Eve suggests taking actions to change their situation. Adam absolves God from the charge of injustice in cursing all mankind, but fails to love him, while Eve proposes the action of barrenness to prevent God's curse from falling upon posterity; Adam acknowledges the justice of God's punishment, but wishes for the death which would end his misery, while Eve proposes the action of suicide to evade God's punishment. Thus Eve shares the sin of Moloch, who defies God, while Adam shares the sin of Belial, who fails to achieve positive dutifulness and virtue, separating himself from God. Lastly, the course of the debate in the infernal council contrasts with the interaction of Adam and Eve during their repentance. The point at which Adam rejects Eve's defiant suggestions is not only a reversal of his actions at the time of the fall and an antithesis to Satan's relapse, during which Satan repeats his fall, but it is also an antithesis to the sort of interaction which is characteristic of the unrepentant; the fallen angels corrupt one another, turning from simple proposals to subtler and more evil ones, while Adam resists evil, prevails upon his wife to do likewise, and returns to piety.

The loyal angels are more essential to the analysis of Adam and Eve; for at the points at which they have the greatest importance, the three incidents in which their ability to resist evil is tried, they indicate by their behavior what Adam and Eve should have done at the time of the fall. (Incidentally, the discussions of the physical nature of angels—their eating [5. 406–33] and their lovemaking [8. 620–29]—aid in this application of angelic conduct to human situations, for the discussions show the essential likeness in the lives of the two sorts of creatures.)

The confrontation of Abdiel and Michael with Satan during the war in heaven, an incident which demonstrates how heresy can be combatted, suggests what arguments Eve should have used against the serpent's heresies. When Eve was incited to determine for herself what laws applied to her, in violation of God's rule, she should not have accepted the idea that a creaturely perfection exists apart from obedience to God's law, but instead should have argued, with Abdiel, that God's pronouncements rather than a creature's opinions determine what is law; and when incited to prove her bravery by disobeying, she should not have accepted the notion that she was free from external control, but should have argued, like Abdiel, that it is weakness rather than strength to disobey. In response to the serpent's deprecations of God's divine attributes, Eve should not have adopted an agnostic doubt, but should have defended those attributes, like Abdiel. When Eve was urged to believe that God had the evil intention of depriving men of their due wisdom, she should not have been seized with suspicion, but should have argued, with Michael, that God is the source of goodness, and that the knowledge of evil does not bring wisdom. And finally, when encouraged to doubt God's punishment, Eve should not have argued herself into skepticism, but should, like Michael, have believed God's threats.

Not only should Eve have been able to answer the serpent's heresies, however, she should have been able to pierce Satan's disguise, like the angels guarding Eden during Satan's first visit to earth. She should, first of all, have been able to defeat Satan's physical disguise. It is true that since Uriel cannot detect Satan when he takes the form of a cherub, Eve could not have penetrated Satan's disguise by simple inspection. But Uriel keeps watch even when there is no cause for suspicion, and thereby catches Satan off his guard; Eve, therefore, should not have been merely surprised by the serpent's speech, but should have been alerted by the unusual circumstance to the possibility of fraud. Once alerted, Eve could have detected Satan by use of reason. When Ithuriel and Zephon find a toad crouching at Eve's ear, they deduce that the toad is Satan in disguise by connecting the toad's interest in Eve with Satan's known interest in man. Eve should have been able to connect the arguments of the serpent with the arguments in her Satan-inspired dream. First of all, elements of the serpent's preliminary personal seduction appear in the dream. The serpent's overestimation of the worth of Eve's beauty coincides with the praises of the tempter in the dream, who tells Eve,

> *Heaven wakes with all his eyes,*
> *Whom to behold but thee, Nature's desire,*
> *In whose sight all things joy, with ravishment*
> *Attracted to thy beauty still to gaze.*
>
> (5. 44–47)

In addition, the serpent's suggestion that Eve needs the adoration and service of the angels is forecast in the tempter's suggestion that Eve should ascend to heaven:

> [B]e henceforth among the gods
> *Thyself a goddess, not to Earth confined,*
> *But sometimes in the air, as we; sometimes*
> *Ascend to Heaven, by merit thine, and see*
> *What life the gods live there, and such live thou.*
>   (5. 77–81)

The serpent's pronouncements about God are also present. The serpent's argument that Eve can attain a happier life by eating the fruit corresponds to a similar assertion in the dream: "[H]appy though thou art, / Happier thou may'st be" (5. 75–76) ; and the serpent's argument that it is brave to disobey is also suggested. The tempter in the dream asks,

> *O fair plant . . . with fruit surcharged,*
> *Deigns none to ease thy load and taste thy sweet,*
> *Nor god, nor man; is knowledge so despised?*
>   (5. 58–60)

He implies that only poverty of spirit could keep a creature from taking the fruit. In addition to attacking God's rule, the tempter advances the serpent's arguments against God's superiority. The argument that others' attainment of wisdom cannot hurt God if he is omnipotent is anticipated in the tempter's assertion that

> *good, the more*
> *Communicated, more abundant grows,*
> *The author not impaired, but honored more;*
>   (5. 71–73)

the argument that God cannot be divine if he is envious is hinted at in the tempter's question, "Or envy, or what reserve forbids to taste?" (5. 61) ; and the conclusion that the fruit can "make gods of men" (5. 70) is broached. Finally, the serpent's aspersions on God's love are anticipated in the dream; the serpent argues that God prohibits the fruit in order to deprive man, and the tempter rejects what is, he implies, an evil prohibition: "forbid who will, none shall from me withhold / Longer [the] offered good [of the tree], why else set here?" (5. 62–63) Since the serpent offers arguments so similar to those of the tempter in the dream, and since that tempter is "One shaped and winged like one of [the angels] from Heaven" (5. 55) , and since (as Eve had learned by the time of the temptation) the foe seeking to tempt man is a fallen angel, Eve should have been able to deduce that the serpent was the angelic tempter in disguise, and that that tempter was Satan.

Eve should also have been able to pierce Satan's verbal disguise, his pretense of friendliness and wisdom. When Gabriel interrogates Satan as to his reasons for being in Eden, he interprets Satan's answers according to God's principles, and therefore is not distracted or lulled by Satan's lies, but instead suspects Satan of duplicity and ill intent. By a like recourse to divine standards, Eve could have discerned the malice behind the serpent's personal advances. When the serpent encouraged Eve to forget the obedience owed to Adam's commands, stressing Eve's sovereignty and minimizing the importance which Adam had placed upon the fruit, and when the serpent encouraged her to forget Adam's superiority, stressing Eve's worth and encouraging her to seek to be envied, Eve should have considered that the serpent was disparaging her husband's guidance and worth, and that he was suggesting that she should abandon her wifely allegiance and respect; she should not simply have made a mild protest at the irrationality of the serpent's praise, but should have suspected that the serpent was attempting to undermine her marriage. And when the serpent approached her with overtones of sexual admiration, and when he proposed that Eve abandon love for sexual vanity, Eve should not have considered him friendly, but should have been angered by the suggestion of adultery and insulted by the suggestion of whoredom—should have considered the serpent a depraved enemy. Similar recourse to divine standards would have exposed the evil behind the serpent's pose of wisdom in his attack on God. Judging the serpent according to his obedience and his acknowledgment of God's superiority, and according to his love and awe, Eve would have found that if his tale were true, the serpent would have learned from the fruit to defy the laws of God with presumptuous self-righteousness, to derogate the creator of the universe, to suspect the motives of the Being to whom he owes gratitude, and to boast his unpunished audacity— results which should at least have caused Eve to doubt the serpent's interpretation of his experience, and which, placing the serpent's character in doubt, should have caused her to wonder whether the whole tale were not a fabrication intended to deceive and corrupt her.

In addition to applying God's standards, Gabriel determines by logic that Satan is lying: Eve could have detected the serpent's hidden purpose by similar means. All the serpent's arguments attack the proper relation of man to God, but they posit different views of God's nature. When attacking God's rule, the serpent argues that God will honor the bravery of a creature who is undeterred in his pursuit of wisdom; the assumption is that God has an indulgent nature. But in attacking divine goodness, the serpent argues that God intends to degrade man; the assumption here is that God is malicious. When doubting God's wrath, the serpent argues that his safety proves the safety of man from God's threat; the assumption is that God would not punish man for what he allows to beasts, that he is not, therefore, arbitrary. But in attacking divine superiority, the serpent argues that God is using his earlier existence to impose the belief that he is the creator; God, it is assumed, is a liar. Since indulgence and malice, reasonableness and deceptiveness are contraries, Eve should have been suspicious of the serpent's argument, and she should have seen that what all his arguments have in common is their end, the justification of disobedience, and she should have wondered why the serpent was so interested in having her disobey that he would use any arguments, however inconsistent, to persuade her to that end. Logic would have led Eve to suspect that the serpent was an enemy intending to ruin her by separating her from God.

These two tests of the angels' ability to resist evil suggest, then, what Eve should have done at the time of her fall; and the incident that ends the second test, God's hanging of his scales in the heavens, suggests what would have happened if Eve had acted as she should. The fact that in his speech upon viewing Eve, Satan confesses to fear of Adam's strength of mind and limb indicates that Satan contemplates violence as well as seduction; if Eve had resisted his seduction, Satan might have attempted force, whereupon God would have intervened, as he intervened to prevent the combat between Satan and the guardians of Eden.

The third angelic test, Abdiel's confrontation with Satan during the fall of the angels, indicates what Adam should have done when Eve tempted him after her fall. First, like Abdiel, Adam should have attempted to reconcile his loyalty to God and his loyalty to creatures. Instead of rationalizing and repeating Eve's heresies, Adam should have proclaimed his loyalty to God by voicing his earlier insights into Eve's transgressions, just as Abdiel refutes Satan's heresies. Then he should have tried to make Eve repent. As Abdiel refers to the causes and effects of Satan's actions to persuade Satan to reconsider, so Adam should have told Eve that she had been deceived and ruined, so as to make her aware of her need for repentance; and as Abdiel sets himself up as the voice of resistance in order to keep the other angels from joining Satan, so Adam should have refused to join Eve, insisting that she join him through penitence.

It is true that Abdiel addresses angels who have not yet fallen, and who are therefore able to change, while Adam would be addressing a fallen Eve. But Eve is not, like the angels, "self-tempted"; therefore she is at least possibly eligible, as they are not, for the grace that would enable her to change despite her fall. Adam could, thus, have succeeded in an attempt to change her, just as Abdiel has a chance of success at the time of his speech. But if forced to choose between allegiances, Adam should, like Abdiel, have chosen the higher allegiance. If Eve had shown herself adamant against repentance, Adam should have answered whatever arguments she had advanced, blamed her obstinacy, and made clear her doom, following Abdiel's example. If this course seems callous, it should be noted that the course chosen by Adam results in a similar action—Adam's retraction of his marriage vow and his banishment of Eve after the Son's judgment. The latter action can more justly be called callous, however, for in the hypothetical case Adam would be acting justly, while in the real case he acts without rational or moral grounds. What consequences Adam's earlier divorce from Eve would have had, the poem does not suggest.

In addition to their direct thematic function, then, the minor characters contribute to the theme indirectly, by aiding in the evaluation of Adam and Eve. The principal actions of the fallen angels relate to the two turning points in the main plot, the fall and the repentance, and serve to complete the analogies and antitheses between the poem's two plots, while the principal actions of the loyal angels relate to the first turning point, suggesting what actions Adam and Eve should have taken at the time of the fall.

The prophecy of Michael relates indirectly to the theme of *Paradise Lost*. The expository structure of the prophecy is connected with, basically, the theological premises and the secondary plot of the poem—with elements, then, which in turn bear on the theme. But in addition, the prophecy has a direct relationship to the theme, for through its incidents it presents versions of the two main defenses of God offered in the poem—moral applications of those defenses, to be exact.

Though Satan's plot defends God by showing the bad effects of denying him, it also has an obvious moral application, serving as a warning to men not to follow Satan's example. (It is true, of course, that Satan's story differs in certain respects from the story of any human sinner, for God denies Satan the grace and the offer of salvation which he grants to man, and logically must punish Satan for something other than rejecting grace and salvation. But human sinners can place themselves in Satan's position by refusing to heed God's call to repentance, and by refusing to have faith in the Savior, whereupon they bring upon themselves Satan's fate.) In like manner, the positive defense of God offered through the main plot serves to exhort men to the Christian life; for, as all men, according to God's curse, must follow Adam and Eve into sin, all may choose, like Adam and Eve, to accept God's gifts and attain salvation. This moral application of the poem's defenses is aided by the minor characters, who function as moral examples at a lower level of abstraction. Abdiel, described as relying upon his knowledge of God's nature in defiance of "number" and "example" (5. 896–903), is a type of the religious man; and the four participants in the debate in hell are clearly intended to be human social types. Moloch is a warrior, and Belial, with his sophistication and inner depravity, is a libertine, a type which includes men of church as well as of court, Belial's followers being priests (1. 492–96) and courtiers (1. 497–505) whose amusements are lechery and brawling. Mammon, admirer of heaven's golden floor—of God's possessions rather than his attributes—is a type of the merchant, while Beelzebub, who, in debating, proposes the conversion of all other interests into spite, is a type of the criminal. The games in hell, recalling the arts, contests, wars, and explorations of the pagan world, suggest that the ends for which unreligious men live are ultimately empty.

The prophecy of Michael contains a final moral application of the poem's defenses of God. The first section of the prophecy, the section on evil, offers an application of the negative defense, a series of examples of how men ought not live. The first part of this section, the part on death, makes relatively little contribution, though Michael's moralizing on violence (ll. 423–28) and intemperance (ll. 530–34) turns the figures of the first two visions, Cain and the inmates of the hospital, into examples of vice. The second part of the section, the part on sin, is more significant; it applies the four stages of spiritual decline to examples of human misconduct. The seduction of pious men is connected with the fall in the vision of the sons of Seth, human warfare with the rebellion in the vision of the giants, human folly and tyranny with the relapse in the account of Nimrod, and men's debauchery with the deterioration in the vision of the contemporaries of Noah. The contrasting second section of the prophecy, the section devoted to good, offers an application of the positive defense of God, a series of examples of how men ought to behave. What each example proves is stated by Adam; for it is from the account of God's plan to rescue mankind that Adam derives his final summary of moral doctrine:

> *Henceforth I learn, that to obey is best,*
> *And love with fear the only God, to walk*
> *As in his presence, ever to observe*
> *His providence, and on him sole depend,*
> *Merciful over all his works, with good*
> *Still overcoming evil, and by small*
> *Accomplishing great things, by things deemed weak*
> *Subverting worldly strong, and worldly wise*
> *By simply meek; that suffering for truth's sake*
> *Is fortitude to highest victory,*
> *And to the faithful death the gate of life;*
> *Taught this by his example whom I now*
> *Acknowledge my Redeemer ever blest.*
> (*12. 561–73*)

In the opening reference to obedience by which Adam indicates what response is due to God the lawgiver, he refers to the example of the patriarchs, the "men / Obedient to his will" with whom God deigned "to dwell" (12. 244–48). In the phrase "to walk / As in his presence" by which Adam indicates what response is due to God the judge, Adam refers to the example of all "the just," who have nothing to fear at Christ's second coming, "the day" for them "of respiration" (12. 539–40). When Adam states what response is owed to God the giver of grace, saying that he has learned to "observe / [God's] providence, and on him sole depend," he refers to the example of the apostles and their converts; for they are the "good" who triumph, the "weak" and the "meek" who overcome persecution and error. Finally, before the proclamation of faith which completes Adam's statement of what response is owed to God the savior, Adam finds in Christ's human life a model for two qualities of the redeemed, their ability to face trial and their ability to meet death in confidence of immortality. In both sections of the prophecy, lastly, the major examples are set off by minor contrasting examples: the rebellious giants are contrasted with the just Enoch, the debauched contemporaries of Noah with the redeemed Noah, the apostles and their followers with their worldly successors.

Thus, though the prophecy of Michael is the least integral element in the poem, it not only has structural and intellectual connections with the other elements, but is directly related to the theme of the poem. By its application of the poem's defenses of God to the moral life of men, it bears on that defense of God through moral analysis of his creatures which *Paradise Lost* offers through its minor characters and through its double plot.[2]

NOTES / INDEX

Notes

Introduction

[1] Joseph Summers, *The Muse's Method: An Introduction to "Paradise Lost"* (London, 1962), p. 177.

[2] Jackson I. Cope, *The Metaphoric Structure of "Paradise Lost"* (Baltimore, 1962).

[3] See E. M. W. Tillyard, *Milton* (London, 1930), pp. 241–43.

[4] Denis Saurat, *Milton: Man and Thinker* (New York, 1925), p. 213.

[5] B. Rajan, *"Paradise Lost" and the Seventeenth Century Reader* (London, 1947), p. 44.

[6] Ibid., pp. 44–46.   [7] Ibid., pp. 45–46.   [8] Ibid., p. 45.

[9] See Walter Raleigh, *Milton* (London, 1900), pp. 81–82.

[10] E. M. W. Tillyard, *Studies in Milton* (London, 1951).

[11] *Milton*, pp. 243–54.   [12] *Studies*, pp. 13–14.   [13] *Milton*, p. 243.

[14] Ibid., pp. 245–46.   [15] Ibid., pp. 249–51.   [16] *Studies*, pp. 44–45.

[17] Ibid., pp. 10–13.   [18] Ibid., p. 12.   [19] Ibid., pp. 13–14.

[20] Ibid., p. 45.   [21] Ibid., p. 50.   [22] *Spectator*, No. 267.

[23] Ibid.

[24] See his account of its "fable" in Douglas Bush, *"Paradise Lost" in Our Time: Some Comments* (New York, 1945), pp. 49–53.

[25] Ibid., p. 64.   [26] *Studies*, p. 50.   [27] Ibid., p. 45.

[28] Ibid., pp. 45–49.   [29] *"Paradise Lost" in Our Time*, p. 74.

[30] Ibid., pp. 62–74.   [31] Ibid., p. 79.   [32] *Studies*, p. 60.

[33] *Milton*, p. 88.   [34] Ibid., p. 87.   [35] Ibid., pp. 132–33.

[36] Ibid., p. 139.   [37] Ibid., p. 133.

[38] On Satan, see William Epson, *Milton's God* (London, 1961), pp. 37–61, 71–89; on Eve, pp. 147–64; on Adam, pp. 182–89.

[39] Ibid., pp. 61–71.   [40] Ibid., p. 53.   [41] *Studies*, pp. 45–49.

[42] *Spectator*, No. 297.   [43] *Milton*, p. 129.   [44] *Spectator*, No. 369.

[45] Dick Taylor, Jr., "Milton and the Paradox of the Fortunate Fall Once More," *Tulane Studies in English* 9 (1959) : 50–51.

[46] Lawrence A. Sasek, "The Drama of *Paradise Lost*, Books XI and XII," *Studies in English Renaissance Literature*, ed. Waldo F. McNeir, Louisiana

State University Studies, Humanities Series, No. 12 (Baton Rouge, La., 1962), pp. 195–96.

[47] "Paradox of the Fortunate Fall," pp. 48–49.

[48] Asserting that even Michael is ignorant of God's full intent ("The Fortunate Fall in *Paradise Lost*," *MLN* 74 [1959]: 103), which, he says, goes beyond the mere "legal transaction" which the angel describes to Adam (ibid., p. 104) —the account, he says, gives Adam "very little to rejoice at" (p. 103) —Madsen argues that God makes the fall a positive benefit to mankind by initiating a "new and higher order of existence" (p. 105). This order, man's "mystical union with God," is, he says (p. 104), announced in the opening colloquy in heaven (3. 281–94, 303–4, 311–17) and reaffirmed in the Son's description of the prayers of the penitent Adam and Eve:

> *Fruits of more pleasing savor from thy seed*
> *Sown with contrition in [man's] heart, than those*
> *Which his own hand manuring, all the trees*
> *Of Paradise could have produced, ere fallen*
> *From innocence.*
>
> (*11. 26–30*)

Madsen argues that the Son here is not contrasting "the easily-won . . . moral fruits of unfallen man" with the "bitter-sweet fruits of moral struggle," but rather the "purely human fruits produced by man's 'own hand' " with the "supernatural fruits produced by man's transplanting in Christ" (p. 105). One objection to this theory is the question of how Michael could be ignorant of a doctrine which God expounds not in a private but in a public exchange: the angels are said to listen with "Admiration" to the dialogue in heaven (3. 271–73). Another objection is the uncertainty of Madsen's reading of the Son's plea for man. The fact that the Son likens grace to God's earlier gift of Eden suggests that he is comparing two instances of gratitude, man's acceptance of grace and the thankfulness for Eden which man shows by his careful tending of the Garden. Thus read, the passage asserts the preciousness of repentance to God, and the interpretation is bolstered by the resemblance of the sentiment to that in the text from Luke: "joy shall be in heaven over one sinner that repenteth, more than over ninety and nine just persons, which need no repentance." The main objection to Madsen's theory, however, is its inherent improbability. It is unlikely that Adam would be shown as rejoicing over a doctrine which Milton thought devoid of comfort, or that God would be shown as concealing from Adam a doctrine which Milton thought God's only adequate defense.

[49] A. O. Lovejoy, "Milton and the Paradox of the Fortunate Fall," *ELH* 4 (1937): 179.

[50] *Milton's God*, p. 191.

[51] Millicent Bell, "The Fallacy of the Fall in *Paradise Lost*," *PMLA* 67 (1953): 880–81.

[52] Ibid., p. 881.

[53] William H. Marshall, *"Paradise Lost: Felix Culpa* and the Problem of Structure," *MLN* 76 (1961) : 17.

[54] Note also:

> *[H]er rash hand in evil hour*
> *Forth reaching to the fruit, she plucked, she eat.*
> *Earth felt the wound, and Nature from her seat*
> *Sighing through all her works gave signs of woe,*
> *That all was lost.*
>
> > *(9. 780–84)*

> *Adam, soon as he heard*
> *The fatal trespass done by Eve, amazed,*
> *Astonied stood and blank, while horror chill*
> *Ran through his veins, and all his joints relaxed;*
> *From his slack hand the garland wreathed for Eve*
> *Down dropped, and all the faded roses shed.*
>
> > *(9. 888–93)*

> *Soon as the force of that fallacious fruit,*
> *That with exhilarating vapor bland*
> *About their spirits had played, and inmost powers*
> *Made err, was now exhaled, and grosser sleep,*
> *Bred of unkindly fumes, with conscious dreams*
> *Encumbered, now had left them, up they rose*
> *As from unrest, and each the other viewing,*
> *Soon found their eyes how opened, and their minds*
> *How darkened; innocence, that as a veil*
> *Had shadowed them from knowing ill, was gone;*
> *Just confidence, and native righteousness,*
> *And honor from about them, naked left*
> *To guilty Shame. He covered, but his robe*
> *Uncovered more.*
>
> > *(9. 1046–59)*

[55] A. J. A. Waldock, *"Paradise Lost" and Its Critics* (Cambridge, 1947), p. 57.

[56] "Milton and the Paradox of the Fortunate Fall," p. 179.

[57] *"Paradise Lost: Felix Culpa* and the Problem of Structure," p. 17.

[58] Ibid., p. 17*n*, quoting Waldock, pp. 91–92.

[59] *Metaphoric Structure*, p. 22.

[60] Arnold Stein, *Answerable Style: Essays on "Paradise Lost"* (Minneapolis, 1953), p. 8.

[61] *"Paradise Lost" and the Seventeenth Century Reader*, p. 72.

[62] Ibid., p. 71.   [63] Ibid., p. 74.   [64] *"Paradise Lost" in Our Time*, p. 47.

[65] Tillyard, *Milton*, p. 262.   [66] Ibid., p. 261.
[67] *"Paradise Lost" and Its Critics*, pp. 57–58.
[68] *"Paradise Lost" in Our Time*, p. 17.
[69] *"Paradise Lost" and Its Critics*, p. 60.
[70] *"Paradise Lost" in Our Time*, p. 52.   [71] Ibid., p. 81.
[72] Ibid., pp. 83–84.
[73] *"Paradise Lost" and the Seventeenth Century Reader*, p. 63.
[74] Ibid., pp. 69–70.   [75] London, 1616, p. 17, quoted by Rajan, p. 70.
[76] *"Paradise Lost" and the Seventeenth Century Reader*, pp. 56–57.
[77] Ibid., p. 67.   [78] Ibid., pp. 63–65.   [79] Ibid., p. 71.
[80] Ibid., p. 78.   [81] *"Paradise Lost" in Our Time,"* p. 84.
[82] See Saurat, pp. 209–10.   [83] Ibid., p. 151.   [84] Ibid., pp. 173–74.
[85] Ibid., p. 160.   [86] See Waldock, p. 33*n*.

1 The Premises

[1] Since I have confined my account of God's nature to those characteristics that bear on his function in *Paradise Lost*, those which are directly involved in the relationship of God and his creatures, I have not handled three topics usually treated when God is discussed—the matter of Milton's orthodoxy, the matter of the defensibility of Milton's philosophy, and the matter of Milton's characterization of God. In the first case the materials lie outside my subject; in the other two cases the topics lie outside it.

In the process of determining what doctrines figured in the judgment of the poem's central characters, I found that the heresies most commonly assigned to Milton were not doctrines of this kind—a fact which explains, I think, why these heresies are so debatably present in the work.

Some heresies, the boldest ones, are demonstrably not present in the poem. Saurat's claim that Milton's God is "identical with the Absolute of nineteenth century philosophy" (*Milton: Man and Thinker* [New York, 1925], p. 113) has long been refuted, and William Empson's theory that God is "an emergent or evolutionary deity" (*Milton's God* [London, 1961], p. 130) is similarly based on misreadings. Empson argues first of all that when the Father announces the elevation of the incarnate Son, he is announcing that he will abdicate "in the sense of becoming totally immanent or invisible" (ibid., p. 139):

> *Therefore thy humiliation shall exalt*
> *With thee thy manhood also to this throne;*
> *Here shalt thou sit incarnate, here shalt reign*
> *Both God and Man, Son both of God and Man,*
> *Anointed universal King. All power*
> *I give thee; reign for ever, and assume*
> *Thy merits; under thee as Head supreme*
> *Thrones, Princedoms, Powers, Dominions, I reduce.*
> *(3. 313–20)*

Empson explains that the Father must be giving the Son his own throne, because the Son could not be rewarded with the gift of what he already owns, and because "the sequence 'this throne . . . here . . . here . . . Head Supreme'" would be "very empty rhetoric if it [did] not refer to the supreme throne" (*Milton's God*, pp. 137–38). But according to Michael's account of the Son's ascension, the Son is to return to his own throne, rather than succeed to the Father's; Michael says that the Son will "enter into glory, and resume / His seat at God's right hand" (12. 456–57). The news, then, is not that the Son is being given a new throne, but that he will occupy his old throne in a new state; and what the sequence emphasizes is not the words "throne" and "here" but the words "thy manhood," "incarnate," and "Both God and Man," the words which designate this new state. What the passage stresses, furthermore, is not the idea of reward (Milton has undercut that reward with his earlier elevation of the Son), but the means by which, as the Father says, the Son's "descending to assume / Man's nature" will be kept from "lessen[ing] or degrad[ing]" his divinity (3. 303–4). The point of the passage is that the enthronement of the incarnate Son raises man to godhood, and so compensates for God's descent to manhood.

The second passage on which Empson's theory relies is the Father's description of the end of the world, in which, Empson says, the Father foretells his final absorption of the creatures:

> *Meanwhile*
> *The World shall burn, and from her ashes spring*
> *New Heaven and Earth, wherein the just shall dwell,*
> *And after all their tribulations long*
> *See golden days, fruitful of golden deeds,*
> *With Joy and Love triumphing, and fair Truth.*
> *Then thou thy regal scepter shalt lay by,*
> *For regal scepter then no more shall need;*
> *God shall be all in all. But all ye gods,*
> *Adore him, who to compass all this dies,*
> *Adore the Son, and honor him as me.*
>
> (3. 333–43)

Empson argues that by using the impersonal verb "shall need" to suggest that the Father as well as the Son will have no need for authority, and by appending the final equation of the Father with the Son to suggest that the Father too will (in a figurative sense) die, Milton converts St. Paul's "autocrat[ic]" text into a "pantheis[tic]" one (pp. 134–35). But Empson omits from his quotation the lines which describe the life of "the just," and those lines make the pantheistic hypothesis less probable than its alternative, for it is easier to make conventional interpretations of the lines about the Son's scepter and merit than it is to explain what sort of "golden deeds" can occur in a world in which creatures have all been absorbed into the deity.

If the most radical heresies attributed to Milton are disprovable from the text, the heresies most commonly attributed to him cannot be finally disproved. These are the heresies of Arianism, materialism, and mortalism, the heresies whose presence in *De Doctrina Christiana* is unmistakable. But, if these heresies cannot be definitely disproved, they cannot be definitely proved, either, despite the parallels that Maurice Kelley draws between the poem and the treatise (in *This Great Argument: A Study of Milton's "De Doctrina Christiana" as a Gloss upon "Paradise Lost"* [Princeton, N. J., 1941]). B. Rajan has noted that the speech of Raphael (5. 469–505) which has been cited as evidence of materialism can be taken as a conventional expression of the idea of the chain of being (*"Paradise Lost" and the Seventeenth Century Reader* [London, 1947], pp. 26–27, 59–62), and that though Adam mentions the doctrine of mortalism in his lament (10. 782–816), the state of the speaker negates his pronouncements (ibid., pp. 27–28).

The case for Arianism is similarly tenuous. The most that Kelley can claim is that most of the passages relevant to the subject are as susceptible to Arian as to Trinitarian interpretation (*Great Argument*, p. 120). Only one passage does he claim to be unmistakably Arian, and on the basis of this passage he argues the Arianism of the whole. The passage is part of the reply of the newly created Adam to God's test of his rationality:

> *No need that thou*
> *Shouldst propagate, already infinite,*
> *And through all numbers absolute, though One.*
> *(8. 419–21)*

Kelley argues that the passage asserts the Arian view of the voluntary generation of the Son as opposed to the Trinitarian view of his necessary generation (pp. 120–21). But, in the first place, Adam must be addressing the Son, for God is visible to him (8. 367–68), and the Son is "he in whose face invisible is beheld / Visibly, what by Deity" the Father is (6. 681–82). This being the case, the phrase "No need that thou / Shouldst propagate" cannot possibly refer to the creation by the Father of the Son. Even if Adam were addressing the Father, his speech could not be interpreted as an assertion of Arianism if God's argument and Adam's entire reply are examined. God argues thus:

> *What thinkest thou then of me, and this my state?*
> *Seem I to thee sufficiently possessed*
> *Of happiness, or not? who am alone*
> *From all eternity; for none I know*
> *Second to me or like, equal much less.*
> *How have I then with whom to hold converse*
> *Save with the creatures which I made, and those*
> *To me inferior infinite descents*
> *Beneath what other creatures are to thee?*
> *(8. 403–11)*

Adam's reply takes the form of an antithesis:

> *No need that thou*
> *Shouldst propagate, already infinite,*
> *And through all numbers absolute, though One;*
> *But Man by number is to manifest*
> *His single imperfection, and beget*
> *Like of his like, his image multiplied,*
> *In unity defective, which requires*
> *Collateral love, and dearest amity.*

> (8. 419–26)

First of all, if Adam is saying that God procreates voluntarily, then the antithesis which he is drawing is that man manifests his imperfection by procreating while God manifests his perfection by procreating when he does not need to. This antithesis is so clumsy that an alternative reading is demanded, a reading in which Adam would be straightforwardly arguing that man manifests his imperfection by procreating, and God his perfection by not procreating. Adam, in this reading, would be using the word "propagate" in the narrow sense of "to reproduce sexually," the sense which is consistent with his later reference to "Collateral love"; he would not be using the word in the sense of "to proceed" or "to emanate," the sense which would apply to the generation of the Son. The reference to divine sexual reproduction would not be pointless, furthermore, for Adam would be demonstrating a prelapsarian insight into God's nature which contrasts with the mistaken notions of his fallen descendants in Greece and Rome.

In the second place, if Adam's reply refers to the generation of the Son, then the Father would have to be referring to the Son in the speech to which Adam is replying; otherwise Adam would be making a strangely irrelevant reply: God would be saying that he has only angels and men to talk to, and Adam would be answering that the Father made the Son voluntarily. If God is referring to the generation of the Son, however, then "creatures which I made" would have to lump the Son together with men and angels; "none I know / Second to me or like" would have to refer to the inferiority of the Son, rather than to the nonexistence of any second god; "those / To me nferior infinite descents / Beneath what other creatures are to thee" would have to mean that not only are men and angels inferior to God, but that even the Son is as inferior to the Father as the irrational brutes are to Adam. These are startling pronouncements even for an Arian deity, and they contrast markedly with the terms with which the Father addresses the Son: "Effulgence of my glory . . . Second Omnipotence" (6. 680, 684), "Son who art alone / My word, my wisdom, and effectual might" (3. 169–70). Furthermore, though Adam's reply would not be irrelevant to such a speech by God, the reply could only mean that man is obliged to procreate (and therefore has to take his chances with his offspring) whereas the Father did not have to make the Son (and therefore should stop complaining if he isn't good company).

Clearly, then, the dialogue has nothing to do with the subject of the Son's generation. God, by way of test, is merely comparing his relation with men and angels to Adam's relation with the animals, arguing that Adam is no more alone than he is. Adam detects the fallacy, and points out the difference between God' and man—that God is self-complete while man is not. The passage does not disprove the existence of Arianism in *Paradise Lost,* but it certainly does not prove its existence, being, in fact, irrelevant to the subject. The case for this heresy is therefore as uncertain as the case for mortalism or the case for materialism.

This is not to say that when Milton defines doctrines he tries to avoid controversial ones. C. S. Lewis claims that Milton excludes his "private theological whimsies" from *Paradise Lost* in order to produce a poem which is "Except for a few isolated passages . . . not even specifically Protestant or Puritan" but "as far as doctrine goes . . . Christian" (*A Preface to "Paradise Lost"* [London, 1942], p. 91). However, because he assumes that Milton's account of the fall follows Augustine (ibid., p. 65), Lewis claims that Milton's views on sexuality are Augustine's (ibid., pp. 68–69), though he thinks that Milton did not adequately render these views (pp. 118–20); and because he views the poem as a *"mimesis* of the Fall" (p. 91), he does not mention the poem's views on grace and salvation. He misses, thus, what A. J. A. Waldock notes (in *"Paradise Lost" and Its Critics* [Cambridge, 1947], p. 62), that Milton is totally rejecting, and not, therefore, misrendering, Augustine's view of prelapsarian sex; and he fails to notice that when he dismisses the questions of grace and election upon which Milton takes an anti-Calvinist stand, and the question of faith and works upon which Milton is anti-Catholic, he is dismissing as the subject of "a few isolated passages" the doctrines that figure in half the main action of the poem. When Milton wants to present not Augustine's literal fall but his own view of human moral perfection, he introduces what Lewis would consider a private theological whimsy; when he needs to define a doctrine which figures in the action of his poem, he defines his position and takes the chance of alienating the doctrinally scrupulous of various sects. In doctrinal matters Milton does not strive for maximum acceptability, and if he leaves ambiguous the questions of Arianism, materialism, and mortalism, the reason must lie in the irrelevance of these subjects to his theme.

The reason, then, that these three heresies are so ambiguously treated in *Paradise Lost* is surely that Milton is not trying to treat them. *Paradise Lost* is essentially a moral work, not a metaphysical one; it deals not with the nature of the universe, like *De Doctrina,* but with the moral development of God's creatures. Because the moral status of Adam and Eve and of Satan is not dependent upon whether they believe that the Son was necessarily or voluntarily created, whether they believe that the universe is composed of one substance or two, whether they believe that when a man dies, his soul' lives on or is temporarily extinguished, Milton has no reason to take a position on these issues. He does not, therefore, even raise them as metaphysical questions, but only touches upon them incidentally to some moral point which is germane to his purpose. Thus, even if the passage that Kelley cites as proof of the Arianism of *Paradise Lost* were in fact concerned with the generation of the Son, the point of the passage would not be the nature of God but the moral status of Adam, who shows that at this time he knows what his place is in the universe. Similarly, in the passage that Kelley cites as proof of materialism, the point is not the physical nature of the universe, but the nature of man's duty and the reward promised for man's obedience; in accordance with God's instructions that he "such discourse bring on, / As may advise [Adam] of his happy state" (5. 233–34), Raphael is paraphrasing for Adam what God announced at the time of his creation of the world, that he plans to elevate mankind after a trial of man's loyalty (7. 150–61). And in the passage which Kelley cites as proof of mortalism, the point is not the nature of death but the moral status of Adam, who is here speculating on matters beyond his knowing instead of attending to his duties. In cases like these, the reason that no definite information on heresies can be elicited is that the heresies involved are not doctrinally relevant to the poem and are, therefore, not the subjects of the passages.

I do not treat the question of Milton's orthodoxy, then, because I have come to believe that the usually mentioned heresies are not doctrines essential to God's function in *Paradise Lost*. The second common subject which I do not treat is the defensibility of Milton's idea of God. I have felt that the principle of suspended disbelief should be applied to this subject, and that a defense of Milton's theology is neither feasible nor desirable.

In the first place, it is doubtful that Milton's theology can be defended to anyone who is at all inclined to doubt it. Much of what critics offer as defense could convince only partisans of their cause. C. S. Lewis quips that "Many of these who say they dislike Milton's God only mean that they dislike God: infinite sovereignty *de jure* combined with infinite power *de facto,* and love which, by its very nature, includes wrath also—it is not only in poetry that these things offend" (*Preface,* p. 126) ; he assumes that a god exists and that this god is the god of classical theism, a procedure which does not answer those who—like Empson in his discussion of God's absolute sovereignty (*Milton's God,* pp. 161–62) —question the validity of those premises. Douglas Bush, defending Milton's God from the charge of harshness and tyranny, says that "Many persons . . . [prefer,] and think that Milton should have preferred, a Browningesque Deity who was all Love and nothing else, an infinitely vague and amiable grandfather" (*"Paradise Lost" in Our Time: Some Comments* [New York, 1945], pp. 40–41) ; he provides no answer to the sort of objection which Empson raises (or revives), that God's wrath is morally evil because God tortures without the intention of inducing reform (*Milton's God,* pp. 19–20).

Even John S. Diekhoff, the most analytic and thorough of the orthodox defenders, sometimes relies on assumptions which no doubter would grant and which come close to begging the question. For example, on the subject of God's curse upon mankind, Diekhoff argues that "for Milton, God's justice is inseparable from his mercy" (*Milton's "Paradise Lost": A Commentary on the Argument* [New York, 1946], p. 114). God's justice, he says, may be rendered suspect by the condemnation of men who, because of the sin imputed from Adam, have never been free, and therefore have never been true moral agents (ibid.) ; but, he says, God's mercy exonerates his justice, in that God restores men's freedom and allows them to choose salvation, balancing the merit imputed from the Son against the imputed sin by which they have been condemned (pp. 122–23). Diekhoff's argument relies for its acceptance on the prior belief in what the argument is supposed to prove, that God is good; for without this prior belief, it is impossible to grant that God is justified in condemning a man who is innocent because he later offers to pardon the nonexistent crimes, or that God is generous in offering conditions of pardon to a man whom he has wrongfully condemned. Furthermore, the argument relies for its acceptance on the prior belief in the reasonableness of God's transactions, another matter which the argument is supposed to prove; for without this assumption, it is impossible to grant that if a man is wrongfully condemned on the basis of a second man's guilt, it is just and right to pardon him on the basis of a third man's innocence.

But even if critics argued in a way which doubters could accept, and even if the doctrines presented were presumed to be defensible, *Paradise Lost* would still be impossible to defend; for the poem itself does not always present valid arguments, and where its proof is defective, no proof by the critic, however valid, can save it. For example, the doctrine of election which is present in the poem, though it is not subject, like the Calvinist doctrine, to the objection that it makes God a despot who arbitrarily saves some and damns others, is nevertheless open to the objection that it makes God a despot who arbitrarily withholds from some the favors which he grants to others. There may be an answer to this objection, but no answer can defend the poem, for in the poem God is represented as establishing the doctrine by arbitrary fiat: "Some I have chosen of peculiar grace / Elect above the rest; so is my will" (3. 183–84). If a critic attempts to defend *Paradise Lost* in matters like this—in places where Milton has taken for granted a challengeable premise or failed to consider an issue—the critic ends by writing what is not in fact criticism of the poem. If Diekhoff's premises about the problem are granted (for further discussion, see note 6 to chapter 2), his explanation of why God does not grant to Satan's followers the grace which he grants to Adam and Eve is a case in point. Arguing that God's explanation is that man was tempted while the angels were not (so he reads God's statement that the angels "by their own suggestion fell, / Self-tempted" [3. 129–31]), Diekhoff claims that God's explanation is defective, in that Satan is shown as tempting his followers as he tempted Eve (ibid., pp. 99–101). After considering alternative explanations, Diekhoff finally suggests that what justifies God's discrimination is the fact that in falling, Satan's followers fail to love good, while Adam and Eve only prefer a lower to a greater good (pp. 103–4). The trouble with this suggestion is that, though it may be more satisfactory than the explanation that God gives (granted Diekhoff's reading), it is not applicable to the poem. When God provides an explanation for his action, that explanation must be taken as the final one; if an alternative is needed, God must either be fallibly offering a faulty argument or deliberately concealing the truth from his auditor, either of which interpretations violates the premises of the poem. In remedying what (given his reading) is a defect, Diekhoff offers a defense which may have merit as theology, but which cannot apply to God the character in *Paradise Lost*.

Not only is the defense of Milton's theology impractical, however, it is also undesirable. The defenders of *Paradise Lost* are anxious to answer Shelley's claim, made in the *Defense of Poetry*, that Milton made his God more evil than his devil (see Lewis, p. 92; Bush, p. 62; Diekhoff, pp. 29–31). To this claim, two answers are possible. One is the religious objection to Shelley's view of the Christian deity, the other the literary objection to Shelley's refusal to accept the postulates of a work whenever these disagree with his own beliefs. Insofar as critics defend Milton's theology, they answer Shelley on religious grounds. The choice is unwise. First of all, it turns what should be a literary dispute into a religious quarrel. When Empson asserts that Milton's "subject cannot be viewed in a purely aesthetic manner" (*Milton's God*, p. 9), and proceeds to argue from every questionable premise and every inadequate argument the wickedness of God (see pp. 93–95, for example), he is proceeding from the premises supplied him by the religious defenders of *Paradise Lost*: if they can argue that the goodness of the God of *Paradise Lost* is to be granted on the basis of the validity of Milton's theology, then he can argue that this goodness is to be denied on the basis of the invalidity of that theology. A comparatively simple interpretive question has been swallowed up in an endless theological dispute, for the subject of debate here is the validity of Christian dogma, and the debate cannot end, by the defenders' own calculations, till the conversion of the Jews.

In the second place, the religious defense puts emphasis on what is secondary in *Paradise Lost*. It may lead, as it does in the work of C. S. Lewis, to the placing of emphasis on what is thematically secondary. Lewis, having defended the theology of *Paradise Lost* against the charge of heresy (*Preface*, pp. 81–90), tells Christian readers that the poem is a "great ritual *mimesis* of the Fall" in which "all Christendom" can join (ibid., p. 91). In accordance with this interpretation, Lewis advises non-Christian aesthetes to accept the poem's idea of obedience "as they accept the inexplicable prohibitions in *Lohengrin, Cinderella,* or *Cupid and Psyche*" or as they accept the theme of the tale of Peter Rabbit, who "came to grief because he *would* go into Mr. McGregor's garden" (p. 70); other non-Christians he tells to try "by an effort of historical imagination" to understand Milton's world view (pp. 70–71). For Lewis, *Paradise Lost* is an account of historical events in Eden, and the reading of it is a religious act, like attendance at Mass. Non-Christian readers are visitors at the Mass: some are children, told to be quiet and listen to the pretty music; others are merely poor ignorant heretics, given pamphlets and tracts so that they can understand the service. Properly, however, the Mass belongs to the believers alone. Lewis misses what Bush sees about *Paradise Lost,* that it is not primarily a history, meaningful only to people who believe in a literal fall as interpreted by a particular theological scheme, but rather an account, fictional in its universality, of man's moral experience, of, as Bush puts it, "the trials and weaknesses of every man and every woman" (*"Paradise Lost" in Our Time*, p. 47). Lewis's approach, thus, is that of a man who reads *Macbeth* as a re-creation of true happenings in ancient Scotland.

But even if the religious defense avoids emphasis on what is thematically secondary, it places emphasis on what is structurally secondary. Although Bush does treat *Paradise Lost* as a "universal example" (ibid.), he stresses acceptance of the theological beliefs which underlie the narrative (see pp. 48, 56–57, for example). This procedure does not misrepresent the work, but it does place weight on its premises rather than on what is built upon these premises, the delineation of moral change in the persons of the central characters. The approach, thus, is that of a man who reads *Macbeth* for its presentation of King James's warnings about witches.

For both C. S. Lewis and Bush, *Paradise Lost* is equivalent to Genesis. Genesis contains the account of events in Eden for which Lewis reads *Paradise Lost*, and it can be read doctrinally by Christians, appreciated as a fairy tale by aesthetes, and studied in connection with Christian theology by studious nonbelievers. Genersis contains the theological lesson for which Bush reads *Paradise Lost*, a warning on the danger of "irreligious pride" and on the necessity for "religious humility" (p. 57). Yet Genesis does not contain what is most impressive about *Paradise Lost*, its depiction of moral change, both of moral deterioration in the early history of Adam and Eve, as well as in the person of Satan, and of moral regeneration in the later history of Adam and Eve. This representation makes *Paradise Lost* as different from Genesis as *Macbeth* is from Holinshed, and though of course there is nothing about the literal belief in Eden or the theology of *Paradise Lost* which precludes the apprehension of what is distinctive about Milton's poem, an insistence on literal belief no more assures such apprehension than an insistence on the historical existence of a King Macbeth or an insistence on the validity of a belief in witchcraft assures the perception that *Macbeth* is a study in the cumulativeness of evil. Thus the religious defense is not critically useful.

If defense of the theology of *Paradise Lost* is neither feasible nor desirable, it is also not really necessary. Milton may have believed in the truth of his theology, but the reader is only obliged to suspend disbelief and see what is being done with these materials. And although analysis of the poem's structure requires that the work be viewed in terms of its own system, there is no reason that, if he likes, the reader may not by the process of abstraction translate its issues into other terms.

C. S. Lewis frowns on this last. In answer to Saurat's idea that a reader should "disentangle from theological rubbish the permanent and human interest of [Milton's] thought" (Saurat, *Milton: Man and Thinker*, p. 111), Lewis argues that the reader should not look for universals but instead should imaginatively adopt the code of the work; "instead of seeing how the courtier would look without his laces," he says, "you can try to see how you would feel *with* his lace; that is, with his honour, his wit, his royalism, and his gallantries out of the *Grand Cyrus*" (*Preface*, p. 62). The trouble with this view is that it allows for no translation of ideas from one frame of reference to another. Either one must learn a set of ideas made hypothetical by the lack of appropriate circumstances—for example, one can learn that honor, wit, royalism, and gallantry would be useful characteristics if only there were courts—or one can literally apply ideas to what are in fact changed circumstances—for example, one can become a follower of dictators, as the nearest equivalents to absolute monarchs; but one cannot ask what the equivalent to the courtier's world view would be in a democratic context. The danger of the first alternative can be seen in the tale of Miniver Cheevy. The danger of the second can be seen in Lewis's own *That Hideous Strength*, where, making a literal transference to modern times of Milton's description of Edenic gardening tools, "such . . . as art yet rude, / Guiltless of fire had formed, or angels brought" (9. 391–92) and Milton's condemnation of the technological sons of Seth (11. 564–73), Lewis contrasts scientific medicine and agriculture with herb lore and family plots, connecting the former with the devil and the latter with God. This sort of application, with its dogmatic indifference to what the seventeenth century did not know about the ability of science to control its plagues and famines, tends to substantiate Empson's assertion that what literalists get from *Paradise Lost* "is evil" (*Milton's God*, p. 277). The alternative of finding universals does necessarily make the issues of the work more abstract, but it need not distort these issues, any more than it distorts *Macbeth* to see it as concerned with something broader than the power of witches.

With or without such abstraction, appeal to the principle of suspended disbelief provides a better answer to Shelley's sort of misinterpretation than assertions of religious faith. In the first place, the literary answer handles a literary question in literary terms. The literary objection to Shelley's claim that the God of *Paradise Lost* is morally inferior to Satan is that, because the theory denies the obvious premises of the poem, it reduces the poem to incoherence. The moral points that are deduced from the speeches are at variance with the authorial commentary, and the plot is at variance with the supposed theme, since it shows liberated man willingly capitulating to the tyrant, the sort of ending which Shelley labeled as "feeble" in his preface to *Prometheus Unbound*: "I was averse from a catastrophe so feeble as that of reconciling the Champion with the Oppressor of mankind." Empson acknowledges the incoherence which this interpretation entails when he states that *Paradise Lost* is "good . . . because of its moral confusions" (ibid., p. 13); he refers in the words "moral confusions" to the theory that Milton gives valid reasons to the rebels while endorsing the god against whom they are rebelling. Because it attributes incoherence to the poem, the theory devalues the poem aesthetically. Empson, it is true, is not derogatory, but the judgment he is passing is moral rather than aesthetic: moral confusion is better than consistent moral blindness. A. J. A. Waldock, however, whose analysis also leads to the conclusion that *Paradise Lost* is incoherent *("Paradise Lost" and Its Critics,* pp. 144–45), makes an aesthetic judgment on the basis of that conclusion, the judgment that *Paradise Lost* would have made a better tone poem than an epic (ibid., pp. 146–47): it is so bad a poem, in other words, that it never should have been attempted. Now, defenders of *Paradise Lost* certainly have a right to argue that it is critically irresponsible to select from various interpretive schemes the one theory which must by its very premises prove that the poem being examined is a literary failure. This kind of argument is more appropriate for critics than the attempt to convert to Christianity all those who do not believe Milton's theology, and it ought to prove more effective.

In the second place, the literary answer avoids the misplaced emphasis of a religious defense while countering the attack on God. By not defending either Milton's accuracy in rendering the events of the historical fall or the truth of Milton's theological system, but by arguing that the system is to be taken for granted because it contains the premises of the poem, the literary argument stresses what is built upon the premises, the delineation of moral change; thus it allows weight to be placed on what is thematically and structurally central to the poem without allowing these matters to be interpreted arbitrarily. For example, when in relation to Eve's decision to disobey,

> *In plain then, what forbids he but to know,*
> *Forbids us good, forbids us to be wise?*
> *Such prohibitions bind not,*
>
> 　　　　　　　　　*(9. 758–60)*

Empson argues that "This means that you ought not to obey a God if your conscience tells you that his orders are wrong" (*Milton's God,* p. 160), a defender can object that if the issues are to be restated, they should be restated in terms which parallel the terms of the work; that the equivalent in the work for Empson's law of conscience is not the argumentation against God but the belief that God deserves to be loved; and that therefore the passage proves that one ought not violate his conscience no matter how tempting the violation seems and no matter how many excuses he can find for it. Such an objection is more critically useful than the objection that Empson doubts the truth of Genesis, or lacks the trust of Abraham.

I do not treat the subject of the defensibility of Milton's theology, then, because it seems to me that it is critically sounder to approach the theology in terms of its literary function, as the premises of the work, to be viewed with suspended disbelief, than to attempt a theological defense of the poem which could be neither effective nor critically useful. The last conventional subject which I do not treat is the topic of Milton's characterization of God. I have felt that the gap between the stated and the presented characteristics of God involves the evaluation rather than the meaning of the character, and that even the evaluative question is of minor importance.

Despite the claims of apologists, the representation of God does not support his stated nature. Jackson I. Cope attempts to defend Milton's characterization by arguing that the opening scene in heaven is sublime, a ritualistic presentation of an awe-inspiring paradox. His first point, however, that "the language [of the divine colloquy] is ritualistic" (*The Metaphoric Structure of "Paradise Lost"* [Baltimore, 1962], p. 170) is invalid. Cope claims that when the Father asks for a volunteer for the office of savior of mankind, his question, "Dwells in all Heaven charity so dear?" (3. 216) is a "rhetorical question" in a "ritual of enacted certainty" (ibid.). But, in the first place, Milton's description of the reception of the question proves that the request is not merely rhetorical:

> He asked, but all the heavenly choir stood mute,
> And silence was in Heaven; on Man's behalf
> Patron or intercessor none appeared,
> Much less that durst upon his own head draw
> The deadly forfeiture, and ransom set.
> And now without redemption all mankind
> Must have been lost, adjudged to Death and Hell
> By doom severe, had not the Son of God,
> In whom the fulness dwells of love divine,
> His dearest mediation thus renewed.
>
> (3. 217–26)

The statements about the angels' failure to answer make sense only on the supposition that the Father's question is real, for the angels would not be expected to answer a rhetorical question or to apply its terms to themselves. Furthermore, the statement of what would have happened had the Son not answered makes sense only on the supposition that the question is a real one, for a ritualistic announcement of the Son's mission would raise no possibility of his failing to answer.

In the second place, the theory would have unwelcome moral consequences. Cope says that in the dialogue "Father and Son are acting out, as clearly as Satan and Beelzebub have done in the infernal debates, a rhetorical and nondramatic ritual" (p. 173). Satan and Beelzebub, however, are not engaging in a ritual but in a piece of political manipulation. This manipulation could be interpreted as a parody of a heavenly ritual, but only if the dialogue in heaven were perceived by its audience to be a ritual. If, as would be the case, the angels were unaware that God was not really asking them to save man, the scene in hell would not be a parody of the scene in heaven but a direct parallel to it; God would be manipulating the angels in the way that Satan manipulates the devils. Cope's theory, thus, would prove that God is a tyrant.

The Father's question, then, cannot be interpreted as Cope interprets it, and the collapse of the interpretation is particularly damaging to the case for ritualism, for upon his reading of the Father's question Cope bases his refutation of the theory that the scene in heaven is not ritual but drama (p. 170).

In addition, the argument by which Cope attempts to prove his theory is fallacious. Cope argues that the ritualism of the divine colloquy is proved by the presence of "reiterative schemes" in its speeches (pp. 170–73). This theory rests on the assumptions that figures which involve repetition of words must have reiteration as their purpose, and that passages which contain repetition must be ritualistic. These assumptions account for the fact that Cope never considers the meanings of the sentences in which "reiterative schemes" appear, and never proves that the passages which contain these figures contain the enumerations and refrains characteristic of litanies; he merely cites examples of figures—e.g., "anaphora ('Should man . . . should man'" [p. 171]) —and assumes that the citations themselves prove his thesis. The fact is, however, that though such figures as anaphora are sometimes used to introduce repetitive phrases, they are sometimes used to introduce logical distinctions or to emphasize emotional points; that though passages containing such figures may be litanies, they may be emphatic expositions or emotional outbursts. Each figure must be examined for its individual effect; and when Cope's examples are so examined, they prove not to be examples of ritualistic repetition.

Some reinforce logical distinctions. Cope points out the antimetabole ("Upheld by me . . . By me upheld" [p. 172]) in these words of the Father:

> *Upheld by me, yet once more he shall stand*
> *On even ground against his mortal foe,*
> *By me upheld, that he may know how frail*
> *His fallen condition is, and to me owe*
> *All his deliverance, and to none but me.*
> (3. 178–82)

What the figure does in these clauses is point up two different aspects of the subject being discussed, God's gift of grace. In the first phrase, emphasis is placed on the word "Upheld," and the clause that follows explains the degree of strength which is being imparted to man; in the second phrase, emphasis is placed on the words "By me," and the clause that follows explains the necessity for man's recognizing the source of this strength. Other instances of what Cope calls "reiterative schemes" are examples of emotional emphasis. He cites the epanalepsis (p. 171) in these words of the Son:

> *[O]r wilt thou thyself*
> *Abolish thy creation, and unmake,*
> *For him, what for thy glory thou hast made?*
> (3. 162–64)

In the echo of "unmake" and "made," a word is opposed to its negatively prefixed form in order to call protesting attention to the reversal of plan which the act of unmaking would entail. These examples (more could of course be cited) suggest that the figures listed by Cope are not used to create the effect of reiteration; and the passages that contain them are not litanies but passages of argumentation and doctrinal exposition. The claim that the rhetoric of the divine colloquy is ritualistic is, thus, untrue.

The end to which Cope says the scene is directed is the presentation of
"the paradox of the *felix culpa*" (p. 174), which he says is the central trope
of the poem (ibid.), and which he says produces the effect of "wonder" ap-
propriate to an epic (pp. 175–76). This theory misrepresents the scene.
Cope claims that the paradox is introduced "at the very beginning of the
dialogue, in God's first speech, when he plays through so elaborate a 'tran-
lacer' upon fall, fell, fallen" (p. 174). The first uses of the word occur
about fifteen lines into this speech:

> For Man will hearken to [Satan's] glozing lies,
> And easily transgress the sole command,
> Sole pledge of his obedience; so will fall
> He and his faithless progeny. Whose fault?
> Whose but his own? Ingrate, he had of me
> All he could have; I made him just and right,
> Sufficient to have stood, though free to fall.
> Such I created all the Ethereal Powers
> And spirits, both them who stood and them who failed;
> Freely they stood who stood, and fell who fell.
> Not free, what proof could they have given sincere
> Of true allegiance, constant faith, or love . . . ?
>
> (3. 93–104)

The second group of examples occurs twenty-five lines later:

> So without least impulse or shadow of fate,
> Or aught by me immutably foreseen,
> They trespass, authors to themselves in all,
> Both what they judge and what they choose; for so
> I formed them free, and free they must remain,
> Till they enthrall themselves: I else must change
> Their nature, and revoke the high decree
> Unchangeable, eternal, which ordained
> Their freedom; they themselves ordained their fall.
> The first sort by their own suggestion fell,
> Self-tempted, self-depraved; Man falls, deceived
> By the other first; Man therefore shall find grace,
> The other none.
>
> (3. 120–32)

One striking fact about these instances is that when the meanings of the
sentences are taken into account, the forms of the word "fall" turn out not
to be the central, rhetorically stressed words in the sentences. In the clause
beginning "I made him just and right," the important words are "just" and
"right," for the clause supplies specific examples supporting the claim made
in the preceding clause, that God gave man "All he could have." The word
"fall" appears in a concessive phrase which does not supply supporting
evidence. In the line "Freely they stood who stood, and fell who fell," there

is no more stress upon "fell" than upon its opposite, "stood," and the central stress goes on the word "Freely." This clause forms the conclusion to the argument that God created his creatures perfect, the conclusion being that not God's making but the creatures' choices account for their differing fates. The word "Freely" is the word that exonerates God and places the responsibility for their fates upon the creatures, and its centrality is shown by the fact that the next sentence explains the necessity for freedom and begins in a way which makes sense only if "Freely" rather than "fell" is the key term: "Not free." In the clause "they themselves ordained their fall," the rhetorical emphasis is upon "they themselves." The sentence as a whole asserts that the fall is to be blamed not upon God but upon the creatures. The first clause states this thesis. The second and third clauses provide the reasons: creatures are guilty because they have freedom of choice, while God could not possibly be guilty because to limit the creatures' freedom would entail a self-contradiction on God's part. The final clause emphatically restates the thesis. The words "they themselves" not only place blame upon the creatures but also serve to exonerate God, for through the antithetical construction whereby the final clause is tied to the preceding words, "the high decree . . . which ordained / Their freedom," the words "they themselves" take on the force of "they themselves and not God's high decree." The rhetorical weight thus falls upon "they themselves" rather than upon "fall"—as, indeed, the use of the intensive modifier suggests. Finally, in the sentence beginning "The first sort," the emphatic words are not "fell" and "falls" but "their own suggestion" and "deceived," for these words distinguish the case of the angels from that of man, and account for the difference in treatment which God is here announcing.

So unemphatically is the word "fall" used in the speech that it is doubtful that the appearances of the word constitute a polyptoton ("tranlacer") at all. For polyptoton to exist, the repeated word must be used emphatically (forms of the word "deduct" appear frequently in the income tax instructions, but no effect of polyptoton is achieved), and the instances of the repeated word must be proximate; without these conditions, the occurrences of the word cannot be heard as a connected series. Now, it is at best an exaggeration to speak of one "elaborate" polyptoton in a speech in which twenty-five lines separate one group of appearances of a word from another group: the most that could be claimed is that the speech contains two not-so-elaborate "tranlacers." And because the instances of the word "fall" do not receive rhetorical stress, it is doubtful that even the proximate instances can be heard as a series.

In order to support his thesis that the divine colloquy embodies the paradox of the fortunate fall, Cope not only exaggerates the prominence of the word "fall" in the Father's first speech but ignores a word which is more prominent than "fall" but which does not relate to the doctrine of the fortunate fall. Forms of the word "free" appear as frequently in the first speech as those of the word "fall"; the appearances are stressed at least some of the time ("Freely" and "Not free"; "I formed them free, and free they must remain"); and the two groups of proximate instances are separated by only fifteen lines (too many for all the appearances to be heard as a single series, but fewer than the twenty-five lines which Cope accepts). If the appearances of "fall" constitute a polyptoton, then the appearances of "free" constitute an even more striking polyptoton, and Cope should say of the Father's first speech that the Father "plays through so elaborate a 'tranlacer' upon free and freedom"—a statement that could not be gracefully connected with "the paradox of the *felix culpa.*"

Cope's theory also has structural consequences. The theory requires that the whole scene develop around one central point, the central paradox, and Cope therefore speaks of it as "unfold[ing]" (*Metaphoric Structure*, p. 175), and interprets two of the Father's speeches as contributing to this linear development. In so doing, he again distorts the evidence.

Cope comments thus upon the lines which end the first section of the Father's second speech: "Milton would seem to be somewhat abusing epizeuxis . . . but this is owing to the fact that the speech is approaching its emphatic climax before the close, and Hoskins explains that epizeuxis 'is not to be vsed but in passion'" (p. 172). Both "climax" and "close" are misleading. "Climax" implies that the speech is an argument or list which advances toward a central point or example; but if the Father's speech is structured in this way, the most important point that the Father has to present is the following epizeuxis:

> But hard [shall] be hardened, blind be blinded more,
> That they may stumble on, and deeper fall;
> And none but such from mercy I exclude.
>
> (3. 200–202)

The fact is, then, that the first section of the body of the speech is not a progressive series but an unclimactic outline of doctrines concerned with the subject of grace. First the gift of grace is announced (3. 173–82); second, the workings of grace are outlined: the elect are divided from ordinary men (3. 183–84) and the nature of the grace given ordinary men is told (3. 185–97); and third, the penalty for rejecting grace is announced (3. 198–202). In relation to the last subject, epizeuxis is used, but the "passion" involved is not the passionate presentation of a climactic point, but simply the wrathful announcement of a divine threat. The word "close" implies that the second section of the body (3. 203–16) logically follows from the preceding materials. The transitional clause, however, implies that a new point is about to be expounded: "But yet all is not done" (3. 203). What follows is not a continuation but the broaching of a new subject, the subject of salvation. Cope needs the structure of climax and close because it suggests that one central point is being developed through an advancing and unified argument. What the Father's speech contains, however, is a first section in which one set of doctrines is unclimactically enunciated, and a second section in which a separate set of doctrines is announced—not the sort of structure that Cope's theory requires.

The Father's third speech, Cope says, "is largely a detailed reiteration of Christ's assertions concerning the results of his own sacrifice—the return of love into eternal joy" (p. 173). This too is misleading. The first section in the body of the speech (3. 281–302) does not repeat the Son's speech, which is a narrative account of his mission as savior; instead it returns to the second section of the Father's own second speech, and explains how the Son's mission will effect the salvation the need for which was announced at that point. The second section of the body (3. 303–41) does not refer to the Son's account, but instead turns to a new subject, the means whereby the incarnation is prevented from degrading the Son; the Father, announcing the elevation of the incarnate Son, describes the Son's supremacy in his office of judge. Cope needs a redundant speech not only because redundancy suits a ritualistic dialogue, but because, after the announcement of the incarnation, there is no place for a discussion of the fortunate fall to go. The speech itself, however, is not redundant, and is neither so restricted in scope or so unified in topic as Cope's theory requires.

The opening scene in heaven is not a ritual but a set of rhetorical speeches; it does not contain a single paradox gradually unfolded but a series of doctrines explaining the four offices of God, first the office of creator and lawgiver, then the office of giver of grace, then the office of savior, and finally the office of judge. It does not produce the effect of sublimity which Cope attributes to it, hoping thereby to answer the charge that God is, in the words of Irene Samuel, "a wooden bore" ("The Dialogue in Heaven: A Reconsideration of *Paradise Lost*, 3. 1–417," *PMLA* 71 [1957]: 601).

Miss Samuel's own reply to that charge is superior to Cope's. Though her description of the Father's speeches as nonrhetorical (ibid., p. 603) was rightly challenged by Cope (*Metaphoric Structure*, pp. 167–70), he did not effectively answer her central thesis, that the scene in heaven is a dramatic episode and not merely an exposition of doctrines (Samuel, p. 601). The question remains, however, whether her theory can accomplish the rehabilitation of God's character which she intends. Miss Samuel defends the characterization of the Father by arguing that his speeches reveal him to be the "omnipotent moral law" and not the "gloating, tyrannical victor" whom Satan depicts (p. 603). She describes the impression made by his speeches with the phrases "flat statement of fact . . . calm analysis and judgment" (ibid.), "passionless logic" (ibid.), "the cold logic of 'thus it is and thus must be'" (p. 605). These phrases do not accurately describe the effect which the speeches produce.

In the first place, the Father does not seem "cold" in the sense of "emotionless": when it comes to threats and denunciations he is warm enough. He seems "cold" only in the sense of "loveless." A. J. A. Waldock comments on the absence of love in the Father's first speech, where the subject of mercy is brought in at the end, "by," Waldock says, "an almost comical afterthought" (*"Paradise Lost" and Its Critics*, p. 103). And even in this afterthought the Father does not seem to be thinking of his creatures; what he talks about is what his mercy proves about him, the giver:

In mercy and justice both,
Through Heaven and Earth, so shall my glory excel,
But mercy first and last shall brightest shine.

(3. 132–34)

God's second speech does not ameliorate the impression left by the first. In the first section of the body of the speech, God turns his description of the effect of grace into a demonstration of his power:

Upheld by me, yet once more [man] shall stand
On even ground against his mortal foe,
By me upheld, that he may know how frail
His fallen condition is, and to me owe
All his deliverance, and to none but me;

(3. 178–82)

then he announces the doctrine of election in a display of arbitrary might: "so is my will" (3. 184); then he describes how grace entails the delivery of perpetual threats:

The rest shall hear me call, and oft be warned
Their sinful state, and to appease betimes
The incensëd Deity, while offered grace
Invites;

(3. 185–88)

and finally he describes how he will punish those who defy him: "hard [shall] be hardened, blind be blinded more, / That they may stumble on and deeper fall" (3. 200–201). The impression created is that God's main interest is the display of his might, his main enjoyment the punishing of his creatures; and when after such an opening God announces that he will not extend his grace unless certain conditions are met ("But yet all is not done" [3. 203]), it sounds as though the painful and difficult conditions are the result of God's reluctance to do anyone a good turn, even when the turn allows him to prove his power and to threaten and punish his creatures. This impression cannot be countered by the argument that Miss Samuel uses, that the "compassion, love, and grace" of the Son "are emphatically equated with the substantial expression of the invisible Godhead" ("Dialogue in Heaven," p. 603); for the question here is not what is doctrinally asserted, but what is dramatically rendered, and the love of the Father is not so rendered.

In the second place, God does not give the impression of being dispassionately logical, of delivering "calm analysis and judgment," because the doctrines are stated not as simple explanations, but as insistently self-defensive, and therefore not disinterested, arguments. Waldock lists the characteristics of the Father's first speech: "The uneasy explanations, the hammering in of key words ('they themselves,' 'they themselves,' 'not I'), the anxiety to meet beforehand all possible lines of attack, the rhetorical pleading, the indignation before the event ('whose fault? Whose but his own? ingrate,' etc." [*"Paradise Lost" and Its Critics*, p. 103]) ; these are not the characteristics of unimpassioned logical explanation.

There is no doubt that God is intended to represent what Miss Samuel says, the "omnipotent moral law," that he is supposed to have the "compassion, love, and grace" she attributes to him, that he is supposed to contrast with Satan's "straw figure of a gloating, tyrannical victor," as she says. But these traits are not dramatically rendered, and no other dramatic elements in the scene can compensate for what is actually presented—a god who is a self-defensive and self-aggrandizing authoritarian, quick to punish but unable to love: "just" (as Empson quips) "what one would expect from a usurping angel" (*Milton's God*, p. 103) .

Though there is a discrepancy between what is said about God (partly in authorial commentary, partly in God's own speeches) and what is shown about him, this discrepancy is not of interpretive importance. Empson says that "if God is to be shown acting in a story, we have something better to do than take his status for granted" (ibid., p. 94) . According to this theory, whatever God reveals about himself can be used to dispute what he says, in the way that C. S. Lewis disputes what Eve says about her love for Adam on the basis of what she reveals about her motivation in offering him the apple (*Preface*, p. 121) . Empson, however, ignores the fact that authorial commentary backs up what God says about himself, and that the qualities thus attributed to God preclude any discrepancy between what he says and the truth about his nature. Thus it is not necessary to analyze God's character in order to determine his meaning. If the presented characteristics of God reinforced the stated ones, they would be relevant, if not essential, to a discussion of his meaning. If they do not, however, it is not God's nature but Milton's portrayal which is to be questioned. And though the discrepancy is a criticism of *Paradise Lost*, the matter is, as E. M. W. Tillyard says, a "detail" (*Studies in Milton* [London, 1951], p. 52) —not so much for the reason that C. S. Lewis gives, that the work is an epic rather than a devotional poem (*Preface*, pp. 127–28) , but for the reason that God's role in the epic is so far from the center of the poem's action—further even than the role of the loyal angels—that the question of characterization is not an important one.

[2] Though the particular subpoints may be idiosyncratic or narrowly sectarian, the broad outlines of what I take to be the premises of *Paradise Lost* are so commonplace that C. S. Lewis, without seeing their place in *Paradise Lost*, lists as the commonly recognized attributes of the Christian deity those attributes that Milton assigns to God: "infinite sovereignty *de jure*, combined with infinite power *de facto*, and love which, by its very nature, includes wrath also" (*A Preface to "Paradise Lost"* [London, 1942], p. 126) . These premises do not, however, correspond to the doctrines of *De Doctrina Christiana*.

Correspondence between the poem and the treatise could be demonstrated only by analyzing each work separately—by determining the importance and the logical connection of the various doctrines in each—and then by showing that the two works not merely contain similar materials, but order these materials in similar ways. Maurice Kelley in his attempt to prove doctrinal congruence does not follow this procedure, but instead merely arranges short passages of *Paradise Lost* under the headings of *De Doctrina*. The case he makes thereby is not convincing.

In the first place, because of his failure to analyze, Kelley offers proofs which are at best not very strong. Ignoring the question of the relative importance and the interconnection of doctrines in each work, Kelley frequently couples a key doctrine in *De Doctrina* with an incidental point in *Paradise Lost*. Even if his proofs for the Arianism of *Paradise Lost* were true, for example, this doctrine, important in *De Doctrina*, would be only incidentally present in the poem (this point is discussed in the preceding note). Such examples tend to prove not that the two works share a common system, but that what is central to one work has no place in the other.

In the second place, Kelley does not produce results which substantiate his claims. In order to prove the correspondence of *De Doctrina* and *Paradise Lost*, Kelley takes fragments out of the epic, and provides no indication as to the function of these fragments in the poem's action or their bearings on the poem's theme. For example, he argues that four lines in Adam's lament (10. 789–92) present the same doctrine of mortalism that is present in *De Doctrina* (*This Great Argument: A Study of Milton's "De Doctrina Christiana" as a Gloss upon "Paradise Lost"* [Princeton, N. J., 1941], p. 154); he does not show that the presence of this doctrine proves anything about Adam or that its presence helps to defend God. Kelley's investigation does not illuminate, therefore, either the point of *Paradise Lost* or the way in which that point is made; instead it reduces the work to a pointless aggregation of unrelated doctrinal minutiae—a result which jeopardizes the claim that comparison with the treatise helps to explain the poem.

In the third place, because he fails to analyze *Paradise Lost*, Kelley admits, without realizing it, that *De Doctrina* does not bear on what is most important in the poem. In discussing the second book of *De Doctrina*, the book devoted to ethics, Kelley says that because *Paradise Lost* "concludes with the departure of the fallen couple from the garden, it has little to say of man's duties to God and to his neighbor" (ibid., p. 185); thus he offers only a few incidental parallels between the poem and this part of the treatise. The action of *Paradise Lost*, however, revolves around Adam and Eve and Satan, and these creatures are treated in terms of their relations to God and their relations to fellow creatures. If the treatise's views on duty do not apply to these relationships, then the treatise does not help in judging the poem's central characters or in determining their changes. This subject is not one that can be lightly dismissed; if *De Doctrina* does not help in understanding Adam, Eve, or Satan, then it does not help interpret the poem.

Though Kelley does not make a convincing case for the correspondence of *De Doctrina* and *Paradise Lost*, the question still remains as to whether the doctrines of the poem correspond to those of the treatise when the importance of the ideas and their logical interconnections are taken into account. The answer, so far as I have been able to determine, is that they do **not**.

³ The connection of conscience with feeling may seem rather arbitrary, especially when, as in the Father's speech, conscience is referred to as the "umpire Conscience" (3. 195). The parallel passage in Michael's prophecy, however, similarly connects conscience ("law of faith"), guidance, and feeling:

> [F]rom   Heaven
> He to his own a Comforter will send,
> The promise of the Father, who shall dwell
> His Spirit within them, and the law of faith
> Working through love, upon their hearts shall write,
> To guide them in all truth.
>
> (12. 485–90)

This interpretation, furthermore, coincides with the nature of the new dispensation as differentiated from the old (see 12. 300–306).

⁴ As in the case of the wrath which God displays in his office of savior, it is possible to make moral excuses for God's action here: Satan, though unable to reform, is able to choose between alternative evils, and so can be held responsible for the sort of evil he chooses. It is also possible to find thematic justification for God's display of wrath: the action tightens the parallel between the fate of Satan and the fate of the unrepentant human sinner for whom Satan serves as a warning. These defenses, however, if they violate no evidence in the poem, cannot be supported by such evidence.

2 The Secondary Plot

¹ Three positions have been taken on the problem of Satan, the position that Satan is a badly rendered character, the position that he is a successfully rendered heroic character, and the position that he is a successfully rendered evil one. I disagree with the first two positions, although they have been argued well, and favor the third.

A. J. A. Waldock attacks the characterization of Satan by arguing that Milton imposes changes upon Satan from without, presenting in the place of a single evolving character a series of discontinuous and technically different portraits (*"Paradise Lost" and Its Critics* [Cambridge, 1947], p. 83). His argument, though forceful, often oversimplifies the evidence, and sometimes interprets it in doubtful ways.

Waldock claims, first of all, that in the opening section of *Paradise Lost* the portrait of Satan consists of a juxtaposition of incompatible elements. He argues, first, that the remorse and the admissions of helplessness and guilt in the Niphates soliloquy are incompatible with the attitudes which Satan reveals in the opening scenes in hell (ibid., p. 86). In these scenes, Waldock says, Satan is characterized by his indominability (p. 77), though Milton tries to undercut his impressiveness by offering unfavorable—and invalid—commentary (pp. 77–81). This argument does not justly describe the opening scenes. In addition to expressions of unchanging defiance, Satan's speeches contain expressions of his awareness of past folly; the opening speech to Beelzebub (1. 84–94), the speech upon first glimpsing hell (1. 242–45), and even the address to the assembled troops (1. 622–26) open with melancholy confessions. Furthermore, the expressions of indominability themselves have elements of display in them, what Waldock calls an "element of bravado" (p. 67). The reason for this bravado Milton explains in the commentary which Waldock dismisses as authorial sneering: Satan is "Vaunting aloud, but racked with deep despair" (1. 126). Thus, what is portrayed is not simple defiance; Satan is shown as having doubts which he does not want to reveal to his followers and which he conceals with defiant proclamations. These doubts are the same doubts which Satan confesses in the Niphates soliloquy; and if the remorse and guilt of that soliloquy are not similarly anticipated, the reason is that hell evinces God's power and brings Satan awareness of his own weakness, while earth evinces God's goodness and brings Satan awareness of his evil.

Waldock also argues that Satan's speech upon first encountering Adam and Eve contains a mechanical juxtaposition of two contrary moods, regret (4. 358–75) and ironic mockery (4. 375–92), and not a convincing conflict of emotion (ibid., pp. 89–90). It can be argued, however, that the details which Waldock sees as ironic—Satan's desire for "League" with man and his offer of a "dwelling" wider than the "narrow limits" of Eden—are instead Satan's self-comforting excuses, and that the objectionably abrupt shift of tone which he sees does not exist. According to the alternative reading, the point of the speech is not conflict, but rather the rationalizations by which evildoers accustom themselves to evil; in the Niphates soliloquy Satan resolved to do evil, and here he seeks to justify to himself a concrete instance of that evil.

The opening section of *Paradise Lost,* then, may be seen as a portrayal of impenitence, which leads up to and away from a central moment of decision, that contained in the Niphates soliloquy; it need not be viewed as a disconnected sequence of incompatible traits. Of the closing section of the poem, Waldock says that the stature of Satan is reduced by progressively inferior modes of presentation. In the second soliloquy, he argues, Satan is allegorized, reduced to a "helpless symbol . . . endowed with the capacity to point his own moral" (ibid., pp. 90–91). This argument, however, overlooks the fact that Satan's allegorization of his imbrutement (9. 163–71), the passage upon which Waldock bases his argument, may be interpreted as a passage of characterization, parallel to Satan's earlier admission of the misery of reigning in hell (4. 86–92) or Satan's pronouncement "myself am Hell" (4. 75); the passage proves that Satan still retains some insight. Furthermore, the soliloquy as a whole is dramatic in its techniques, not expository. Satan is characterized more by what he reveals than by what he announces— by his self-contradiction, by his failure to act upon his own insights, by the comparative feebleness of those insights. The characterization is aided, furthermore, by reminiscences of the first soliloquy, which help both to show the continuity in Satan's development and to define the changes which have taken place in him.

Waldock also attacks the final scene in hell, arguing that its pattern, the undermining of a confident villain through a "practical joke," is the technique of a "comic cartoon" (pp. 91–92). This argument is stronger than the others, for the transformation scene is obviously a bad one, but Waldock's emphasis on the comedy in the transformation is misleading. In the first place, the return of Satan and his transformation parallel Satan's confidence of victory in the second battle in heaven and his overthrow in the third battle; yet the pattern of the earlier scene produces no comic effect (for Arnold Stein's argument on the comedy of the war in heaven, see note 4 to this chapter). Furthermore, the transformation is not merely a physical punishment, but a symbolic exemplification of Satan's moral state; thus the scene is not a simple, comic, indignity. The transformation is objectionable not for any comic debasement of Satan, but for its crude restatement of what he has already been shown: the blindness of Satan is evident from his behavior, and not only is the refutation of his words unnecessary, but the physical exemplification of Satan's errors tends to distract attention from the main point, his spiritual deterioration. Waldock's claim, moreover, that comic debasement is a substitute for characterization is false. The scene of Satan's return is more than a buildup preceding a comedown: Satan's speeches and actions refer to his second soliloquy and the speech preceding the temptation, to his speech ending the debate in hell, and to the battle in heaven, and thereby establish the full course of Satan's development. The final section of *Paradise Lost*, then, does not abandon characterization for allegory and elementary comedy; it deserves to be taken seriously as a delineation of a character in the process of rapid disintegration.

As to the second school, that which views Satan as a successfully rendered heroic character, the early Satanists need no comment, William Empson having revived their case with much more textual evidence and analysis of character than they had offered. Empson argues that the "hunger [of orthodox critics] to argue that [Satan] is very bad from the start" obscures their perception of his "gradual . . . degradation" (*Milton's God* [London, 1961], p. 71). His own contention is that Satan has a plausible case in his fall (ibid., pp. 71–89) but that upon seeing earth, he finds that he has been mistaken in denying God's metaphysical claims, and that "only harm can follow from the success of his heroic effort" (pp. 61–62). Empson's distinction between mistaken belief and conscious error is more applicable to *Paradise Lost* than the interpretations of many orthodox critics. His evaluation of these two states, however, disregards the premises of the work. Satan's mistaken doubt is to be viewed as morally culpable. Empson may accept an analogy to his own belief that the enjoyment of another being's suffering is evil (p. 260) : a man who tortures another man because he sincerely doubts that his action is evil is not exonerated by his sincerity. Satan's persistence in the face of the disproof of his position is, of course, an aggravation of this original offense. Furthermore, Empson's emphasis on the effect upon Satan of the sight of earth is somewhat misleading. Earth does remind Satan of God's goodness, but before that, the sight of hell has convinced him of God's authority, and has initiated the self-doubt whose beginning Empson places no earlier than the Niphates soliloquy.

My own argument is a version of the third position taken on the problem of Satan, the position that Satan is a successfully rendered evil figure. C. S. Lewis, who argues this position, explains neither the pattern nor the nature of the degeneration of Satan, which he describes thus: "From hero to general, from general to politician, from politician to secret service agent, and thence to a thing that peers in at bedroom or bathroom window, and thence to a toad, and finally to a snake—such is the progress of Satan" (*A Preface to "Paradise Lost"* [London, 1942], p. 97). B. Rajan, who also argues the position, contends that Satan's decline follows the "reading order" of the events rather than their chronological order; although he defends the poem on the grounds of the effectiveness of each portrayal of Satan in its particular context (*"Paradise Lost" and the Seventeenth Century Reader* [London, 1947], pp. 104–6), his theory denies the coherence of Satan's development as surely as Waldock's outright attack. My argument is intended to defend the characterization of Satan and to explain the pattern and nature of his development.

² I accept the traditional view of the events of Satan's fall, but reject a traditional approach to his fall, that of exploring Satan's motivation.

William Empson has advanced a novel theory as to the events of Satan's fall. He argues that Satan and his "regent powers" (5. 697) had long been questioning God's place (*Milton's God* [London, 1961], p. 58), that the birth of Sin took place at some preliminary council of leaders (ibid.), and that the elevation of the Son only brought the rebellion to a head (ibid., p. 72). This seems to me a very unlikely theory. Empson argues that the events which Sin describes could not have taken place in the interval between Abdiel's departure from Satan's camp and the end of the war in heaven; quoting from her description,

> *Amazement seized*
> *All the host of Heaven; back they recoiled afraid*
> *At first, and called me Sin, and for a sign*
> *Portentous held me; but familiar grown,*
> *I pleased, and with attractive graces won*
> *The most averse, thee chiefly, who full oft*
> *Thyself in me thy perfect image viewing*
> *Becam'st enamored; and such joy thou took'st*
> *With me in secret, that my womb conceived*
> *A growing burden. Meanwhile war arose,*
>
> (2. 758–67)

Empson argues that "war arose late in [Sin's] pregnancy and after a general change of sentiment" (pp. 58–59). "Meanwhile," however, is not "thereafter"; Sin is not saying that war broke out after she was pregnant, but that the public events were contemporaneous with the private ones. Though this account makes Sin's gestation period a short one, she is a supernatural creature, not a human being, and there is evidence of the brevity of her terms: her "Hell-hounds" were "hourly conceived / And hourly born" (2. 796–

97). Furthermore, Empson slightly misquotes the phrase describing Sin's reception. The phrase he uses, "when familiar grown" (p. 59), suggests that there was an appreciable interval of acquaintanceship, while the text itself, "familiar grown," focuses on the time of acceptance rather than on the interval before it, and suggests no long debate. Finally, Empson's theory requires that only Satan's commanders be present at the earlier councils which he posits, for Abdiel clearly knows nothing of any earlier plotting. Yet, if Sin's phrase "all the Seraphim with thee combined / In bold conspiracy" (2. 750–51) can be read as applying only to Satan's commanders (and the emphasis in the phrase is on the numerousness, not the exclusiveness, of that assembly), the synonymous phrase which Sin uses later, "All the host of Heaven," can refer only to Satan's entire army. Thus the evidence for Empson's theory is not strong enough to establish the existence of so many unnarrated events, especially when—given the peculiar nature of Sin's reproduction—nothing in her account makes impossible the obvious conclusion that she was born after Abdiel's departure from Satan's camp. My own account, therefore, presumes that Satan's fall begins with his thoughts after the Son's elevation, proceeds with his seduction of Beelzebub and his speeches to his assembled legions, and concludes with the birth of Sin shortly after Abdiel quits the assembly.

It is conventional in analyses of Satan's fall to discuss his motivation. For example, in order to prove that the "source of all evil" is "passion triumphant over reason," Denis Saurat (in *Milton, Man and Thinker* [New York, 1925], p. 150) argues that Satan falls from pride, but adds that his fall is associated with lust, the passion par excellence, not only through Satan's incestuous relationship with Sin, but through his conception of her (he cites James: "Then when lust hath conceived, it bringeth forth sin" [ibid., pp. 154–55]). Less philosophically and more orthodoxly, C. S. Lewis, developing a hint by Charles Williams, argues at length that egotism, the "sense of injured merit" (1. 98), is the cause of Satan's fall, as well as his central trait (*A Preface to "Paradise Lost"* [London, 1942], pp. 92–94, 99–100). One trouble with such attenton to motive is that Milton does not focus on the subject. A. J. A. Waldock warns against "prob[ing] into the cause of . . . disobedience" to find "some offense in the background" to supplant the offense of disobeying (*"Paradise Lost" and Its Critics* [Cambridge, 1947], p. 57), and the principle applies to Satan as well as to Adam and Eve. Milton presents as his account of Satan's fall a scene in which Satan makes heretical pronouncements to his followers. His central concern is thus the pronouncements themselves, the demonstrations of a creature's doubts about God's attributes. If Milton were interested in motivation, he would have narrated what he only refers to, the scene in which Satan meditates on the Son's elevation (5. 657–71) and (though Lewis does not mention this aspect) in which he begrudges God's gifts (4. 46–53); and had Milton been interested in emphasizing the passional aspect of Satan's fall, not only would he not have made the birthplace of Sin Satan's head, and not only would he not have made Satan's lust an allegorical love of Sin (for the existence of Sin as a character does not negate her allegorical meaning), but he

would not have detached the evidence of passion from the central account of
Satan's fall.

A second trouble with the hunt for motives is that *Paradise Lost* is not
structured around likenesses and differences in motivation. Waldock, citing
the Hebraic interpretation of Williams and the Hellenic one of Greenlaw,
notes the difficulty of finding a theory of motives that will unite the case of
Satan with the case of Adam and the case of Eve (*"Paradise Lost" and Its
Critics,* pp. 58–61). That the unifying principle lies not in the motives of
the characters but in the denials of God which they make is suggested by the
results of E. M. W. Tillyard's revised analysis of the structure of *Paradise
Lost.* Tillyard says that the first stage of the characters' development is con-
cerned with "the motives prompting revolt" (*Studies in Milton* [London,
1951], p. 45), but when he discusses motives, he cannot find an adequate
likeness in the cases; the most he can say is that "Adam and Eve fell for a
variety of reasons, of which pride was one," while "Pride, pure and simple,
was the single and sufficient motive" of Satan's fall (ibid., p. 46). When
Tillyard does find a likeness, it lies not in motivation but in the "single
divine command" which is "antecedent to each motive or set of motives"
(ibid.). The likeness he finds is a likeness in the conditions governing the
creatures' relationship to God, and the existence of this kind of likeness sug-
gests that what unites the two plots is a comparison of the moral states of
the poem's three protagonists.

Thus, instead of approaching Satan's fall from the standpoint of his moti-
vation, I have approached it from the standpoint of his moral status. The
passages usually cited for their bearing on motive I have interpreted as
indicating simply what is Satan's major, and what his minor, lapse.

[3] It is not necessary to accept the argument advanced by A. J. A. Waldock
(in *"Paradise Lost" and Its Critics* [Cambridge, 1947], p. 71) and elaborated
by William Empson (in *Milton's God* [London, 1961], pp. 82–83), that
Satan could not argue that the theory of creation advanced by Abdiel were
new unless it was new, and that therefore God must have denied to some
angels the knowledge given to Abdiel. The theory of divine creation is
presented as a self-evident doctrine—Adam reveals that as soon as he was
created, he deduced that God made him (8. 273–82); and it is logical to
assume that the angels, who live within sight of God's throne, have learned
something about the roles of the divine persons. Thus when Satan says that
Abdiel's argument is a "Strange point and new" (5. 855), he is saying not
that he never heard the point before, but that he wants to examine as if it
were a new theory what everyone has always taken for granted. This inter-
pretation is consistent with the lines that follow; having announced his
intention to doubt, Satan demands evidence:

> *Doctrine which we would know whence learned. Who saw*
> *When this creation was? Remember'st thou*
> *Thy making, while the Maker gave thee being?*
> (5. 856–58)

Satan's argument is effective, then, not because he resists a change in doctrine, but because he offers a new way of looking at old tenets; not Abdiel but Satan is the theological innovator.

As to what the speech proves about Satan, I agree with Empson (*Milton's God*, pp. 84–89) that C. S. Lewis is wrong in claiming that Satan's view of his creation is meant to seem ridiculous (*A Preface to Paradise Lost* [London, 1942], pp. 95–96). Unlike Empson, however, I think that Satan is supposed to appear evil in his doubts, and the mock surprise of the opening of the speech (as I interpret it) would contribute to the impression of blasphemy: "That we were formed then say'st thou? and the work / Of secondary hands . . . ?" (5. 853–54).

⁴ Dr. Johnson complained that the "confusion of spirit and matter" filled the account of the war in heaven "with incongruity"; citing Milton's statement that without armor, the angels could have "evaded" the cannon shot "By quick contraction or remove" (6. 595–97), he argues that despite that armor the angels could have avoided injury, contracting to escape their garments, and fleeing ("John Milton," in *Lives of the English Poets*). C. S. Lewis answered this objection by arguing that Dr. Johnson had misunderstood Milton's metaphysics; Milton, he argued, had not encased spirits in material armor, but had provided arms of denser substance for angels composed of "subtle" matter (*A Preface to "Paradise Lost"* [London, 1942], p. 109). Lewis's argument was answered by A. J. A. Waldock, who pointed out that Dr. Johnson's objections were as valid for creatures composed of subtle matter as they were for spiritual creatures. He attacked the account of the war on the grounds that Milton had assigned Homeric modes of warfare to creatures for whom these modes were inappropriate, and had compounded the difficulty by emphasizing both the nonearthly qualities of the warriors and their earthly modes of warfare; Waldock also complained of the strained quality of the writing in all but the closing incident (*"Paradise Lost" and Its Critics* [Cambridge, 1947], pp. 108–12). This line of argument Arnold Stein attempted to undercut with the claim that the war in heaven was not to be taken at face value. He argued, in the first place, that the war was "epic comedy" (*Answerable Style: Essays on "Paradise Lost"* [Minneapolis, 1953], p. 23), citing as evidence first the presence of verbal ridicule on the part of God and of the loyal and disloyal angels (ibid., pp. 20–22), and second (pp. 22–26) the presence of action that was "intended to induce laughter in the reader" (p. 22), namely the wounding which renders Satan "physically ridiculous" (ibid.), the toppling of the bombarded angels, the uprooting of the hills, "made comic by controlled excess" (p. 23), and the expulsion of the disloyal angels, which makes them "appear . . . ridiculous" (p. 25). Stein argued, secondly, that the incidents of the war were symbolic —"part," as he put it, "of a complex metaphor" (p. 17). Approaching the war in terms of the concept of discipline, he argued (pp. 32–37) that the angels' armor represents God's disciplinary limitation of might (the ridicule that the loyal angels endure as a result of their arms is thus, he explained, a part of their trial). Satan's invention of cannonry, he argued, represents the violation of discipline, and the angels' retaliation "breaks from the

discipline altogether and returns more completely to fundamental material force" (p. 34). Chaos results, which God undoes by intervening; God, according to Stein, uses force to fulfill the moral order in a reversal of Satan's attempt to usurp right with might; his restoration of discipline is indicated by the fact that the Son's chariot shakes everything but the throne of God, and by the fact that the Son limits his might so as not to annihilate the rebels. On the basis of this interpretation, Stein argued that the physical incidents of the war in heaven symbolized the rational sins of Satan and the retribution unintentionally set in motion by him. J. B. Broadbent replied to Stein's defense, accepting the contention that Milton intended the war to be comic, but criticizing the episode on the grounds that Milton had not sufficiently distinguished good from evil power. He claimed that Milton had failed on one hand to demonstrate sufficiently the evil of Satan, and on the other hand had unwisely adopted a militaristic conception of God; and he argued that despite Milton's ironic qualifications, he had been drawn by the desire to rival Homer into writing battle poetry which bore no relation to his moral point, and that Milton's story, because it prevented his opposing peace to war and required him to present superior power as the cure for violence, prevented his criticizing the immorality of war, and limited him to attacking its inefficiency (*Some Graver Subject: An Essay on "Paradise Lost"* [London, 1960], pp. 218–28). Joseph H. Summers, on the other hand, defended the episode on new grounds suggested by Stein, but without fully accepting the comic interpretation. He argued that the effectiveness of the narration lies in the surprises that it introduces not only for the rebellious and the loyal angels, but for the reader who expects a conventional battle; he denied, however, that all the surprises are comic, arguing that the reader is called upon to share not only God's comic view, but the heroic perspective of the loyal angels and the tragic one of the rebels (*The Muse's Method: An Introduction to "Paradise Lost"* [London, 1962], pp. 122–37).

The first question raised by this dispute is whether Milton's account relies on unconventionality for its effectiveness. The theory of Stein, that the war in heaven is comic, is dubious. First, it is questionable that the evidence of comedy is strong enough to establish what is not a surface quality of the scene. It is true that any physical indignity can be made the object of laughter, but the presence of indignity is not in itself evidence of comedy: if it were, Adam would be portrayed as giggling at the inhabitants of the lazar-house (11. 477–99). Stein claims that the combat with the hills is narrated in such a way as to elicit laughter. Citing the passage of description,

> *From their foundations loosening to and fro*
> *[The angels] plucked the seated hills with all their load,*
> *Rocks, waters, woods, and by the shaggy tops*
> *Uplifting bore them in their hands. Amaze,*
> *Be sure, and terror seized the rebel host,*
> *When coming towards them so dread they saw*
> *The bottom of the mountains upward turned;*

> *Till on those cursëd engines' triple-row*
> *They saw them whelmed, and all their confidence*
> *Under the weight of mountains buried deep,*
> *Themselves invaded next, and on their heads*
> *Main promontories flung, which in the air*
> *Came shadowing, and oppressed whole legions armed,*
>
> (6. 643–55)

Stein argues that the reader's standpoint is not that of a participant but that of a detached onlooker, because the phrase "Amaze, / Be sure, and terror seized the rebel host" serves to place the reader outside the action; he compares the reader to the viewer of a custard-pie bombardment (*Answerable Style*, pp. 23–24). Stein omits, however, the description of the effects of the bombardment:

> *[The rebels'] armor helped their harm, crushed in and bruised.*
> *Into their substance pent, which wrought them pain*
> *Implacable, and many a dolorous groan,*
> *Long struggling underneath, ere they could wind* .
> *Out of such prison, though spirits of purest light,*
> *Purest at first, now gross by sinning grown.*
>
> (6. 656–61)

This description destroys the custard-pie analogy: once pain is introduced, the bombardment cannot be seen as comic; it can only be viewed with empathetic pain or with vindictive pleasure. The presence of pain also destroys any potential comedy in the incidents of the wounding of Satan and the expulsion of the rebels.

Stein's remaining example of comic indignity is that of the loyal angels' retreat under cannon fire. Stein argues that the "verbal derision" of Satan and Belial serve to "cap" an "unsparing" description of the angels' comic-plight (ibid., p. 23):

> *Foul dissipation followed and forced rout;*
> *Nor served it to relax their serried files.*
> *What should they do? If on they rushed, repulse*
> *Repeated, and indecent overthrow*
> *Doubled, would render them yet more despised,*
> *And to their foes a laughter; for in view*
> *Stood ranked of Seraphim another row*
> *In posture to displode their second tire*
> *Of thunder; back defeated to return*
> *They worse abhorred.*
>
> (6. 598–607)

It is doubtful, however, that Raphael's purpose in detailing the angels' dilemma is to render himself and his fellows ridiculous; rather Raphael is explaining to Adam why the angels' retreat is no reflection on their zeal. The laughter of Satan, furthermore, serves to keep the reader from laughing, since the reader ought not share the delight of an aggressor in the overthrow of his victims. The physical indignities which Stein cites, then, are not evidences of comedy, and the case for the comic effect of verbal ridicule is even more tenuous. Not only, as Stein observes (p. 21), are taunts conventional in epic battles, but the taunts here are mostly Satan's blasphemies about God's nature and his sneering rejections of the love of his neighbor—the sort of laughter which causes the reader to reject the speaker, not the sort which causes him to share the speaker's mirth.

In the second place, the episode, interpreted as comic, would not achieve its end, not would it be compatible with parallel episodes elsewhere in *Paradise Lost*. If the war is, as Stein says, "terribly funny," "like . . . a scherzo, a kind of great scherzo" (p. 20), it should not be disconcerting to think of the Father addressing the Son thus:

> *Two days are passed,*
> *Two days, as we compute the days of Heaven,*
> *Since Michael and his powers went forth to mock*
> *These disobedient: hilarious their fight,*
> *As likeliest was when two such foes met armed.*
> *Two days, then, are passed; the third is thine;*
> *For thee I have ordained it, and the farce*
> *Have ordered, that the glory may be thine*
> *Of capping this great jest, since none but thou*
> *Can cap it.*

The events are those of Stein's interpretation and the fifth line meets Dr. Johnson's (and A. J. A. Waldock's) objection to angelic armor, but the address does not seem consonant with a divine refutation of heresy whose culmination is, as the Son declares to the Father, a terrible chastisement: "[W]hom thou hat'st, I hate, and can put on / Thy terrors as I put thy mildness on" (6. 734–35). Furthermore, a comic war would not be consonant with two analogous episodes in Michael's narration, the war of the giants (11. 638–59), which imitates the angels' war, and the last judgment (12. 537–51), of which the war in heaven is a type. Adam is shown as weeping at the sight of the human war (11. 674), and the last judgment is treated as an awesome display of power, the day of "vengeance to the wicked" when the Son, "revealed / In glory of the Father," will "dissolve / Satan with his perverted world" (12. 541, 545–47).

The less radical version of the theory that the war in heaven is unconventional, Joseph Summers's claim that the war strikingly violates literary conventions, is also open to doubt. In such matters as the violence of the angelic combats and the Son's unusual mode of warfare, matters in which, Summers says, the war exceeds expectations (*Muse's Method*, pp. 131–35), there is no reason to assume that the effect sought is that of novelty rather than that of epic grandeur. The cases in which conventions are rejected are the crucial cases, and here Summers's examples are weak. He argues, first of all, that Raphael's vague reference to "infinite" deeds and his refusal to name the "thousands" of heroic angels (6. 240–41, 373–85) constitute an undercutting of the "old heroic tradition," a rejection of conventional descriptions of deeds and catalogues of heros (p. 129). Since, however, Raphael does describe in detail the heroic deeds of Abdiel and Michael (6. 189–98, 296–343) and does list other heros (6. 354–72), there is no very striking departure from custom in his account as a whole.

Summers also argues that the narrative of the war contains a surprising rejection of the usual glorification of arms. He cites the fact that the classical weapons are said to be diminished by the imagery comparing them to heavenly bodies (6. 310–15); the fact that cannonry prevents the display of prowess and makes arms a hindrance; and the fact that arms are cast away when the angels hurl mountains (pp. 129–31). The images, however, may be seen not as reversing classical precedents but as overgoing and thus honoring them; and the other details must be placed within the pattern of the war as a whole, a pattern which is that of historical development: classical weapons give way to modern and modern to future. The hurling of the hills is usually interpreted in James H. Hanford's way, as a regression, the abandoning of "civilized arms" for "crude missles," a return (indicated by the allusion to the Titans' war) to "primitive combat" ("Milton and the Art of War," *Studies in Philology* 18 [1921]: 259). But the Biblical phrase, "they shall say to the mountains, Cover us; and to the hills, Fall on us," implies that burial is the worst imaginable condition, preferable only to facing God's wrath; and the phrase is always applied to a future time. Thus warfare with hills is not primitive warfare but warfare carried as far as a creature can carry it, and warfare of a future age; the reference to the Titans merely heightens the account and provides a historical justification for it, the pagan tale being what Adam's descendants remembered of Raphael's report. The change, obsolescence, and abandonment of arms, then, is one means of showing the evolution of warfare, and the narrative of the war works not by the surprising repudiation of heroic conventions but by the assembling of all military lore into what Hanford calls "an epitome of war in general" (ibid., p. 258).

If the unconventionality of the war in heaven is denied, however, the absurdity of the episode need not be conceded. It is probable that all flaws in it cannot be explained away, despite Summers's laudable attempts to remove inconsistencies (*Muse's Method*, pp. 125–26). The limitation on the size of the loyal army is not only weakly explained, but it places in doubt the Father's honesty in declaring that "none but [the Son] / Can end" the war (6. 702–3), for the Father has prevented the angels from using all their resources against the rebels; and the Father's statement that he has delayed the rebels' deterioration is not only unexplained, but it is contradicted by Raphael's assertion that the loyal angels had physical "advantages" because of "their innocence," the advantages of being "Unwearied" in battle and "unobnoxious to be pained / By wound" (6. 391–405), and by Raphael's statement that the rebellious angels, though once "spirits of purest light," had grown "gross by sinning" (6. 660–61) .

Though flaws may exist in it, however, the episode is certainly not as bad as A. J. A. Waldock says, nor could it be improved by J. B. Broadbent's suggested means. Waldock's criticisms assume that realism is the only means of lulling disbelief; he ignores the fact that angels with swords are conventional, and he condemns as absurd the warfare with hills (*"Paradise Lost" and Its Critics,* p. 112) for which Milton has Biblical precedents, precedents which he recalls in his paraphrase of the cry of the wicked in Revelations, who "said to the mountains and the rocks, Fall on us, and hide us from the face of him that sitteth on the throne": when the Son rides over them, the rebel angels "[wish] the mountains now might be again / Thrown on them as a shelter from his ire" (6. 840–44) . Even the juxtapositions of earthly and nonearthly details of which Waldock complains can be accepted without questioning because of their familiarity. Raphael's technique of "likening spiritual to corporal forms" (5. 573) is that of the Bible according to the theory of accommodation, and the nonearthly details are like exegeses in which the commentator notes the limits of the Bible's analogical representation.

As to Broadbent's assertion that "Milton should have abandoned his pretense of describing the war in terrestrial terms and treated it all as science fiction" (*Graver Subject,* p. 223), it is hard to see how a battle in which Satan contracted to escape the attacking Abdiel and dodged to avoid a blow from Michael would have prevented disbelief and allayed ridicule. But more important, it is hard to see how such a battle would have contributed to the poem as a whole. Milton's battle account differs from Homer's in that moral significance is primary in it, rather than physical events: the taunts of Milton's warriors contain theological arguments, and the battles are given theological and moral significance. The oddness of the events in a science fiction battle would have focused attention on the literal happenings and taken it way from the issues and from the significances of the happenings; the resultant battle, however convincing, would not, thus, have contributed to the ends of the poem.

The final question raised by the controversy over the war in heaven is that of its meaning. Stein's theory, which relates the war to the concept of discipline, is an improbable one. His contention that the limitation on the size of the angelic army and on their weaponry is a test of discipline is unproven. Raphael does say that God had "overruled / And limited [the angels'] might" (6. 227–29) , but the succeeding phrase, "though numbered such" (6. 229) , suggests that the limitation referred to is only the limitation of numbers, not any limitation on weaponry. Furthermore, no reason is given for the limitation but what is suggested by the preceding clause, which tells of the angels' power to "disturb / Though not destroy, their happy native seat" (6. 219–26) , an explanation which parallels God's reason for breaking off the war, that it "makes / Wild work in Heaven, and dangerous to the main" (6. 695–98) . Nothing at all is said about armor, therefore, and nothing is said about discipline in relation to God's restrictions on the size of the army. Furthermore, Stein's interpretation of the progress of the war does not accord with the evidence in the text. If Satan's invention of gunpowder is a breach in discipline and the angels' retaliation an abandonment of discipline, then the loyal angels have been reduced to Satanic evil in their attempts to combat that evil. This sophisticated notion is not present in the poem, for Raphael does not apologize for the uprooting of the hills, nor does God rebuke it: "behold the excellence, the power, / Which God hath in his mighty placed!" says Raphael of the incident (6. 637–38), and the Son tells the angels that their "warfare" has been "Faithful" and "of God / Accepted" (6. 803–4).

Summers's interpretation of the episode, less specific than Stein's, has more validity, and his general approach can be used to answer Broadbent's attack on the war. Summers derives his thematic summary from the lessons learned by the rebellious and the loyal angels (*Muse's Method*, pp. 136–37), and this point of departure suggests what is wrong with Broadbent's complaint that God and Satan are insufficiently contrasted: looking for contrast in figures who are not comparable, Broadbent misses those moral contrasts that are present. The speeches of the loyal and the rebellious angels are used primarily to define contrasting sets of beliefs. Summers centers his summary around the "results of 'warfare' against the Almighty and His Messiah" (ibid., p. 136), and this subject suggests what is wrong with Broadbent's complaints that the episode is morally irrelevant to the poem and that it fails to attack the immorality of war: assuming that the episode ought to be an ironic comment on war itself, Broadbent misses its point, the judgment that this particular war passes on the beliefs of the two groups of warring creatures. The outcomes of the battles are used to refute the claims made by the rebellious angels. Satan's claim that he can uphold self-made laws and his doubts of God's superiority to himself are refuted when he bows to Abdiel's blow (6. 189–98), and his value of glory and his doubts of the existence of hell are answered by the wound he receives from Michael, which brings shame instead of glory, and inflicts the pain which foretells the pains of hell (6. 323–43). The rebels' confidence during the second battle is answered by the loyal angels' retaliation, which deprives the rebels of their weapons and inflicts upon them the sort of overthrow which their weapons had previously inflicted (6. 646–61). The third battle refutes the rebels' claims in full. The loyal angels, on the other hand, are vindicated. Two expedients prevent their being blamed for not winning the war, the limitation by God on the size of the loyal army and his delaying of the impairment that sin would otherwise cause in the rebels (6. 690–92) —the first weakly explained, the second not explained at all; these expedients turn a two-to-one battle against enfeebled foes into an equal fight. (Denying the limitation on the size of the army, William Empson makes the sneer which Milton is anxious to circumvent, that "the loyalist angels could not defeat Satan's army, though twice their number" [*Milton's God* (London, 1961), p. 112]. Empson argues that when God tells Michael and Gabriel to lead forth angels

"Equal in number to [the] godless crew" of rebels [6. 44–50], he is sending out all the loyal angels, and is reassuring these angels that they are not outnumbered; "Equal . . . to" means merely "no less in number than," Empson argues [ibid., p. 41n]. Empson overlooks, however, Satan's claim that his troops had defied "What [God] had powerfullest to send . . . from about his throne" and had "judged / Sufficient to subdue" them [6. 423–28]; the phrases imply that God sent only selected troops, fewer than the total number available.) Blame is thus removed from the loyal angels, and they are shown as winning the "fame in Heaven" they desire (6. 374–76), God's approval of their fidelity (6. 803–4), and as winning that approval not by pragmatic success but by loyalty alone.

⁵ On this rather unimportant point, critics have been misled by Samuel Johnson. Dr. Johnson assumed that Satan "animate[d] the toad" and hid his spear inside it ("John Milton," in *Lives of the English Poets*). C. S. Lewis in replying to Dr. Johnson accepted his assumption, arguing that Satan's "subtle body" was able to "penetrate" the "grosser body" of the toad (*A Preface to "Paradise Lost"* [London, 1942], p. 109). In refuting Lewis, A. J. A. Waldock accepted the assumption also, merely noting that Lewis had neglected to answer Dr. Johnson's query as to how Satan had disguised his spear (*"Paradise Lost" and Its Critics* [Cambridge, 1947], p. 110). Arnold Stein worked the supposed imbrutement into his analysis of Satan's character, arguing that one of the signs of the loss of insight which is part of Satan's punishment is the fact that, having imbruted himself previously without indignation, Satan is suddenly indignant at having to imbrute himself in the serpent (*Answerable Style: Essays on "Paradise Lost"* [Minneapolis, 1953], pp. 8–9).

The first objection to the theory that Satan imbrutes himself in the toad is that there is no evidence for it. The episode occurs as the last of a series of disguises: first Satan "change[s] his proper shape" and appears as "a stripling cherub" (3. 634–36); then he "s[i]t[s] like a cormorant" on the tree of life (4. 194–96); next he approaches Adam and Eve disguised as "A lion" and "as a tiger" (4. 401–8); and finally he is found "Squat like a toad" at the "ear of Eve" (4. 799–800). There is no more reason to assume that Satan imbrutes himself in the toad than that he imbrutes himself in the other beasts, and no more reason to assume that he imbrutes himself in the beasts than that he possesses some wandering cherub: it is within the power of an angel to assume whatever shape he chooses (angels can "limb themselves," Raphael says, "as they please . . . and color, shape or size / Assume, as likes them best" [6. 351–53]), and if the cherubic disguise is nearer to Satan's natural shape than the animal ones, the reason is not imbrutement but the usefulness of an angelic disguise for deceiving Uriel (there was, after all, no alternative) and the effectiveness of an animal disguise for spying on Adam and Eve (an angel would have been received as a guest, and therefore could not have eavesdropped). The description of Satan, furthermore, suggests that he is disguised rather than imbruted. The phrase "Squat like a toad" means not "inside a squatting toad" but "hunched in a toad's likeness," and the line "So started up in his own shape the Fiend" (4. 819) means not "Satan stepped out of the toad and expanded himself" but simply "Satan appeared in his proper shape instead of his disguised one."

The second objection to the theory that Satan imbrutes himself in the toad is that it makes Satan's behavior at the time of the second soliloquy very strange. If Satan is imbruting himself for the first time in the serpent, then it is easy to understand why he hesitates, taking the step only "after long debate" (9. 87–88) and after venting his "inward grief" (9. 97–98), and it is easy to understand why he feels a vivid sense of disgust at this new necessity:

> O foul descent! that I who erst contended
> With Gods to sit the highest, am now constrained
> Into a beast, and, mixed with bestial slime,
> This essence to incarnate and imbrute,
> That to the height of deity aspired.
>
> (9. 163–67)

If, however, Satan has imbruted himself previously, nothing short of Stein's rather awkward theory of amnesia can account for these responses—and even this theory cannot account fully for Satan's behavior, for it cannot explain why Satan in a less debased earlier state should be indifferent to an action whose moral implications strike him forceably in his later, less aware state.

It should be noted, however, that the reinterpretation of Satan's disguise does not clear up all the angelological difficulties. Milton does not say that angels' weapons share their owners' plasticity, and thus there is no warrant for the supposition that Satan disguised his spear as Froggy's customary sword and buckler.

⁶ The conversation of Satan with Beelzebub brings up the question of Satan's role in his followers' apostasy. On this question, I have assumed that Satan does tempt his followers, but I have redefined the significance of that temptation.

William Empson holds one extreme position on the seduction, the position that Satan does not tempt his followers, but only voices their discontents. He argues that the fact that Satan does not need to develop his arguments and the fact that his followers rapidly assent to them proves that Satan only expresses the hatred which all the rebellious angels feel (*Milton's God* [London, 1961], pp. 27–28). The opposite extreme, the position that Satan seduces his followers, is held by John S. Diekhoff, who cites as evidence the fact that Satan alone is the father of Sin (2. 747–58), that he is said to influence Beelzebub, who in turn influences others (5. 694–704), and that he is said to "allure" his followers (5. 708–10) (*Milton's "Paradise Lost": A Commentary on the Argument* [New York, 1946], pp. 99–101). One compromise position is taken by Arnold Stein, who argues that Milton "never tries to make dramatically real" what he posits, that the angels' fall is a "spontaneous mass contagion" (*Answerable Style: Essays on "Paradise Lost"* [Minneapolis, 1953], p. 75). If it were not for the possibility of a superior solution, I would support the opposite compromise, the position that Milton means to make Satan the seducer of the angels, but confuses the issue with a faulty explanation of God's bestowal of grace.

Ordinarily, I believe, Diekhoff's evidence would be thought decisive, for Empson's is more tenuous and more susceptible to reinterpretation, but one important passage has always been taken as proving the contrary view, the passage in which God explains his bestowal of grace; God says in that passage that he will not give grace to the angels but will give it to man because "The first sort by their own suggestion fell, / Self-tempted, self-depraved" while "Man falls, deceived / By the other first" (3. 129–31). If this statement is taken to mean that each of the angels tempted himself (so Stein [*Answerable Style*, p. 75] and Diekhoff [*Milton's "Paradise Lost,"* p. 99] construe it), then the critic, caught with contradictory evidence, must decide whether independence or seduction is more essential to the work as a whole, and must choose in what place to locate the flaw. I believe that the represented action is more important than the rather incidental theoretical statement.

It may be, however, that the passage of explanation has been misinterpreted, for if the word "self-tempted" is taken in a distributive sense and interpreted as meaning that each angel tempted himself, then the parallel words "deceived / By the other first" should also be taken in a distributive sense, and should mean that each man was deceived by an angel. The fact that this idea is contradicted by the case of Adam suggests that the whole antithesis may have some other meaning. The most satisfactory explanation, I think, is that God's distinction centers on the source of the original impetus to sin. The point made is that man would not have fallen without the intervention of a different, and more clever, kind of creature, who supplied him with heretical arguments, while the angels fell without the intervention of any other sort of creature. According to this explanation, the angels as a group (the words "The first sort" name them as a species) fell "by their own suggestion," that is, by temptations of angelic origin; and they are "Self-tempted" and "self-depraved" in that their temptation and fall were not initiated by any other kind of creature. This explanation is compatible with the theory that Satan seduced his followers, for it sees the pronouncement as referring only to the source of heresy, not to the way in which each individual creature came to accept the heresy.

As to the significance of the seduction, I reject Diekhoff's contention that Satan's temptation of his followers is analogous to his temptation of Eve (*Milton's "Paradise Lost,"* p. 99). Diekhoff's analogy overlooks the total pattern of relationships in *Paradise Lost:* Satan is the inventor of heresy and the seducer of his followers as Eve is the original acceptor of heresy and the seducer of Adam; Satan first violates the proven relationship with his followers as Eve first violates her proper relationship with Adam. In both the religious and the personal sphere, Satan, in so far as he initiates his followers' apostasy, resembles not himself when he tempts Eve, but Eve when she tempts Adam and when she disrupts domestic harmony with her suggestions for gardening.

3 The Main Plot

¹ This idea of the creatures' responsibilities to God, as well as the corollary responsibilities to other creatures, relies upon the principle of hierarchy, expounded at length by C. S. Lewis (in *A Preface to "Paradise Lost"* [London, 1942], pp. 72–80).

The fact that an idea is more abstract or logically prior does not make it structurally more important in a poem; though the principle of hierarchy underlies the notion of the creatures' responsibilities, I have viewed the responsibilities themselves rather than the idea of hierarchy as the concept central to *Paradise Lost*. For reasons I have given in my Introduction, the alternative view, which takes the idea of hierarchy to be central, does not seem to me to lead to satisfactory interpretations.

² The claim that Adam and Eve are never portrayed as innocent is the result of critics' insistence on judging the characters not by the conception of innocence presented in the work, but by their own notion of what innocence means.

Despite lapses in detail (like Adam's parenthetical comment about death: "Whate'er death is, / Some dreadful thing no doubt" [4. 425–26]), Milton portrays unfallen man as a creature who has not sinned, rather than as a creature who is not liable to sin, and as a perfect example of humankind as presently constituted, rather than as a being with attributes different from and more perfect than those of his fallen descendants. Innocence is defined in Adam's famous pronouncement on sin:

> *Evil into the mind of god or man*
> *May come and go, so unapproved, and leave*
> *No spot or blame behind.*
>
> (*5. 117–19*)

Sin, according to this pronouncement, resides not in the contemplation of evil but in the decision to act evilly; and the pronouncement is not merely casual, for it underlies Milton's account of the fall of Satan. Satan is not portrayed as fallen when he broaches his heresies to the assembly in heaven, for Abdiel considers that Satan can still turn back (5. 845–48); only when the decision is made to embrace these heresies does sin occur, the occasion being marked by the birth of Sin. (William Empson's contrary theory on the order of these events is discussed in note 2 to chapter 2.) Because Milton conceives of innocence as extending through the conscious contemplation of heresy, he can without inconsistency ascribe such attributes as the capacity for passion to innocent creatures.

The choice of this definition of innocence is inevitable, given the didactic purpose of Milton's account of life in Eden. Critics—for example, Maurice

Kelley (*This Great Argument: A Study of Milton's "De Doctrina Christiana" as a Gloss upon "Paradise Lost"* [Princeton, N. J., 1941], p. 150) and E. M. W. Tillyard (*Studies in Milton* [London, 1951], p. 10) —have proposed a dramatic justification for Milton's portrayal of Adam and Eve, arguing that the attributes assigned to the pair effect a transition from innocence to sinfulness. Douglas Bush, however, remarks that the picture of the unfallen Adam and Eve is Milton's representation of the Puritan ideal of marriage (*"Paradise Lost" in Our Time: Some Comments* [New York, 1945], p. 75), and if nothing else, the didactic prophecy of Michael suggests that Milton is interested in such moral applications. The exemplary function of Adam and Eve provides a reason other than the dramatic for Milton's portrayal of the pair, for it is impossible to make moral models out of people who are incapable of conceiving of sin and who possess attributes unknown to modern men.

C. S. Lewis assumes that Milton is attempting to portray such innocents, that he is attempting to render that state of innocence envisioned by St. Augustine in which man had the power to consciously direct all of what are now his involuntary physical responses (*A Preface to "Paradise Lost"* [London, 1942], p. 69). In accord with this assumption, Lewis criticizes Milton for inadequately rendering the mysteriousness of prelapsarian sexual feeling, which was, he says, "both very like and totally unlike anything a fallen man could possibly feel" (ibid., p. 120). If, however, Milton were to present the Adam and Eve which Lewis describes, he would have to offer as models for fallen humanity people whose feelings were "totally unlike anything a fallen man could possibly feel." He would, for example, have to hold up to a lecherous son of Adam the example of a man who had no sexual responses except those which he decided to have; or to a gluttonous daughter of Eve the example of a woman who did not salivate unless she chose (the example is derived from Lewis, p. 69n). The ineffectiveness of such examples reveals how necessary it is to Milton's purpose that Adam and Eve be portrayed as meeting with perfect but human capacities temptations which they can and do resist but to which they could succumb.

The critics who claim that Adam and Eve are not portrayed as innocent quite openly reject the poem's pronouncements. Tillyard argues that the idea that evil may enter a good mind "cannot work in concrete literary presentation"; "Dramatically," he says, "the mere fact of entrance implies some pre-existing sympathy" (*Studies in Milton*, p. 11). This argument implies that it is permissible for a critic to interpret a scene in a way that is contrary to the principles affirmed in the work. Millicent Bell argues that Adam "is not convincing when he says 'Yet evil whence? In thee can harbour none, / Created pure'" ("The Fallacy of the Fall in *Paradise Lost*," *PMLA*, 68 [1953]: 871). What Mrs. Bell means is not that there is evidence in the text that the character is not reliable, nor that there is a contradiction such that a critic is forced to disregard one position, but simply that a critic may disregard material in a work if he decides that he doesn't agree with it. Both these critics judge Adam and Eve by their own conceptions of innocence. When Tillyard says that Eve is "on the far side of the line that divides innocence from experience" (*Studies in Milton*, p. 12), his use of the word "experience" suggests that he thinks of innocence as the inability to conceive of evil, while Mrs. Bell explicitly invokes the criterion of "liab[ility] to temptation" ("The Fallacy of the Fall," p. 864). These critical procedures are evident in the arguments by which the two critics support their thesis about Milton's portrayal of Adam and Eve.

The critics' arguments about the morning quarrel of Adam and Eve can be disregarded here, in that this episode should not be thought of as part of the state of innocence (this point is argued in note 12 to this chapter). Mrs. Bell's argument on Adam's speculations about the stars, however, and her argument about Eve's gazing at the reflection in the pool reveal her insistence on judging characters by her own assumptions rather than by those of the work. Detecting an "instinct of waywardness" (ibid., p. 872) in the psychological operations which Adam describes (8. 188–95) in his reply to Raphael's remarks on speculation, Mrs. Bell argues that Adam's "title to perfection . . . is none too clear" because "the outcome of the tale" proves that this instinct is not able to be disciplined by warning (p. 872). As to Eve's love for her reflection and her rejection of Adam (4. 449–80), Mrs. Bell argues that these reveal "a dainty vanity" in Eve, and prove that she has "an ego that might respond to the impulse for self-advancement" (p. 871). Even if the existence of Adam's instinct and Eve's vanity are granted (an alternative interpretation of Eve's trait is proposed in note 5 to this chapter), all that Mrs. Bell proves is that Adam and Eve are not innocent if innocence is defined as the inability to conceive of sin. She does not prove that they are not innocent if innocence is defined as the absence of sinful choice. In Eve's case, Mrs. Bell ignores the fact that Eve's final decision (4. 481–91) is a conscious rejection of error, and in Adam's case she decides, in defiance of all the statements in *Paradise Lost* about free will, that Adam's later failure to control his impulses proves that these impulses are inherently uncontrollable and therefore guilty.

Both Mrs. Bell and Tillyard treat Adam's confession of passion and Eve's dream, and though their arguments differ, their conclusions rely upon the same critical presuppositions. Tillyard argues that when Adam describes his attraction to Eve as "commotion strange" (8. 523–33), he has "admitted to feelings alien to the angelic" (*Studies in Milton*, p. 12), and he argues that in replying (8. 596–617) to Raphael's rebuke, Adam is not "straightforward," for by arguing that Eve's manner rather than her beauty affects him, he is, according to Tillyard, ignoring Raphael's condemnation of his doting; and in asking Raphael about angelic love, he is, Tillyard says, "counterattack[ing]" with "something near impudence" (p. 12). Mrs. Bell argues that the reactions to Eve which Adam describes to Raphael (8. 551–56) are "idolatrous," and reveal that Adam is "subject to temptations and excesses" ("The Fallacy of the Fall," p. 873). Some of these arguments are based upon misreadings. Tillyard's interpretation of Adam's question is rendered unlikely by Raphael's response; Raphael would not answer an impudent counterattack "with a smile" (8. 618–19). Both the claim by Tillyard that Adam is ignoring Raphael's condemnation and the claim by Mrs. Bell that Adam's love is idolatrous overlook Adam's defense from the charge of idolatry:

> *I to thee disclose*
> *What inward thence I feel, not therefore foiled,*
> *Who meet with various objects, from the sense*
> *Variously representing; yet still free,*
> *Approve the best, and follow what I approve.*
> *(8. 607–11)*

But when Tillyard claims that Adam is not innocent because he experiences passion and when Mrs. Bell claims that he is not innocent because he is "subject to temptations and excesses," they are both claiming that innocence is the inability to conceive of sin, and they are both disregarding the fact that Adam has not given conscious approval to any overvaluation of Eve and undervaluation of God.

In analyzing Eve's dream, Tillyard argues that Eve's perturbation (5. 9–11) shows that she has "passed from a state of innocence to one of sin" (*Studies in Milton*, p. 12). This argument relies upon the Freudian notion that if a man is disturbed by a story, he subconsciously wishes to perform the actions represented in it, but is inhibited by his conscious principles. Mrs. Bell warns against such an analysis, arguing that the "modern proneness to suspect the sleeper of wish- or anxiety-phantasies" must be avoided ("The Fallacy of the Fall," p. 871); but her own analysis is also dependent upon a psychological premise. Mrs. Bell argues that, "knowing already the outcome of the story," "we cannot believe" Adam's assertion that evil "May come and go" and "leave / No spot or blame," and that Adam "is not convincing" when he argues that Eve cannot be the source of evil (ibid.); Mrs. Bell states that "we suspect [Eve] receptive to the Tempter's choice flattery and to his adroit fanning of [her] ego" (ibid.). This argument relies upon the assumption that actions are the signs of previous subconscious motives; assuming that such motives exist, Mrs. Bell discounts Adam's pronouncements on Eve's innocence. The psychological assumptions of Tillyard and of Mrs. Bell ought not be granted, for both contradict evidence in the text (Tillyard's argument is treated in more detail in the succeeding note); but even if the assumptions are granted, the arguments would still only prove that Eve is not innocent in the sense of being unable to conceive of sin. The wishes and subconscious motives ascribed by the critics would not remove Eve from the state of innocence as that state is defined in the poem.

The critics who claim that Adam and Eve are never portrayed as innocent, then, do not prove that Milton has no definition of innocence capable of distinguishing that state from the state of sin, nor do they prove that Milton violates his definition; they merely prove that Milton does not use the same definition of innocence that they do.

[3] I reject the common notion that Eve's dream is an anticipation of her

fall. One form of this interpretation views the dream as a revelation of Eve's own evil propensities. Despite his dislike of Freud (see *"Paradise Lost" in Our Time: Some Comments* [New York, 1945], p. 48) and of psychologists in general (he raps them with a spoonerism for "pull[ing] habits out of rats" [ibid., p. 46]), Douglas Bush attributes Eve's dream to her subconscious, arguing that what he calls the "uncensored dream" reveals the "seeds of vanity and ambitious pride" in her (ibid., p. 76). In a variant of this position, E. M. W. Tillyard argues that Eve's perturbation shows that she has a "pre-existing sympathy" with Satan's suggestions (*Studies in Milton* [London, 1951], pp. 11–12). The second form of this theory holds that Eve's dream partially corrupts her. John S. Diekhoff argues that Eve's "desires" are "aroused" by the dream, and that the dream is responsible for her plan to garden separately from Adam (*Milton's "Paradise Lost": A Commentary on the Argument* [New York, 1946], p. 56). Both forms of the theory are combined by Arnold Stein, whose interpretation is particularly sophisticated. Arguing that Eve's dream reveals her own self-love, he claims, first of all, that Satan tempts Eve with her own way of viewing the world, that the style of his speeches is her own style; and secondly he argues that when Satan presents his temptation to self-love as an external temptation, in order to make it seem less guilty, Eve shows her own weakness by attributing the flattering voice to Adam (*Answerable Style: Essays on "Paradise Lost"* [Minneapolis, 1953], pp. 84–89). Stein also argues that Eve's dream is the second of three progressive steps toward her apostasy (ibid., pp. 92–94), and he compares these to three parallel anticipations which he finds in Adam's actions before the fall (pp. 101–3).

Underlying the idea that the dream prepares for Eve's fall is the assumption that since the incidents in the dream clearly foreshadow the later temptation, the purpose of the dream must be to establish causal connections with that temptation; from this assumption come the two proposed links, that the dream reveals the characteristics that cause the fall, or that it contributes to the fall by corrupting Eve. Yet the presentation of the dream itself provides strong evidence that neither of these connections exists. In addition to the obvious facts that Satan is shown as inspiring the dream, that the dream is identifiable as Satan's handiwork by its resemblance to his later temptation speeches, and that Eve is shown as horrified by it, the ending shows that Eve is neither responsible for nor influenced by the dream:

> *Forthwith up to the clouds*
> *With him I flew, and underneath beheld*
> *The Earth outstretched immense, a prospect wide*
> *And various. Wondering at my flight and change*
> *To this high exaltation, suddenly*
> *My guide was gone, and I, methought, sunk down*
> *And fell asleep; but O how glad I waked*
> *To find this but a dream!*
>
> (*5. 86–93*)

This ending is not Satan's doing, since Satan would not have any reason to remove the angel and return Eve anticlimactically to earth, and since the return reneges on what Eve was promised, which was not only flight (5. 78–79) but the power to "Ascend to Heaven . . . and see / What life the gods live there" (5. 79–81); the "sudden" disappearance of the guide reflects, clearly, the fact that Satan was "surprised" at his work by the guardian angels (4. 813–14). Now, the fact that Eve's mind does not on its own continue with Satan's promptings, not even to complete an episode whose plot has already been outlined, shows that what Satan tells Eve is alien to her own mind's workings; and the fact that not only does Eve upon waking reject what Satan has caused her to dream, but that even her sleeping mind does not assimilate and build upon his promptings, shows that Eve is untouched by the thoughts which he has given her.

The arguments supporting the theory that Eve's dream anticipates her fall are not compelling. Bush's psychological theory of Eve's guilt relies on the assumption that Eve is responsible for the dream, and that assumption is strongly contradicted by the text. Tillyard's interpretation of Eve's distress involves sophisticated psychological notions (the preceding note discusses this point) which do not fit the evidence. If Milton had intended Eve's agitation to show her sympathy with Satan's suggestions, he would not have ended her dream with proof that her mind does not embellish Satan's suggestions with fantasies of its own. It is much more consistent with the text to interpret Eve's distress as the horror of a good mind witnessing evil.

Stein is much more careful than Bush or Tillyard, but his argument is not indisputable. In the first place, his stylistic point is undercut by his own accurate analysis of the style of the tempter in the dream. Citing the angel's description,

> [*N*]*ow is the pleasant time,*
> *The cool, the silent, save where silence yields*
> *To the night-warbling bird, that now awake*
> *Tunes sweetest his love-labored song; now reigns*
> *Full-orbed the moon, and with more pleasing light*
> *Shadowy sets off the face of things,*
>
> (*5. 38–43*)

Stein comments: "In [the] invitation to the 'walk by Moon' the solemn bird of night now sings a 'love-labor'd song'—as in the poetry of the fallen world. The light of the moon is now beautiful in a sophisticated way, setting off the face of things by shadow—a notion more proper to a world where good is known by evil" (*Answerable Style,* p. 87). As Stein's references imply, this description of the nightingale and the moon contrasts with the description by Eve—"silent Night / With this her solemn bird and this fair Moon" (4. 647–48); and though Stein argues that Satan is "heighten[ing]" Eve's "verbal sensuousness" (ibid., p. 87), it is simpler to see the style as the Petrarchan style of Satan's later temptation speeches. Furthermore, Stein's suspicions of Eve's attribution of the speech are ungrounded. Stein argues that Eve does not take the "gentle voice" in the dream for Adam's (5. 35–37) simply because he is "the only possibility," for, says Stein, "there are the angels 'By us oft seen' " (p. 84). The gentleness, however, is what Eve goes by, the fact that the voice is speaking to her affectionately and privately; there is no reason to suppose that at this time Adam and Eve have had any close contact with angels—Adam speaks only of having heard the angelic guardians hymning God (4. 680–88) —and even if there has been contact, no angels would have spoken to Eve affectionately or even privately: during his whole visit, Raphael addresses only one brief salutation to Eve alone (5. 388–91). That Eve should think of Adam is, thus, inevitable.

As to the arguments concerning Eve's corruption, the claim, first of all, that Eve's dream is responsible for her plan to garden separately is a doubtful one. Stein argues that "there is nothing back" of Eve's plan "that cannot be traced to the experience of the dream, which is now beginning to be approved" (p. 94). His case is at least overstated, for Eve does not plan to do what she did in the dream, look for Adam or walk to the tree of knowledge, and she does plan to do something not suggested by the dream, tend her flowers; the similarity which Stein finds is very abstract, involving the condition of "isolation from [Adam] in the dream" (ibid.). Diekhoff's argument is even more improbable. Diekhoff suggests that Eve's "dream is in the background of her experience when she later insists upon the separation from Adam in order . . . to subject herself to temptation" (*Milton's "Paradise Lost,"* p. 56). The suggestion that Eve formulates her plan with temptation in mind not only violates the progress of the morning quarrel— there is no evidence that Eve thinks about temptation before Adam's warning (9. 251–69) —but it does not accord with Eve's behavior, for had Eve intended to be tempted, she would have gone to the forbidden tree, the spot where the temptation in the dream took place. (Eve's plan is discussed in note 12 to this chapter.)

In the second place, the structural plan proposed by Stein is dubious. Stein compares Eve's looking in the pool (4. 449–91) to Adam's words upon the creation of Eve (8. 491–99). Yet whereas Eve's error is explained by God (4. 467–75) and her own initial reaction to Adam repudiated by herself (4. 488–91), Adam is not rebuked by God, nor is he apologetic about his words, as he is about the reactions to Eve which he subsequently describes to Raphael (8. 521–59). Furthermore, Stein's two causal chains—Eve's gazing, dream, and plan to garden; Adam's words, confession about passion, and approval of Eve's plan—leave out two events which are clearly meant to bear on the fall, Eve's question about the stars (4. 657–58), which is firmly corrected by Adam (4. 660–98), and Adam's question about the stars (8. 13–38), which is rebuked by Raphael (8. 66–178). In his anxiety to find patterns of development, Stein overlooks a nondevelopmental pattern whereby parallel limitations are ascribed to Adam and Eve through parallel materials: Eve's description of her creation and reactions to Adam is matched by Adam's description of his creation and reactions to Eve, and Eve's question about the stars is matched by Adam's.

The assumption that underlies the idea that Eve's dream prepares for her fall is, I think, faulty. There is no reason to assume that the dream establishes causal connections when the presentation minimizes these connections, and when there is an alternative explanation which the presentation does not contradict. Eve's dream can be approached from the standpoint not of what it indicates causally but of what it proves morally. Its significance in this case is the opposite of the one generally assumed: the fact that Eve is carefully shielded from blame for her reactions to the dream and for its origins indicates that the point of the episode is Eve's blamelessness. According to this interpretation, the dream is a preliminary temptation, and Eve demonstrates, along with Adam, the way in which temptations should be handled.

⁴ Jackson I. Cope connects the ending of Eve's dream, the evening prayer of Adam and Eve, and the pair's lovemaking with two of the major sets of symbols which he finds in *Paradise Lost*. The dream he connects with what he calls the "vertical pattern," the imagery of rising and falling (*The Metaphoric Structure of "Paradise Lost"* [Baltimore, 1962], p. 114); the prayer he associates with the imagery of light and dark (ibid., p. 113); and the lovemaking he treats in connection with the sexual imagery (pp. 82–83), which constitutes a subclass of the images associated with rising and falling (pp. 79–80). The way in which Cope handles these materials reveals the dubiousness of his claim that *Paradise Lost* is not a narrative but an "atemporal, nonsequential structure" of recurrent metaphors (pp. 75–76).

To prove that *Paradise Lost* contains the consistent, comprehensive, and coherent system of images that his structural theory requires, Cope disregards and distorts evidence and extrapolates extravagantly upon very slight pretexts—faults to which every systematic interpreter is liable, but of which Cope is far more guilty than are those earlier narrative critics whose work he dismisses as "ephemeral" (p. 3). Interpreting Eve's dream, Cope cites the passage in which Eve says that she "flew" with the angel "up to the clouds" and then "sunk down / And fell asleep" (5. 86–92); the ascent and descent are, he says, a "visible emblem in little of the fall" (p. 114). The trouble with this interpretation is that it overlooks the reason for Eve's descent, the fact that her sinking down is a sign that her mind has been released from Satan's influence (this point is discussed in the preceding note); the example contradicts the symbolic meaning that Cope imposes upon it.

Because he associates night and evil, Cope finds sinister overtones in the evening prayer of Adam and Eve; "If there is a hymn to the night," he says, "it is prelude to the pre-temptation of Eve in her dream" (p. 113). This interpretation distorts the arrangement of episodes in the poem. Cope's theory, if taken seriously, would turn the evening prayer into an irony: Adam and Eve thank God for the sleep during which Eve is tempted. Milton, however, is always careful to dispel any doubts of God's power and love—sometimes heavy-handedly careful, as when he explains how Satan could escape from the fiery lake (1. 210–20). In this case he creates no doubts, first of all because he connects the prayer not with Satan's preliminary temptation but with the activities of Adam and Eve; the prayer comes near

the end of an episode in which Adam and Eve converse on their way to the
bower (4. 598–775), an episode which ends with their prayer and love-
making, after which Milton emphatically takes his leave of the characters
and turns to a different scene:

> *These lulled by nightingales, embracing slept,*.
> *And on their naked limbs the flowery roof*
> *Showered roses, which the morn repaired. Sleep on*
> *Blest pair; and O yet happiest if ye seek*
> *No happier state, and know to know no more.*
>   *Now had night measured with her shadowy cone*
> *Half way up hill this vast sublunar vault,*
> *And from their ivory port the Cherubim*
> *Forth issuing at the accustomed hour stood armed*
> *To their night-watches in warlike parade,*
> *When Gabriel to his next in power thus spake.*
>   *(4. 771–81)*

Milton, furthermore, separates the prayer from the dream with the scene of
the guardian angels' encounter with Satan; he does not focus in this scene
upon the effects of Satan's attempt, and he treats the episode as a defeat for
Satan. Cope distorts the evidence in order to bring into closer harmony with
his theory a speech in which night is connected emphatically not with Satan
but with God.

Cope treats the lovemaking of Adam and Eve as an exception to a sym-
bolic pattern; sexuality is the "chief image of evil at crucial points in
Paradise Lost," he says (p. 80), but the sexuality of Adam and Eve is "con-
doned in the bower scenes of Book IV" (p. 82). There is one very strong
objection to Cope's symbolic theory, the fact that Milton clearly and em-
phatically states that sex is not evil:

>   *[Adam and Eve] eased the putting off*
> *These troublesome disguises which we wear,*
> *Straight side by side were laid, nor turned, I ween,*
> *Adam from his fair spouse, nor Eve the rites*
> *Mysterious of connubial love refused;*
> *Whatever hypocrites austerely talk*
> *Of purity and place and innocence,*
> *Defaming as impure what God declares*
> *Pure, and commands to some, leaves free to all.*
> *Our Maker bids increase; who bids abstain*
> *But our destroyer, foe to God and Man?*
>   *(4. 739–49)*

It is interesting to see how Cope deals with this disproof. First of all, he
misrepresents the offending evidence. By using an impersonal construction
("Their sexuality is condoned"), he conceals the fact that Milton makes an

authorial pronouncement about sex. By saying that sexuality is condoned "in the bower scenes," he conceals the fact that Milton is talking not about prelapsarian sex but about sex in general; the words "commands to some, leaves free to all" cannot apply simply to Adam and Eve. By using the word "condoned," Cope conceals the fact that Milton says not that God excuses an evil, but that God commands a good. Milton's pronouncement is thus triply attenuated.

Then, to cover the exception to his theory, Cope supplies a speculative argument on God's motives. He argues that man's sexuality is "God's reaction to Satan's active seduction of and by Sin" and that sin is "patterned into the inevitable but not yet unfolded imperfection of the fallen world created in consequence of the first fall" (pp. 82–83). For the idea that God modeled man's sexuality on the example of Satan and Sin, Cope can provide no evidence from the text, and Milton's silence on the matter is suggestive: if sex is viewed as evil, then its bestowal needs excuse, but if it is a good, as Milton insists, then its bestowal requires no explanation. Cope's theory, furthermore, is hardly the simplest available. Raphael explains that angels express their love by interpenetrating (8. 626–29); the God who gave the angels a physical expression of love would naturally give such an expression to man. Raphael also says that angels experience man's corporeal enjoyments "In eminence" (8. 622–24); man is a denser creature than angels, and therefore God had to give him a kind of physical union different from the higher creatures' interpenetration. As for Cope's contention that sexuality is a sort of prefiguring of the "inevitable . . . imperfection of the fallen world," that suggestion is repeatedly contradicted in the poem: God insists that the fall of the world is not inevitable (3. 117–19), he plans the world without intending that man fall (7. 154–61), and he makes the world "entirely good" (7. 549). Cope defends his theory with an extrapolation which is completely unsupportable.

Cope explains his system of symbols by appealing to literary models, like *Finnegans Wake,* which, he says, uses "the interplay of light and dark tones" and "movement upward and downward" for "both the formal and the meaning pattern" (p. 75); "the cyclical rhythms of rise and fall," he says, constitute a "myth of man's history" and a "reification of his individual domestic, physical, sexual, and spiritual experience" (p. 77). He also appeals to religious anthropology, mentioning the Christian, Manichean, and Platonic symbolism of light and dark (p. 79), and the pagan and Christian mythology of fall and resurrection, which he connects with "nature's rhythm of seeding and rising out of earth" and with "man's own sexual rhythms" (p. 80). It is one thing, however, to conceive of a literary procedure and to justify a system of symbols; it is another to demonstrate that a particular poem uses the procedure and contains the symbols. The way in which Cope handles the state of innocence of Adam and Eve reveals how far his theory is from the materials of *Paradise Lost.*

[5] I have placed much less than the usual weight upon the incident of Eve's gazing in the pool, and I have not interpreted it in either of the usual ways, as evidence of Eve's credulity, or as evidence of her self-love.

The theory, argued by Maurice Kelley, that Eve's error about her reflection "foreshadows her later credulity" (*This Great Argument: A Study of Milton's "De Doctrina Christiana" as a Gloss upon "Paradise Lost"* [Princeton, N. J., 1941], p. 150), does not adequately account for the materials of her speech. Eve's speech contains not only her error over her reflection (4. 460–75) but her initial rejection of Adam (4. 475–80) and her subsequent surrender to him (4. 481–91). These events are all part of a single story, but the last two have nothing to do with credulity. The theory that Eve's gazing at her image reveals her self-love is more plausible, but it is based, I believe, upon false analogies. Arnold Stein compares Eve to a "beautiful woman opening her eyes to look into the mirror that happens to be there" (*Answerable Style: Essays on "Paradise Lost"* [Minneapolis, 1953], p. 93). This comparison overlooks the fact that Eve does not know that she is looking at an image of herself, and therefore cannot be accused of even harmless vanity. When Douglas Bush claims that the "first hint of [Eve's] vanity" is contained in the scene's "veiled" allusion to the "myth" of Narcissus (*"Paradise Lost" in Our Time: Some Comments* [New York, 1945], p. 76), he does not examine the allusion carefully enough. Milton alludes specifically to Ovid's account of Narcissus (4. 460–69 recall *Metamorphoses* 3. 435, 457–62), and he makes no reference to the climax of this account, wherein Narcissus recognizes that he is looking at himself and persists in his passion though it means his death (*Metamorphoses* 3. 463–73). When Milton suggests a comparison of Eve's case to that of Narcissus, then, he omits the material which makes Narcissus an emblem of self-love.

Eve's attraction to her image proves not that she is vain, therefore, but merely that she is attached to beauty. Beauty is Eve's attribute, and she responds to it in the way that others respond. Stein remarks (*Answerable Style*, p. 92) that Eve's reaction resembles the response which Adam has upon first seeing her (8. 474–77), and Eve's beauty moves everyone else as well; it distracts not only Satan (9. 445–62), but Raphael and Adam, who watch Eve leave before resuming their conversation about the stars (8. 39–43, 59–63). What the allusion to Ovid explains, then, is that Eve is affected by the attribute which affects her viewers; Narcissus at the pool is said to be the victim of the features which made him loved (*Metamorphoses* 3. 423–26). Love for beauty, furthermore, figures in the other events of Eve's tale. When she first sees Adam, Eve judges him by the standard of beauty and grace, and therefore she undervalues the love which God has ordained. Later she learns that spiritual qualities are more valuable than physical ones, and therefore that physical beauty is less valuable than wisdom, and graceful gestures less valuable than what Eve calls "manly grace" (4. 490), the physical revelation of men's spiritual loftiness. Learning this, Eve can love Adam properly, and can therefore feel the proper gratitude—the gratitude she expresses earlier (4. 444–48) —for what God has given her.

The emphasis placed upon the incident of Eve's viewing of her image has been excessive, and critical errors have, I believe, resulted from it. Kelley (*Great Argument*, p. 150) and Bush (*"Paradise Lost" in Our Time*, pp. 76–77) see Eve's gazing and Adam's confession of passion (8. 521–59) as the two passages foreshadowing the fall, and neglect Eve's (4. 657–58) and Adam's (8. 13–38) questions about the stars; though Stein's analysis is more elaborate, his emphasis and omissions are the same (see Stein, pp. 92–94, 101–3). Emphasis on Adam's confession is not entirely misleading, for the confession does relate to Adam's primary sin in falling; but Adam's reply (4. 660–80) to Eve's question about the stars suggests that the question reveals a serious limitation in her. Emphasis on Eve's reactions to her reflection, therefore, may obscure what is central to her fall. Such an obscuration is present in Stein's analysis. When Stein reaches the topic of Eve's fall, he subsumes under the heading of self-love Eve's desire for godhead (p. 103) and her worship of the tree of knowledge (p. 97); he thereby eliminates as a separate subject the creature's acknowledgment of divine authority, and ignores as a separate factor in Eve's fall the insufficient thought which figures in her rejection of that authority and which is revealed in her question about the stars. Stein thus not only subordinates what ought to be a coordinate topic, but subordinates what is in this case the more important of two topics; for what Kelley calls Eve's "credulity" may not be foreshadowed, as he claims, in her love for her reflection, but it is, as he suggests, central.

⁶ I have not approached Milton's representation of the fall in either of two usual ways, by treating the fall in terms of its causes, or by denying that any unifying pattern can be found in the representation.

Two arguments advanced by A. J. A. Waldock seem to me valid objections to the causal approach to the fall. The first is the effect of such an approach on the characterization of God. Waldock argues that the penalty levied against mankind seems severe even when the crime for which it is levied is disloyalty to God; reducing the crime to some lesser, causal sin—Waldock cites Tillyard's "gregariousness" but others could be substituted—makes God seem irredeemably cruel (*"Paradise Lost" and Its Critics* [Cambridge, 1947], pp. 57–58).

The second objection is the inability of any single cause to apply to the cases of Satan, Adam, and Eve. Waldock analyzes several unsuccessful causal theories (ibid., pp. 58–61), and his arguments could be applied to theories later than those he mentions (this point is touched on in note 2 to chapter 2, which deals with Satan's fall). Even the atypical interpretation of Arnold Stein does not disprove his claim. Stein says that both Adam and Eve fall through self-love (*Answerable Style: Essays on "Paradise Lost"* [Minneapolis, 1953], p. 103), and he argues (rather sketchily) that Satan's fall is analogous both to the fall of Adam (ibid., pp. 109–10) and to the fall of Eve (p. 116). Whereas other critics seek fairly specific causes for each apostasy, and therefore find no satisfactory likeness between the separate cases, Stein attempts to trace different surface phenomena back to identical root causes. Thus, when he discusses the fall of Eve, Stein argues that Eve's "attempt to embrace what is above her, deity" is "self-love, which requires the debased transfer of devotion to the Tree of Knowledge as a mirror of self" (p. 103), and when he discusses the fall of Adam, he includes under the heading of self-love Adam's "trust in himself and in his knowledge," his "preference of the image he has begotten to the image in which he is begotten," and his "withdrawing from self-transcendence upward to embrace his finite being as creature" (p. 109)'.

The trouble with this approach is that the text will not support Stein's broad application of the concept of self-love. For example, there is no evidence in the poem that Eve's worship of the tree is an instance of self-love. Commenting upon the introduction to Eve's speech after eating the apple: "Thus to herself she pleasingly began" (9. 794), Stein argues (p. 95) that Eve's "hypnotized intellectual posture" recalls the earlier incident of her gazing at her reflection in the lake (4. 449–67). If, however, this argument is persuasive, what persuades is not the evidence in the poem but the force of Stein's metaphoric explanation: the words "hypnotized" and "posture" create the link. Continuing with the lines in which Eve is said to do "low reverence . . . as to the power / That dwelt" within the tree (9. 834–38), Stein argues that the words "as to" indicate that "if it is not the tree as tree that Eve is worshipping, neither is it unambiguously the power that created the tree" (p. 96); the implication is that Eve is also, as Stein says earlier, worshiping herself, the tree being "a convenient external correlative of self" (p. 95). Even if "as to the power" means "as if to the power," however, the connection to self-love is very remote, and the line may mean only "to the power that dwelt within, as it were," the word "as" expressing doubt as to the existence of the "power" being worshiped. The idea that Adam's love for Eve is a love for himself is even further from the text. When Raphael warns Adam about his love for Eve, he mentions two dangers, the danger of sensuality (8. 561–94) and the danger of preferring love for man to love for God (8. 633–35). Clearly this warning is meant to indicate the nature of Adam's later weakness, and that weakness is not defined in terms of self-love. If the term "self-love," then, cannot be justifiably applied to all the phenomena to which Stein applies it, Waldock's claim that there is no single cause which can unite the apostasies of Satan, Adam, and Eve still holds true.

In the case of Satan's fall, there is not enough evidence and emphasis to justify a causal approach (this point is discussed in note 2 to chapter 2); evidence does exist in the cases of Adam and Eve, but the pertinent material is not such as to justify only a causal approach. I have viewed this material, first of all, as contributing to the definition and portrayal of sin. The foreshadowings and warnings point up the element of conscious decision which is the sine qua non of sinning. The foreshadowings show the difference between the ability to sin and sinful choice, and the warnings suggest the alternative courses open to the sinners at the time of their mischoosing. In the accounts of the falls themselves the causal elements function simply as parts of descriptions of sinful acts; one kind of sin is illustrated by the choice of a delusive self-advantage over a real duty, another by the choice of a nearer and more obvious good in place of a higher one. I have also viewed the material usually treated in terms of causality as differentiating major from minor faults (this point is discussed in the two succeeding notes). Thus I have absorbed the topic of cause into a moral framework, and have eliminated it as a separate subject, one important in itself.

I have not, however, adopted the view propounded by other critics of the causal approach, the view that because the fall is meant to include a multiplicity of sins, the representation of it is not supposed to display any unity of design. The classic case is presented by Maurice Kelley. Citing the rather random list from *De Doctrina Christiana* (1. 11) by which Milton proves that the fall comprised all sins, Kellley argues that *Paradise Lost* treats the fall in the same way, and he offers as proof eighteen short passages which name eleven different sins in connection with the fall (*This Great Argument: A Study of Milton's "De Doctrina Christiana" as a Gloss upon "Paradise Lost"* [Princeton, 1941], pp. 144–46) . On the basis of this evidence, Kelley concludes that the "failure to recognize . . . Milton's concept of the manifold nature of the fall vitiates—if it does not render valueless—" studies which "oversimplify" the fall by "reducing [it] to [a] simple formula" (ibid., p. 150*n*) . This argument is very weak. Kelley makes no attempt to show that the eleven sins he names account for the contents of the major speeches of the fall and explain why the fall is foreshadowed in the way that it is; and in fact the eleven sins he names are not structurally significant, some of them, like disobedience, being so general that they include all the specific categories into which sins are divided, and some of them, like gluttony, being so trivial that they are treated as aspects of greater transgressions. Kelley's list of eighteen random passages only proves that the sins listed in *De Doctrina* have no bearing on the fall as it is treated in *Paradise Lost*. Furthermore, Kelley is self-contradictory in his comments about the poem. He says that "Milton is careful to indicate the predominant weaknesses which will lead to [the] undoing [of Adam and Eve]," namely "credulity" and "uxoriousness" (p. 150) . In this statement, he accepts the basic argument of those whom he accuses of oversimplifying, the argument that through devices like foreshadowing Milton singles out certain sins as central ones. He does not see that such an admission vitiates the claim that in narrating the fall, Milton lists a multiplicity of sins instead of formularizing them.

The claim that Milton does not organize his depiction of the fall is, I think, false; the trouble with the causal argument is not, as Waldock says, that it searches "for a unifying principle deeper than Milton's" (*"Paradise Lost" and Its Critics*, p. 61) , but rather, I believe, that it searches for a unifying principle different from Milton's; the organizing principle is to be found not in the causes of each fall, but in its nature, in the violations of the creaturely responsibilities to God which each apostasy entails.

[7] This account of Eve's fall affirms the view that intellectual inadequacy is the chief cause of Eve's fall, though it greatly subordinates the question of causality, and it affirms the view that Eve's guilt is adequately demonstrated in the poem.

A. J. A. Waldock's claim that no formula can be assigned to Eve's fall is not valid. Waldock argues that because Eve's fall consists of a "chain of events" (*"Paradise Lost" and Its Critics* [Cambridge, 1947], p. 33) —he mentions her dream, her insistence upon gardening separately, and the temptation scene itself—any cause derived from the temptation scene alone misrepresents her case (ibid., pp. 30–37). Waldock's list can be questioned (the causal connection between the dream and the fall is disputed in note 3 to this chapter), but the central fallacy in his argument is the idea that the series of events constitutes an inevitable sequence, as the words "chain of events" imply. It is true that Eve's plan of gardening both weakens her resistance and her defenses, and increases the likelihood for temptation, but Eve is still, at the moment of her choosing, "Sufficient" to stand, "though free to fall" (3. 98–99). Despite her previous actions, she is capable of repulsing the serpent, and therefore it is legitimate to ask why at the time of her decision she fails.

Textual evidence supports the view that the chief cause for Eve's fall is what Maurice Kelley calls "credulity" (*This Great Argument: A Study of Milton's "De Doctrina Christiana" as a Gloss upon "Paradise Lost"* [Princeton, N. J., 1941], p. 150) and what E. M. W. Tillyard calls "triviality of mind" (*Milton* [London, 1930], p. 260). Two inducements are mentioned in the passage of description that precedes Eve's speech of decision, the seeming reasonableness of the serpent's arguments to the "too eas[ily]" assenting Eve, and the attractiveness of the fruit to her "longing eye" (9. 733–43). It is reasonable to connect these inducements with the two episodes that foreshadow the fall, Eve's question about the stars (4. 657–58) and her gazing at the reflection in the lake (4. 449–91). The episode of the gazing has nothing to do with Eve's attraction to the fruit if that episode is interpreted as revealing her vanity, but if it is interpreted as revealing her love of beauty (the interpretation is argued in note 5 to this chapter), then it does relate to her attraction to what the description emphasizes is an object pleasing to sight and smell. The question about the stars clearly reveals some kind of intellectual weakness, and is easily connected with her later error. In the temptation scene, the intellectual failure is clearly primary—for one thing, the whole situation revolves around disguise and deception—and the priority there is matched in the foreshadowing episodes, where Adam's sharpness in answering Eve's question (4. 660–80) reveals the primary seriousness of the limitation disclosed by it; analysis of Eve's speech of decision supports this view.

The question of causality must be put in its place, however, and here two formulations by Tillyard should be examined. The first is his earlier contention that Adam and Eve "are punished with a doom out of all apparent proportion to their crime. To their crime, yes," Tillyard says; "but not to the mental triviality that accompanied it: by their miserable inadequacy before the issues of life mankind have deserved their fate" (*Milton*, p. 289). The second is Tillyard's later argument that "such disobedience" as is displayed in the fall "is near to what is now popularly described as the acts of disregarding the facts of existence, going against the nature of things, or refusing to come to terms with the conditions of one's environment" (*Studies in Milton* [London, 1951], p. 24). Both of these arguments translate the religious sin of "falling off / From" one's "Creator" (1. 30–31) into Darwinian terms of adaptation and survival (whatever the merit of the particular analogies, the process is legitimate enough: the question is argued in note 1 to chapter

1) , but the first argument shifts the focus of the narration from the sin of dis-
obedience to the cause of sin, while the second focuses upon the sin itself.
The latter view is clearly superior (the deficiency of the causal interpretation
is argued in the preceding note) : what is important about Eve's fall is not her
credulity and her attraction to beauty, but the fact that because of the former,
Eve questions her duty to God, and that because of the latter, Eve is
strengthened in her doubts of God's goodness.

Eve's fall has been extenuated on intellectual and on moral grounds; on
neither ground can Eve be justly defended. The intellectual arguments are
defective particularly in that they overlook the suggestions in the poem as to
how Eve should have responded to her temptation. The first defense offered
is that Eve displays adequate reasoning in her decision. J. B. Broadbent ar-
gues that, granted its premise, Satan's argument is "intellectually unanswer-
able," and that therefore Eve could not be expected to "counter-attack"
(*Some Graver Subject: An Essay on "Paradise Lost"* [London, 1960], p.
258) , and Waldock argues that Eve's "reasoning is quite sound" (*"Paradise
Lost" and Its Critics*, p. 37) , and that therefore she does not deserve to be
blamed for "triviality of mind" (ibid., p. 40) . Broadbent's claim is refuted by
Waldock's excellent analysis of the conflicting conclusions about God posited
by Satan's arguments (ibid., p. 37*n*) : Satan's speech is blatantly sophistical,
and the suspicion that Satan's illogicality engenders in Gabriel (4. 947–49)
indicates what effect the sophistry should have upon Eve. Waldock's claim
suffers from his failure to see that Gabriel's logical examinations of Satan's
arguments (4. 917–23, 947–49) set standards for Eve: instead of logically
building upon the serpent's propositions, Eve should be performing the
more demanding task of analyzing his arguments.

The second defense offered is that Eve's errors are excusable ones. Broad-
bent argues that Eve has "no reason to suspect the serpent," who is not a
"blatant" tempter (*Graver Subject*, p. 289), and Waldock says that Eve is, "na-
turally, bewildered" by the serpent's arguments, and that her "only defence"
would have been "a closed mind" (*"Paradise Lost" and Its Critics*, p. 36) .
Broadbent's argument ignores the warnings of danger which Eve has been
given, and it overlooks the example of Ithuriel and Zephon, whose discovery of
Satan when he is disguised as a toad (4. 797–800) indicates that Eve should
have been able to detect Satan imbruted in the serpent. (All the points
about the bearing of the angels' behavior on the evaluation of Eve are dis-
cussed at greater length in chapter 5.) Waldock's argument ignores the
standards of judgment suggested in the work. Adam corrects the sinless
improprieties in Eve's question about the stars (4. 660–88) , but Waldock is
tolerant of Eve's "bewilder[ment]" even when it contributes to her fall; Eve's
reaction to her Satan-inspired dream shows that Eve is capable of rejecting
evil ideas (this interpretation is defended in note 3 to this chapter) , but
Waldock is tolerant when, failing to close her mind, she accepts the argu-
ments that doom her.

The moral defenses offered by William Empson are no more valid than
these intellectual ones. Empson badly misreads Eve's soliloquy before the fall,

and as a result he substitutes for the moral issues of the poem issues of his own devising. Empson claims, first of all, that Eve falls primarily because she believes that God is testing her courage rather than her obedience (*Milton's God* [London, 1961], pp. 159, 163). For proof he argues the sublimity of the motive, citing "the principle of Mr. Rajan that the characteristic virtue of [*Paradise Lost*] is sublimity"; he admits that the argument "is not prominent" in Eve's speech before the fall, maintaining that "if it had been, Milton would have had to call [Eve] justified" (ibid., p. 159). One objection which can be raised to this argument is its strange premises about critical procedure. When Empson argues that Eve's real motive is a motive which Milton could not assign her, he attributes to Eve an existence apart from her existence in the poem; and when he supports his interpretation with an observation by a critic while admitting that the interpretation is not upheld by the text, he accepts a critical generalization in preference to the material upon which it is based. In presenting his theory of motivation, Empson defies the evidence in the text; his theory, therefore, can hardly be said to interpret the poem.

Furthermore, even if Eve's motive were what Empson claims, her conduct would not be guiltless by the standards in the work. If Eve were to set aside God's command on the grounds that it really meant the opposite of what it said, she would be acting as Adam does when he sets aside the command on the grounds that God does not really mean to enforce it (9. 938–51); according to the standards of the work, she would be speculating upon the intentions of God in order to disobey him. Granted these standards, the moral condition which Adam's action illustrates, and which Eve's action would illustrate were her motive what Empson says, is a moral condition which Empson himself condemns in other contexts; it is the condition of the Christians whom Empson blames for finding ways of reconciling torture with the command to love one's neighbor (p. 252).

Secondly, Empson defends Eve's decision not to obey God's prohibition. He argues that Eve is impatient with God for setting her "such a difficult puzzle about his intentions," but that her impatience is not guilty because she does not conclude that God is bad, only irritatingly hard to understand; Empson says that Eve decides what to do by appealing to the principle that one ought not act contrary to his conscience, whatever the threatened punishment (pp. 159–60). Empson's contention that Eve does not pronounce God wicked is untrue. Her argument proceeds with increasing suspiciousness until she decides that God is the forbidder of good, that he is, in other words, evil, whereupon she indignantly rejects him. The central fault in Empson's argument, however, is that it ignores the poem's premise that God is good, a premise asserted in Eve's own pronouncement on his generosity (5. 329–30). Given the premise, Eve is pursuing what she desires by rationalizing that the values which stand in the way and which she has accepted before are really bad values. The moral process that is illustrated is one, again, which Empson himself condemns; he censures pious "high officials" who, acting, he suspects, from obscure sadistic motives, claim that it is good to prevent the use of mechanical contraceptive devices, and who disregard the alternative and more compelling good of preventing famine and war (pp. 265–66).

Finally, Empson defends Eve's assertion of ignorance of good and evil. He argues that when Eve refers to her "ignorance . . . of law or penalty" (9. 774–75), she is maturely recognizing her ignorance of the "moral sanction behind [the] law" and of "the meaning of the repeated obscure threats of a penalty" (p. 162). Empson reads the line as if it presents a list: "What do I know about God, law, death, or penalties?" But the line is structured as a pair of alternatives: "God or death—law or penalty." Read this way it proves not to be an inquiry into sanctions and meaning, but a skeptical doubt of recognized laws and known penalties: Eve is claiming not to know whether eating the apple would prove lawful (contrary to what God says) or whether it would prove punishable (as God claims). What is illustrated is the convenient skepticism that excuses violations of duty; and though Empson's subject leads him to discuss examples of obedience to perverted principles rather than examples of immoral skepticism, he does mention the case of Stalin's persecutions, which, he says, were shocking to George Orwell particularly in that they were not, like the persecutions of Christianity, the results of "a system of torture-worship" (p. 235). Stalin's cynical disregard of morality is close enough to Eve's skepticism to show that even a nonbeliever can accept as one of the postures of evildoers the moral attitude that Eve exemplifies here.

[8] This account, though it subordinates the question of causality (in ways and for reasons stated in note 6 to this chapter), affirms the theory that there is an admixture of sensuality in the love for Eve which leads to Adam's fall, and it presumes that Adam's guilt is adequately demonstrated in the poem.

There is much less debate over the cause of Adam's fall than over the cause of Eve's, but the question of whether Adam can justly be accused of sensuality has been debated. A. J. A. Waldock claims that Adam shows only an exemplary kind of love. He argues that Adam's statement of how Eve affects him (8. 521–59) is a "curious mixture," revealing Milton's differing attitudes to love (*"Paradise Lost" and Its Critics* [Cambridge, 1947], pp. 42–43), and that Raphael's condemnation of sensuality (8. 561–94) simplifies and distorts what Adam has said (pp. 43–44). Waldock argues, secondly, that Milton's statement that Adam falls "overcome with female charm" (9. 997–99) is an attempt to compensate for and to neutralize his own portrayal of the event (pp. 49–50), a portrayal which shows Adam's motive to be "love as human beings know it best . . . true love . . . the kind of love that Raphael has told Adam 'is the scale / By which to heav'nly Love thou maist ascend'" (p. 52).

The central fault with this interpretation is that it takes at face value seven lines in one of Adam's speeches, and substitutes the issue stated in these lines for the issue raised by the episode as a whole. The lines are these:

> [W]ith thee
> *Certain my resolution is to die;*

How can I live without thee, how forgo
Thy sweet converse and love so dearly joined,
To live again in these wild woods forlorn?
Should God create another Eve, and I
Another rib afford, yet loss of thee
Would never from my heart.

(9. 906–13)

On the basis of these lines E. M. W. Tillyard speaks of Adam's refusal "to forsake Eve in her extremity" (*Milton* [London, 1930], p. 262), and Waldock commends Adam for "not want[ing] the company of anyone, even the company of another Eve" but for wanting *"this* Eve" (*"Paradise Lost" and Its Critics,* p. 47). The trouble with this formulation is that Eve's "extremity" is not only that she is "to death devote," but that she is "Defaced" and "deflowered" (9. 901), and that therefore Adam no longer possesses the wife whose "sweet converse and love" he remembers. Adam faces an Eve who is as changed as one gone suddenly mad, and this change is not merely announced (Waldock refuses to credit authorial commentary) but is rendered in Eve's blasphemies (9. 861–77), in Eve's new insincerity (9. 853–55), and in the horror with which Adam listens to her words:

Adam, soon as he heard
The fatal trespass done by Eve, amazed,
Astonied stood and blank, while horror chill
Ran through his veins, and all his joints relaxed;
From his slack hand the garland wreathed for Eve
Down dropped, and all the faded roses shed.
Speechless he stood and pale.

(9. 888–94)

Adam is portrayed, then, not as simply joining through loyalty an endangered wife, but as betraying his own values to take on those of a person whose spiritual corruption he can see, and as ignoring the changes in a person whose past qualities he values. Milton's explanation for this conduct is Adam's attraction to Eve's unaltered beauty, and this explanation he offers in his comments upon Adam's fall and presents through Raphael's rebuke.

Misinterpreting the situation, Waldock misappraises all the material connected with Adam's fall. Because he oversimplifies the scene he dismisses Milton's commentary on the fall, and he is likewise mistaken in dismissing the foreshadowing episode. Waldock holds up as evidence of Milton's ambivalence a speech which reveals contrary elements in the speaker, Adam. Adam explains the strength of sexual attraction (8. 528–33), and in connection with this subject he blames nature as the cause of his weakness (8. 534–37); then he moves to a second, though related, subject, the feelings that Eve's beauty arouses in him, and he treats this subject by contrasting what he knows (8. 540–46) with what he feels (8. 546–59). The differences of attitude in this speech simply reveal the difference between rational analysis and self-excuse, doctrinal knowledge and feeling. Waldock then condemns as "untruthful" and "unpleasant" (p. 43) a speech by Raphael which only replies to points previously raised and emphasizes doctrines already admitted. Raphael rebukes Adam's self-excuse by invoking Adam's own rational assessment (8. 561–66), replies to Adam's description of the effects of beauty by reinforcing Adam's judgment in opposition to his feelings (8. 567–78), and treats the subject of sexual passion by contrasting the lesser value of passion (8. 579–85) with the higher value of rational love (8. 586–94). If this reply is concerned with sensuality, the reason is not Raphael's distortion of Adam's speech, but Waldock's own sentimentalization of it. Adam is not, as Waldock says, "giving the plainest possible exposition" of the nature of 'true love'" (p. 44): he is explaining, in the last part of his speech, how Eve's "loveliness" affects him (8. 546–47).

Finally, Waldock's assessment of Adam's relation to Eve during the fall is inaccurate. Citing as evidence of love for Eve Adam's decision to "share her fate," Waldock speaks romantically of the "supreme of moments when life and death hang in the balance" (p. 47), thereby calling up associations which have nothing to do with the case. Adam is not Alcestis, giving up a life to save a life, for Adam's action cannot help Eve; and he is not Romeo, ending a life made empty by the (supposed) death of his beloved, for Eve is in a position to be helped. Adam does not think of Eve's welfare when he decides to "share her fate," and that failure diminishes the nobility of his act. When Waldock equates Adam's love with the love that Raphael describes, furthermore, he is inverting the case. If Adam's love were the recommended love of soul (8. 586–87) which leads to the love of God (8. 589–92), Adam would be concerned with restoring Eve, and would trust God to help him; instead, in speaking of his unwillingness to lose Eve's "sweet converse," Adam blinds himself to the fact that Eve has been "defaced," and in "Submitting to what seemed remediless" (9. 919), he neglects to think of God's aid. His actions are the sensual ones against which Raphael warns.

Adam has been justified by two kinds of argument, literary and moral, neither of which is valid. There are two major literary arguments, both of them replies to C. S. Lewis's claim that "If the reader finds it hard to look upon Adam's action as a sin at all, that is because he is not really granting Milton's premises" (*A Preface to "Paradise Lost"* [London, 1942], p. 123). The first reply is that there are limits to what can be granted in the way of premises. Waldock argues the general case by means of a hypothetical example, the example of a story which proves that "Might is Right" and whose plot concerns men in a lifeboat who "fight amongst themselves," after which "the strongest, who are the ones left, grab the food and push the women and children overboard" (*"Paradise Lost" and Its Critics*, pp. 53–54). Waldock argues that a reader, told to grant the premises, would feel that "something" had been "overlooked," namely "an unbearable collision of values," in that the reader could not grant such premises "without anaesthetizing, temporarily, nine-tenths of [his] emotional nature" (p. 54). The trouble with this argument is that it confuses the attributes of the literary work with those of the reader, and the interpretation of the work with a moral evaluation of it.

A critic who separates those factors would analyze a story by interpreting its events according to its own value system. He would, for example, explain how altruism is attacked in the person of the ship's tailor (to expand Waldock's example), who voices lofty sentiments in order to persuade the muscular sailors to spare his life, but who thereafter suggests that the women and children be thrown overboard to conserve supplies. He would also explain how the lyrical description of the play of the sailors' muscles when they throw the children overboard contributes to the defense of might. In addition to analyzing, however, the critic might evaluate the story according to his own value system, pointing out the wickedness of its ideas and the technical flaws that result from their dramatization. He might, for example, complain that the portrait of the ship's tailor constitutes an unwarranted generalization, and that the description of the sailors' muscles dodges moral considerations by substituting aesthetic ones.

Critics like Waldock and Empson, who do not grant a work its premises, proceed quite differently. When Empson justifies Satan and Eve, he inverts a story to make it agree with his own morality. He is the critic who cites the scene in which the sailors throw the children overboard as proof that might is not right, and who disregards the fact that the description of the sailors' muscles serves to praise rather than to blame them. When Waldock argues that the portrayal of Adam's fall demands contradictory responses of sympathy and disapproval (pp. 55–56), he attributes to a work the contradiction which exists in his own responses to it. He is the critic who, impressed by the altruistic speeches in the story, argues that these demand approval and that they contradict the author's denigration of the tailor.

Waldock's attitude to premises, then, can only produce interpretations that misrepresent their subjects. More accurate criticism would result from separating literary analysis from evaluation, and granting premises for the former, though not necessarily for the latter.

Waldock also argues that in the specific case of *Paradise Lost* the reader cannot grant the premise that an Adam who, acting in the way proposed by C. S. Lewis, "chastised Eve and then interceded with God on her behalf" (Lewis, p. 123) would be more admirable than "the Adam who impulsively, uselessly, nobly stood by Eve and accepted, without further ado, her fate" (Waldock, p. 56); he cites as proof the description by Harriet Byron in *Sir Charles Grandison* of such an Adam (ibid., p. 53). One trouble with this argument is Waldock's assumption that if the reader dislikes the judgment made of Adam, then the work itself is confused: "the central situation of *Paradise Lost*" is one which "tugs against itself" (ibid., p. 54). But more particular objections can be made to Waldock's case. One is the dubiousness of his value judgments. It is not at all certain that a man who indulges in impulsive and useless heroics is nobler than one who keeps his head in emergencies and thinks of how best to protect his wife and children. Another objection is the unfairness of Waldock's proof. Milton's Adam cannot be justly compared to Harriet Byron's unsympathetic portrait; he must be compared to a sympathetic portrait of an unfalling Adam by Milton himself (if that can be imagined).

The second, and stronger, literary defense of Adam argues that, whatever

C. S. Lewis says about Milton's premises, these premises are nowhere repre-
sented in the scene of Adam's fall. Waldock asserts that no one "responding
naturally" feels that Adam is faced with a conflict of values (p. 55), and
William Empson elaborates that claim, stating that neither of the two
speeches that Adam makes in falling contains "any recognition that obedience
to God is a higher 'value'" than love for Eve (*Milton's God* [London, 1961],
p. 185). There is only one place in which Adam could be expected to recog-
nize the value of the love of God, however, and in that place that recognition
does occur. When Adam decides to follow Eve, he blinds himself to her
change (9. 908–16), and afterwards, because of his decision, he follows her
into metaphysical absurdity (9. 921–51). In these displays of willful blindness
no recognition of true value could be expected. In Adam's initial correct as-
sessment of Eve's state, however, (9. 900–905), recognition could be expected,
and Adam shows it when he says that Eve is "Defaced" and "deflowered."
These words acknowledge the prior value of the love of God, for they imply
that a person who loses this love loses all spiritual worth, and assert that the
Eve whom Adam loved has been ruined.

Furthermore, though in the greater portion of Adam's speeches there is no
recognition of any higher value than the love of Eve, the existence of such a
value is nevertheless asserted. First of all, it is asserted by the contrasting
episodes that suggest what Adam should have done—the scene in which Adam
guides Eve after her dream (5. 100–128), the episode in which Raphael warns
Adam (8. 70–178, 561–94, 633–43), and the account of how Abdiel reacted to
Satan's fall (this last is discussed in detail in chapter 5). Furthermore, as
Tillyard observes, Eve's response to Adam's decision (9. 961–89) serves to
judge it (*Studies in Milton* [London, 1951], pp. 29–30): her blasphemous
approval indicates the folly of the action. When, therefore, Adam argues as
though the love of Eve were the highest value that exists, his argument is not
treated as though it were true.

The literary defenses of Adam do not hold, thus; and the moral defenses
are no more valid. The first such defense is the argument that Adam is
presented as choosing the lesser of two evils. Tillyard uses as an analogy the
man "who hates war yet consents to fight"; the "self-righteousness" of pursu-
ing "narrowly personal" moral ends is more guilty, he says, than the accept-
ance of "an incrimination it is as yet impossible for any human being to be
free of." He notes that this analogy is easily disprovable from the doctrines of
Paradise Lost, but argues that it is "a true analogy as dictated by the poetical
effect" (ibid., p. 29). Even if doctrinal pronouncements are excluded, how-
ever, Tillyard's analogy is not valid, its central fault being the restriction of
"poetical effect" to the effect of certain of Adam's lines when these are sa-
vored as a love lyric in isolation from the situation and the characters in-
volved. Specifically, the choice of the love of God would not be here a "nar-
rowly personal" choice: it is "narrowly personal" of Adam to join Eve, since
the act does not benefit Eve and ruins Adam's descendants; it would not be
"narrowly personal" for Adam to consider how his wife could be saved and the
penalty to his children averted. It is true, of course, that ultimately Adam

would be expected to abandon Eve for God, if that choice were the only one possible, but Adam is not yet pushed to this extremity. Furthermore, the "incrimination" of participating in a war is not an adequate image for Adam's guilt. Tillyard's wording suggests that he is thinking of an Englishman fighting the Nazis; in this case most people would not find fighting a crime, reasoning by analogy to killing in self-defense. When the case is shifted to a German's decision to aid his countrymen in their attempt to conquer the world and to enslave or annihilate its people, however, not many people would be willing to dismiss the refusal to fight as an act of "self-righteousness." What Adam is choosing in choosing to join Eve is made very evident in the characteristics displayed by Eve in her seduction speech, and Adam is initially aware of these characteristics; even if he were forced to abandon her, it is not clear that he would be merely self-righteous in refusing to embrace her complete moral inanity. It should be noted, incidentally, that these objections to Tillyard's analogy are not drawn from the doctrines of the poem but from the action seen in relation to other episodes which suggest Adam's alternatives, and from the character of the participants in the scene—from the "poetical effect" when the poetry is seen as epic rather than lyric in nature.

The second, and more persuasive, moral argument is that Adam's action is not a moral crime. Citing the passage in which Adam guesses that God will not give Satan satisfaction by destroying man (9. 938–51), Empson comments that the passage is convincing, especially because God said that he was creating man in order to keep Satan from boasting that he had "dispeopled Heaven" (7. 150–61), and Empson concludes from the passage that Adam's decision involves no moral considerations: "There is no question of harming God by eating the apple, only a question of how best to handle his vanity and bad temper" (*Milton's God*, p. 185). The argument is persuasive in that it brings up a genuine abstract philosophical question, that of the consequences of the independence that classical theism attributes to God, and in that it cites a genuinely faulty speech, one which would justify Satan's claim that God made man to spite the angels (9. 143–51, 176, 178). But as explication of the poem the argument is invalid. Whatever the abstract merit of the poem's philosophy, the obedience and love of God are considered moral imperatives within that philosophy, and Adam and Eve in their state of innocence are portrayed as acknowledging those imperatives. However bad God's speech may be, it cannot be used to justify Adam's speculations when those speculations are the most tenuous in a series of rationalizations; when they contradict Adam's own initial judgment that disobedience is not an inexpedient act but an immoral one, a "transgress[ion]" (9. 902–3); and when they are foreshadowed by such incidents as Raphael's warning against speculation (8. 70–78). The passage does not prove that Adam is sinless but shows, rather, how unreasonable his action is—so unreasonable that he must rely for justification on guesses of a kind which he has previously repudiated and against which he has been warned.

⁹ Both Adam's confession and God's reply have been questioned by de-

fenders of Adam. Their claim that the two speeches are factually inaccurate is justifiable, though not unanswerable; their moral objections, however, are invalid.

The moral objection to Adam's confession is offered by A. J. A. Waldock, who claims that Adam's defense is "mean-spirited" and at variance with his nobility at the time of the fall (*"Paradise Lost" and Its Critics* [Cambridge, 1947], p. 50). This objection is partly the result of Waldock's overestimation of Adam's nobility. Feeling that Adam's intention of "st[an]d[ing] by Eve and accept[ing] . . . her fate" (ibid., p. 56) is "extremely honourable" (p. 50), Waldock believes that Milton is depriving Adam of his best defense (ibid.). Waldock, however, wrongly denies that sensuality is involved in Adam's fall, and he fails to see that in deciding to join Eve, Adam is failing to consider her spiritual welfare (Waldock's treatment of Adam's fall is discussed in the preceding note); when these aspects of the fall are taken into account, the gap between the act and Adam's later extenuation of it is greatly diminished. Partly, however, the disparagement of Adam's defense is the result of Waldock's failure to see its point. Waldock believes that when Adam says that he could "suspect no ill" from Eve, he is both discrediting her and denigrating his own conduct (ibid.); thus he finds the speech a "miserable, hang-dog performance" (ibid.). He misses what William Empson sees, that Adam is defending both himself and Eve by laying blame on God "for making human nature what it is" (*Milton's God* [London, 1961], p. 186).

The moral objection to God's reply is made by Empson, who argues that in his speech God fails to "consider the real question, which is whether Adam was wrong to disobey him so as to share [Eve's] punishment" (ibid., p. 187). This objection is dependent upon Empson's analysis of what the "real question" is. Empson argues that there is no moral evil in disobeying God because God cannot be hurt by man's eating of the apple (p. 185), while on the other hand, Adam does have a moral duty to (in the words of Genesis) "cleave unto his wife" (p. 187). Concluding that Adam has rightly chosen a moral over an expedient act, Empson feels that God owes Adam if not a pardon at least a complex moral explanation. The trouble with this argument is that it not only sentimentalizes Adam's actions (the interpretation is similar to Waldock's, discussed at length in the preceding note), but it ignores the fact that in the poem, love for God is considered a higher moral duty than love of man—Raphael, for example, tells Adam to "love, but first of all / Him whom to love is to obey" (8. 633–34) (this point is also discussed in the preceding note). According to the standards of the poem, the "real question" about Adam's fall is whether Adam should have let his passional attachment to Eve prevail over his love for God and his concern for Eve's spiritual state. This question God does not ignore.

The factual objections to Adam's confession and God's reply are better grounded. With regard to the confession, Empson comments that in "so far as [Adam] implies that [Eve] persuaded him at the time," he is "lying" (p. 186); and it is true that if the lines "from her hand I could suspect no ill" and "Her doing seemed to justify the deed" (10. 140, 142) are taken as de-

scriptions of Adam's reactions at the time of the fall, they are contradicted by
Adam's initial awareness of the seriousness of Eve's sin (9. 896–905) and by
Milton's statement that Adam fell "not deceived" (9. 998). It is possible,
however, to take Adam's statements as general examples rather than as spe-
cific descriptions of the fall. Adam does not say, "Because I suspected no ill
and felt that Eve was justified, I ate the apple which she gave me." Instead he
merely identifies the agent who gave him the fruit with an appositive de-
scription of Eve's power: "This woman whom thou mads't . . . She gave me
of the tree" (10. 137, 143). It is possible, therefore, to argue that Adam is
first of all blaming passion for his fall by describing Eve's power over his feel-
ings, and that he is secondly shifting all blame to God by framing his descrip-
tion in terms which recall God's words at the time of Eve's creation (8. 450–
51). This interpretation saves Adam's words from the charge of untruth, for
it makes his statements about lulled suspicions and suspended judgment
general instances, equivalent to the examples of his feelings which he earlier
gave to Raphael:

> [W]hen I approach
> Her loveliness, so absolute [Eve] seems
> And in herself complete, so well to know
> Her own, that what she wills to do or say
> Seems wisest, virtuousest, discreetest, best.
> (8. 546–50)

With regard to God's reply, both Waldock ("Paradise Lost" and Its Critics,
p. 50) and Empson (Milton's God, p. 186) complain that God endorses
Adam's inaccurate description of the fall. Citing God's opening words, "Was
she thy God, that her thou didst obey / Before his voice, or was she made thy
guide" (10. 145–46), Waldock argues that God is accepting Adam's errone-
ous report and is wrongfully accusing Adam of having obeyed Eve and of
having been guided by her (p. 50). In the first place, however, it should be
noted that even if God's words are taken at face value, the gap between them
and the truth is so small that it can be accounted for as a matter of emphatic
expression. Adam did "heark[en] to the voice" of Eve (10. 198), for her
picture of the separation which might result from her elevation (9. 881–85)
inspired Adam's picture of the separation which would result from her death
(9. 908–10). Furthermore, though Adam did not obey Eve, he did value her
before the God "whom to love is to obey," and though he did not accept Eve's
guidance, he did neglect to guide Eve toward a proper love for God, yielding
instead to empathy for her fright.

It is possible, however, to argue that God's opening words ought not be
taken at face value. The second half of God's speech is a direct comment on
Adam's faults, and must therefore refer to Adam's conduct at the time of the
fall. In this section of the speech, however, God does not accuse Adam of
obeying Eve or of accepting her guidance; instead he refers to those same con-
sequences of passion against which Raphael previously warned. When he says
that Eve was "lovely to attract / [Adam's] love, not [his] subjection," he ac-
cuses Adam of overvaluing Eve through sexual attraction; Raphael similarly

warned Adam that Eve's beauty deserved "love" but not "subjection" (8. 567–70). When he says that Eve's

gifts
Were such as under government well seemed,
Unseemly to bear rule, which was [Adam's] part
And person, [had he] known [him]self aright,
(10. 153–56)

he accuses Adam of neglecting his superior's responsibilities; Raphael similarly urged Adam to show a proper "self-esteem" and to exert a superior's influence over Eve (8. 570–78). In this section of the speech, God's charges do not exceed the facts (the view of the fall which justifies them is defended in the preceding note).

In the first half of his speech God does talk of Adam's obedience to Eve; here, however, he may not be referring to Adam's conduct. God at this point may be doing what Raphael did when he warned Adam not to "Accuse . . . Nature" for his weakness in the face of beauty (8. 561–66): he may be refuting Adam's excuses, and thus may be referring not to Adam's deeds but to his logic. In this reading, the rhetorical questions with which God opens his speech constitute a reply to Adam's contention that passion excuses his fall. When God asks, "Was she thy God, that her thou didst obey / Before his voice," he means not that Adam has obeyed Eve, but that his eating would be justified only if he could appeal to Eve's command, and could prove that Eve was more important in the universe than God. When he asks, "[W]as she made thy guide, / Superior, or but equal," he means not that Adam has accepted Eve's guidance, but that his eating would be justified only if he could appeal to her guidance and could prove that she was his "guide / And head." The two questions constitute a reduction to absurdity of Adam's excuse. The remainder of God's opening words form, in this reading, a refutation of Adam's claim that the attributes which God assigned to Eve are responsible for Adam's fall. When God says that Eve was "made of" Adam (10. 149), he is, according to this view, reminding Adam that Eve does not have the Creator's attributes which would justify a primary allegiance to her, and when he says that Eve was "made . . . for" Adam (10. 149–50), he is reminding Adam that Eve does not have the superior's attributes which would justify subservience. Having claimed that Adam's action would be lawful only if Eve were God or Adam, God is pointing out that he did not give Eve the attributes of God or Adam. Read in this way, the lines counter Adam's appeal to what God said at the time of Eve's creation. The first section of the speech can be seen, then, as a refutation which, because it does not refer directly to Adam's conduct, does not misdescribe that conduct even to the extent of rhetorically exaggerating it.

Even if this reading is not granted, however, the critics' complaint that God's speech relies on the dubious statements in Adam's confession is not warranted. When God discusses the consequences of passion, he does not refer to Adam's statements about his lack of suspicion and his suspension of judgment; and when God says that Adam has obeyed Eve and accepted her

guidance, he is at worst only blaming Adam for having neglected his alle-
giance to God and for having neglected his superior's responsibilities toward
Eve, a reproach which does not rely upon any dubious statements by Adam,
but which simply invokes those principles applicable to the case of a hierar-
chical superior whose inferior has defected from God. Thus, even if God's
condemnation inaccurately describes Adam's actions, the inaccuracy is an
isolated fault, not an element in a consistently faulty episode.

[10] The commonly expressed view that Adam's lament is the first stage in his
regeneration is not valid.

In the first place, the relation of the lament to other speeches proves that
Adam's self-blame is a sign of sinful despair, rather than, as is often claimed,
a sign of repentance. The nature of the self-blame is indicated first of all by
the fact that Adam's lament is followed by his denunciation of Eve
(10. 867–908). If Adam were properly accepting blame in the lament, then
the violent denials of guilt which he subsequently makes to Eve would be
psychologically inexplicable. The scene would be incoherent, and so it ap-
pears in Douglas Bush's account: "Adam tries to make God the cause of his
sin and fate, but cannot escape the fact of his own responsibility, though he
still accuses Eve" (*"Paradise Lost" in Our Time: Some Comments* [New
York, 1945], p. 85). If, however, Adam's self-blame is taken as evidence of
despair, then his later self-excusing denunciations of Eve make sense psycho-
logically. Adam is miserable, and because he cannot end his misery in the
legitimate way, by submitting himself to God's authority and trusting in his
love, he vents his misery in an illegitimate way, by placing all the blame
upon his wife. Adam's later behavior thus shows that his earlier self-blame is
not a virtuous acceptance of responsibility.

The relation of Adam's lament to Eve's suggestions for the remedy of their
plight (10. 967–1006) also proves the sinfulness of the self-blame. John S.
Diekhoff (in *Milton's "Paradise Lost": A Commentary on the Argument*
[New York, 1946], p. 120) argues that Adam's wish for all of God's wrath
to fall on him is parallel to Eve's idea of petitioning God to place all the
guilt on her (10. 930–36). Diekhoff misses what William Empson sees about
Eve's plea for reconcilement with Adam, the speech in which Eve's proposal
appears—that in this plea, Eve expresses no guilt at disobeying God, but
only guilt for having disregarded Adam's counsel. Eve's "first repentance,"
says Empson, "is towards Adam only, and she regards God as someone she
might badger till he let Adam off" (*Milton's God* [London, 1961], p. 168).
Adam's self-blame is parallel not to Eve's expression of contrition toward
him, but to what Eve says when she offers suggestions for the future, sugges-
tions which do reveal her attitude toward God. Adam's wish to prevent by
his death the propagation of a depraved race anticipates Eve's proposal
that she and Adam remain childless in order to prevent the sufferings that
must befall their children (10. 979–91). Eve's suggestion is clearly not a sign
of redemption, and this fact prevents any pious construction of Adam's
analogous wish.

Finally, the relation of Adam's lament to his speech of repentance

(10. 1013–96) proves that his self-blame is not a step toward redemption. Maurice Kelley argues that Adam demonstrates in his lament the "conviction of sin" which is the first of the five stages of repentance listed in *De Doctrina Christiana* (*This Great Argument: A Study of Milton's "De Doctrina Christiana" as a Gloss upon "Paradise Lost"* [Princeton, N. J., 1941], p. 168). If this interpretation were true, however, the passage of self-blame would have to anticipate those later passages in which Adam's complete repentance is shown. In fact, though, Adam's lament contrasts with his speech of repentance; in repenting, Adam thinks not of dying but of trusting in God's love to ease his life (10. 1056–85). The sort of self-blame that Adam exhibits in his lament, therefore, must be not the pious "conviction of sin" mentioned in *De Doctrina,* but rather a sinful failure to trust in God.

The structure of the lament itself, furthermore, proves that the point of the speech is Adam's despair, and disproves J. B. Broadbent's charge that the speech presents a forced and mechanical resolution to Adam's problems. Broadbent claims, first of all, that the lament lacks drama, being both repetitious and unclimactic. He describes the speech as "misery's sluggish whirlpool—Why was I born? Why don't I die?—stirred for 125 lines," and he complains that "The resolution," Adam's admission that he is "Forced" to "absolve" God, "does not come by insight but submission" (*Some Graver Subject: An Essay on "Paradise Lost"* [London, 1960], p. 265). It is true that Adam's lament returns again and again to the same point; every section of it ends with Adam's despair—the introduction with Adam's cry that "lasting woes" have followed the "fleeting joys / Of Paradise," the first section of the body with Adam's declaration of how "glad" he would be to die, the second section with his fear that he and Death are "found eternal, and incorporate both," and the third section with his assertion that he is "miserable / Beyond all past example and future"; the speech concludes with Adam's statement that he has been "driven" into an "abyss of fears / And horrors . . . out of which / [He] find[s] no way" (10. 842–44). The very fact of this continual return to despair, however, denies the premises under which Broadbent attacks the speech. The complaint about repetition relies on the assumption that Adam's lament is supposed to contain a dynamic struggle of guilt and grace in which grace finally triumphs. The fact that every subject which Adam touches upon leads him to despair shows that, on the contrary, the speech is supposed to represent a guilty creature's ineffectual attempt to combat his despondency. The complaint about the "resolution" of the speech relies on the assumption that Adam's exoneration of God is supposed to be the climax of Adam's victorious struggle. The fact that the section of the speech and the speech as a whole end not with this exoneration but with Adam's declarations of hopeless misery shows that the exoneration is supposed to be only a temporary and inadequate effort at piety. Thus the speech is not an unsuccessful picture of Adam's triumph over evil but rather an effective portrayal of Adam's unending gloom.

Broadbent also complains that Adam's pious pronouncements are con-

trived indications of his salvation through grace. He argues that Adam's
references to God, which begin with his assertion that "God made [him] of
choice his own," "culminate in" Adam's wish that God's "wrath" might
"light" on him—a wish in which Broadbent finds "an echo of the Son's offer
of redemption" (p. 264). Broadbent complains, however, that these refer-
ences are "weakly abstract" and "external" and give the impression of being
merely a "rhetorical device, a technical manifestation of theological grace"
(ibid.). Broadbent's interpretation of Adam's wish is farfetched: the situation
of Adam, who desires a death he deserves, and who distrustfully plans to
end the race of man, is not like that of the Son, who takes upon himself
a death he does not deserve in order to save that race. If the verbal echo
which Broadbent notes is strong enough to connect the Son with Adam, the
connection can only prove that man's view of God is an ironic inversion of
God's loving concern for man. But even if the wish is included among
Adam's pious statements, the placement of those statements refutes the idea
that Adam's lament is intended to show his salvation. As soon as Adam
reconciles himself to God's punishment—"I submit, his doom is fair"—he
lapses into a wish to avert that punishment by dying; as soon as Adam con-
tents himself with what "human reach" can know, he falls into further specu-
lations; as soon as Adam voices his noble resolve to sacrifice himself (to grant
the reading; otherwise the piety resides in the preceding exoneration of God),
he rejects the wish and pronounces his case hopeless. All the pious pronounce-
ments are subsequently undercut; what they must prove, therefore, is not that
Adam has been saved, but that he is far from salvation; and if the pronounce-
ment seem "weakly abstract" and unconvincing (what Broadbent calls "ex-
ternal"), the reason is not that they are mechanically imposed solutions to
Adam's doubts, but that they represent the feeble insights of a despondent
creature. Again, what Broadbent interprets as defective evidences of Adam's
regeneration are in fact effective evidences of his despair.

[11] Noting that by her apology to Adam (10. 914–36) Eve changes the fate
of mankind all by herself, William Empson praises Milton for assigning
great dignity to man in general and to Eve in particular (*Milton's God*
[London, 1961], pp. 165–68). Two points which he makes, however, tend
to qualify this praise. Empson suggests that Eve's accomplishment is not
afforded sufficient credit, and he argues that God is indirectly responsible
for Eve's repentance. Both of these points can be questioned, and the praise
of Milton accordingly increased.

First of all, Empson assumes that Eve's apology is only supposed to be
seen as an inadequate act of penitence toward God. He argues that the fact
that Adam begins his reply to Eve with a rebuke (10. 947–57) and the fact
that later Adam himself works out the proper method for repenting (10.
1086–92) show that "God would not regard [Eve] as repentant until Adam
had redirected her impulses" (pp. 166–67). This argument is sound as far as
it goes, but because Empson misses the function of Eve's speech, he under-
estimates the amount of credit that is given her. As Empson himself says,
"Eve's first repentance is toward Adam only" (p. 168). What follows from

this fact is that Eve's speech proves not that she is inadequately penitent toward God (this fact is the point of a later speech [10. 967–1006]), but rather that she is adequately penitent toward Adam. The adequacy, furthermore, can be seen even in the rebuke that Adam gives her, for Adam's just correction of Eve contrasts with his previous unjust diatribe against her and women generally (10. 867–908), and it demonstrates, thus, the effectiveness of Eve's apology in restoring the proper relationship of husband and wife.

Empson also argues that God is responsible, if indirectly, for Eve's action. Empson acknowledges that Milton believed man did not lose all goodness at the time of the fall, but he argues that Milton nevertheless believed man could not do good without divine aid. Glossing the Son's image of "implanted grace" (10. 23) as a comparison of grace to a seed, Empson argues that God's grace, like his curse, is conceived of as acting "in a kind of biological way" (p. 168); presumably, then, Eve's change of heart is a product of this grace. The trouble with the argument is that Empson derives his definition from a highly metaphoric passage. When a more nearly literal passage is examined, a different conception of grace emerges. In the opening colloquy in heaven, the Father, describing grace, says that he will "call" men, "soften" their "stony hearts," and give them conscience (3. 185–97). The grace that he describes is a direct divine influence which supplements man's natural powers, and in the case of Adam and Eve this influence is manifested in Adam's decision to repent (10. 1028–96), a decision which is marked by a sudden influx of hitherto unremembered facts and by a sudden emergence of contrite feelings and of confidence in God. Eve's crucial apology, therefore, is the product of man's unaided power, as is Adam's acceptance of Eve (10. 958–65) and Adam's later correction of Eve's despair (10. 1013–28). Though Milton shows that God's intervention is needed for man's complete repentance, thus, he also shows how heroic are man's unaided moral efforts. (In this view of regeneration, incidentally, *Paradise Lost* is parallel to *Samson Agonistes,* which shows how Samson on his own overcomes his doubt of God and his self-doubt, after which he is given the grace which enables him to vindicate himself and God—though, of course, in the matter of what God says to man, the two works are very different.)

¹² Three issues are raised by this interpretation of the quarrel of Adam and Eve, the structural question of the place of the incident in the development of Adam and Eve, the psychological question of Eve's motive in wishing to garden separately from Adam, and the moral question of the guilt of the pair's actions.

In identifying the morning quarrel of the pair with the fall in their personal relationship, I rely upon points which have been noted by other critics. Millicent Bell, referring to the list of sins which Milton applies to the fall in *De Doctrina Christiana* (1. 10), points out that in the quarrel, Eve shows what Milton in the treatise calls "a want of proper regard for her husband," and that Adam shows what Milton calls "uxoriousness" ("The Fallacy of the Fall in *Paradise Lost*," *PMLA,* 68 [1953]: 868–69). E. M. W. Tillyard notes that after the prologue in which Milton announces that he is changing his "notes to tragic" (9. 1–47), he portrays Adam and Eve as more nearly like fallen people than they have been up to this point (*Studies in Milton* [London, 1951], p. 13). A. J. A. Waldock, finally, points out that there is a "crucial" connection between the fall and Adam's weakness in letting Eve go off alone, and he notes that Eve later (9. 1144–61) blames Adam for this lapse (*"Paradise Lost" and Its Critics* [Cambridge, 1947], p. 34).

The critics, however, interpret these points as proof of Milton's intentional or unintentional inconsistency. Waldock contends that Milton is unintentionally incriminating Adam when he connects Adam's weakness with the fall. He asserts that when Adam gives his "incensed" (9. 1162) reply to Eve's reproach (9. 1163–86), Milton is "thoroughly *with* Adam . . . bitterly, weepingly with him"; and he says that it is "amusing" to note that Eve is nonetheless "perfectly right" according to "Adam's tenets and . . . Milton's own" (*"Paradise Lost" and Its Critics*, pp. 34–35). Tillyard claims that in order to make a transition from innocence to guilt, Milton "fakes" by attributing fallen characteristics to the innocent Adam and Eve (*Studies in Milton*, pp. 10–11), and he cites the morning quarrel along with Eve's dream and Adam's confession of passion as instances of this "faking" (ibid., pp. 11–13). With regard to the quarrel, Tillyard argues that Milton's prologue is a "smoke-screen" under cover of which he advances Adam and Eve further "into the realms of experience" (p. 13). Mrs. Bell, finally, asserts that Milton never portrays Adam and Eve as innocent ("The Fallacy of the Fall," p. 864), and she contends that the uxoriousness displayed by Adam in the quarrel and the lack of respect for her husband displayed by Eve prove that the pair are fallen before they eat the forbidden fruit (ibid., p. 870).

Strong objections can be raised to these interpretations. Waldock's condescending theory is flatly contradicted by the text. Waldock fails to notice that Milton appends to Adam's "incensed" reply the comment that "neither" Eve or Adam is "self-condemning" and that their "mutual accusation[s]" achieve nothing (10. 1187–89). The comment proves that Milton does not support Adam's claim that his actions during the morning quarrel were blameless. Waldock also fails to notice that as soon as Adam repents, he admits that he has "exposed" Eve to danger and is therefore responsible for her fall (10. 952–57). The episode proves that Milton is aware that both his and Adam's "tenets" were violated by Adam's earlier conduct. The chief fault in Tillyard's analysis is his failure to analyze the difference between the morning quarrel and the episodes preceding it which reveal the limitations of Adam and Eve (that the dream is one of these episodes is disputed in note 3 to this chapter). Tillyard does not see that in the earlier episodes improper ideas and feelings were rejected while in the quarrel these ideas and feelings issue in improper actions, and he does not connect this difference with Adam's pronouncement that evil "leave[s] / No spot or blame behind" so long as it is "unapproved" (5. 117–19). When these facts are taken into account, it is evident that Milton in his prologue is announcing rather than concealing a change in the characters of Adam and Eve. Mrs. Bell, finally, fails to examine the nature of the sins displayed by the pair during their quarrel. Because she assumes that the presence of any of the sins listed in *De Doctrina* is proof that Adam and Eve have fallen, Mrs. Bell does not notice that "a want of proper regard for [one's] husband" and "uxoriousness" differ from such other of the listed sins as "distrust in the divine veracity": the former involve only the relationship of creatures to one another, while the latter involve the relationship of creatures to God. This distinction provides a basis for denying that Adam and Eve commit in their quarrel the same sort of sin which they commit in eating the forbidden fruit.

The points by which these critics seek to prove Milton's inconsistency I take as evidence of Milton's structural intentions. From the fact that Adam's weakness in letting Eve depart is the subject not only, as Waldock says, of later condemnation but also of later repentance, and from the fact that Eve's desire to garden separately is similarly condemned (9. 1134–42, 1175–77; 10. 873–79) and repented (10. 914–36, 11. 176–78), I deduce that the morning quarrel is not meant to be seen as innocent: innocent mistakes may be cursed and regretted, but they cannot be reproved and repented. From the fact that Milton prefaces the quarrel with a prologue announcing the fall, I deduce that the quarrel is meant to be part of Adam and Eve's apostasy. The interpretation is bolstered by the fact that the behavior of the pair during the scene does not simply, as Tillyard says, mark an advance over their earlier displays of potential sinfulness, but in fact contrasts with those displays in being actually sinful; and by the fact that their behavior contrasts with such earlier evidences of uprightness as Adam's instructions to Eve in dutifulness (4. 432–39) and Eve's assertion that no natural beauties would please her without the presence of Adam (4. 639–56). Finally, from the fact that Adam and Eve display in their quarrel not simply, as Mrs. Bell contends, fallen behavior, but fallen behavior in the particular realm of husbandly and wifely responsibilities, I deduce that the scene is intended to represent the fall specifically in the sphere of personal relationships. The interpretation is bolstered by the fact that elsewhere in the poem Milton treats personal and religious matters separately—Eve's speech after eating the apple, for example, falls into two halves, the first concerned with her relationship to God (9. 795–816), the second with her relationship to Adam (9. 816–33); and Adam makes one speech that reveals his impenitence with regard to God (10. 720–844), another speech that reveals his impenitence with regard to Eve (10. 867–908). The materials prove, then, that Milton intends the morning quarrel to represent the fall of man in the sphere of his duties to his fellow creatures.

On the matter of Eve's reasons for wishing to garden separately from Adam, I feel that the evidence does not warrant the complex and profound motivation that critics have attributed to Eve, and that some simpler and less subtle explanation for her conduct should be sought.

Eve's actions after her departure from Adam disprove the most sinister construction of her motives. John S. Diekhoff contends that Eve proposes to garden alone in order to "subject herself to temptation" (*Milton's "Paradise Lost": A Commentary on the Argument* [New York, 1946], p. 56), and Mrs. Bell says that in her persistence Eve sounds as though she "*expected* to meet someone rather interesting in the shade of the fruit trees" and as though she were planning to "deceive her husband" ("The Fallacy of the Fall," p. 870). If Eve wanted to be tempted, however, she would have gone to the tree of knowledge, the place where the temptation in her dream took place (5. 50–56). Instead she goes to the stand of roses (9. 424–27) which she had pointed out to Adam (9. 217–19), and while gardening there she is so far from expecting an interruption by someone "interesting" that she does not even look up when the serpent rattles the leaves near her (9. 518–19). Eve's behavior thus shows that she does not have temptation on her mind.

Though the most common explanation of Eve's motive, that she desires independence, cannot be finally disproved, it is nevertheless open to question. Mentioned by Waldock (*"Paradise Lost" and Its Critics*, pp. 30–31) and by William Empson (*Milton's God* [London, 1961], p. 150), the theory is presented in its most developed form by Arnold Stein, who argues that Eve's desire for independence harks back to her separation from Adam in her dream (5. 35–92), and is a development of the vanity revealed by her earlier fascination with her image in the lake (4. 449–91). This desire is revealed, Stein says, in Eve's argument about efficiency; "in valuing an external for its own sake," he states, Eve "is really valuing it for her sake: because she has nominated the value, because it represents her wish, because she has made it the means and end for her will, and so made it a mirror of self" (*Answerable Style: Essays on "Paradise Lost"* [Minneapolis, 1953], pp. 94–95). In part this argument relies on particular interpretations of Eve's dream and of the incident of her gazing in the pool, and these interpretations are in one case doubtful (the doubt is expressed in note 3 to this chapter), in the other case at least challengeable (the challenge is offered in note 5 to this chapter). Insofar as the argument involves the first speech of the morning quarrel, however, it can be questioned with regard to the deductions upon which it is based.

It is doubtful, in the first place, that Eve's argument on efficiency can be used to prove either her vanity or her desire for independence. First of all, the fact that the argument is, as Stein says, an "opportunistic pretext" (ibid., p. 95) proves that Eve is not making work a value. Eve has proposed that she tend her flowers and that Adam work somewhere else. Needing a supporting reason, she argues that joint labor produces bad results. The flimsiness of the argument shows that Eve is interested not in it but in the proposal which it supports. What she values is not work, thus, but the uninterrupted enjoyment of her flowers. Secondly, the fact that Eve depreciates the "Looks" and "smiles" which she shares with Adam proves that she does not desire separation from him as an end. If Eve had been thinking about the pleasure of being away from Adam, she would have been careful not to tell Adam so by derogating his company, for her whole speech is clearly designed to gloss over her reasons for desiring solitude. Only inattention can account for the clumsiness of Eve's excuse. Preoccupied with the flowers and needing a reason for not asking Adam to accompany her to them, Eve does not think of the moral implications of her depreciation of love, just as she does not consider the fallacies in her appeal to work. If, then, Eve is interested not in a self-established value, work, but in a real value, beauty, her argument does not prove her vanity; and if Eve desires Adam's absence not as an end but as a means, her argument does not prove her desire for independence.

In the second place, it is doubtful that, however the argument of efficiency is taken, it can be used to determine Eve's motivation. There are two reasons for believing that Eve's reference to her flowers reveals the motive behind her plan. First of all, the passage must indicate what Eve was thinking about before she spoke to Adam, because Eve is very positive about where she intends to spend her morning. Secondly, the passage must reveal Eve's own interests, because the reference to the "spring of roses" does not contribute to the persuasiveness of her argument. The opening of Eve's speech contrasts to this passage in the second of these respects. Because Eve's description of the untidiness of Eden paraphrases Adam's speech recommending sleep (4. 623–33), her words do have, as Tillyard says—referring, however, to the speech as a whole—the "air of having been thought out beforehand" (*Studies in Milton*, p. 17) ; the description, thus, does grow out of Eve's preliminary meditations. The fact that she refers to Adam's words, however, indicates that Eve devised this opening to win Adam's approval; it does not, therefore, like her reference to the flowers, reveal her interests. The end of Eve's speech also contrasts with her reference to the flowers, though in a different respect. A spur-of-the-moment invention, Eve's closing argument on efficiency does not stem from her previous thoughts, and therefore it provides no clue as to what moved her. Only the reference to the flowers, thus, reveals Eve's motive, and it suggests not that Eve had thoughts of independence, but that she wished to contemplate her flowers without the distraction of Adam's company.

A third theory of motivation, the elaborate theory offered by E. M. W. Tillyard, cannot be supported from the text. Quoting Eve's repentant statement that "the field . . . calls" her and Adam "To labor" (11. 171–77), Tillyard argues that since this statement is meant to be the opposite of Eve's original proposal, the fact that Eve is later "really anxious" to "do as much as possible" proves that the earlier proposal is "not sincere." According to Tillyard, Eve advances her plan in the hope that Adam will refuse her by declaring that he cannot bear her absence (p. 17). Adam, however, "disappoint[s]" her with his abstractions and his self-praise (pp. 17–18), and only when he finally asserts his masculine leadership is Eve satisfied, having had, according to Tillyard, the "satisfaction of rousing Adam and of obtaining a degree of attention she had never expected" (p. 19). At this point, however, Adam's "chivalr[ous]" offer to "meet her half way" forces Eve to go, though now she would "like," Tillyard says, "to yield" (p. 20) .

Analysis of Eve's repentant speech does not support this theory of her initial motive. First of all, the passage that Tillyard cites does not bear on Eve's proposal. The fact that Eve refers to the "sweat imposed" upon the "labor" to which she and Adam are called (11. 172) shows that she is thinking not about her plan but about God's speech of judgment, and therefore about her speech encouraging Adam to disregard God's threats (9. 961–89); she is repenting her lack of awe, thus, rather than any insincerity about work. Furthermore, when later in the speech Eve does (in passing) refer to her proposal, what she says does not support the theory. Saying, in a line not quoted by Tillyard, that she will not leave Adam's side "where'er [their] day's work lies, though now enjoined / Laborious, till day droop" (11. 177–78), Eve does repudiate the first speech of the morning quarrel. Promising to go "where'er" the "day's work lies," she apologizes for her insistence on visiting her flowers. Promising to stay by Adam even though the "work" is "now enjoined / Laborious," she retracts her argument on efficiency, stating that she will not advance it even though the present circumstances make it appropriate. Promising to stay "till day droop," she takes back the proposal that she and Adam separate for the morning. This recantation proves that Eve did not wish her plan to be refused, for if she had not intended to go off alone, she would not need to apologize, as she does, for planning an unaccompanied visit to her flowers, and if she had intended to elicit compliments, she would have to offer what she does not, an apology for trying to test Adam's love.

The descriptions of Eve, furthermore, do not support Tillyard's account of Eve's changes of feeling. First of all there is in the description of Eve's reaction to Adam's first speech no evidence that she is "disappoint[ed]" in the way that Tillyard suggests. Milton says that Eve replies to Adam with "sweet austere composure" (9. 272), "As one who loves, and some unkindness meets" (9. 271). "Unkindness" is an appropriate word only if Eve thinks that Adam is, on inadequate grounds, denying her what she wants; if Adam is neglecting to pay her a compliment while refusing what she knows to be a foolish request, then his manner might be thought boorish (Tillyard says that Adam behaves like a man who is "sleepy" or "not at [his] best" [*Studies in Milton*, p. 17]), but his refusal could not be termed "unkind." The "composure" of Eve, furthermore, is easier to explain on the theory that she has set her heart on a plan and is determined to carry it out than it is on the theory that she is piqued and is perversely insisting upon a plan in which she does not believe. Secondly, the description of Eve's reaction to Adam's last speech directly refutes Tillyard's claim that, won over by Adam's display of authority, Eve is forced into an unwilling departure. Milton appends to Adam's speech the comment, "So spake the patriarch of mankind but Eve / Persisted" (9. 376–77). The comment clearly indicates that Eve is ignoring Adam's warning, not responding to his assertiveness, and that Eve is bent on carrying out her proposal, not reluctantly assenting to a plan which she never wanted and would like to abandon.

The theory which I have proposed, that Eve wishes to garden separately from Adam because she wishes to give undivided attention to her flowers, is, I believe, warranted by the evidence. It can be deduced from the contents of Eve's first speech; it is consistent with Eve's subsequent absorption with her gardening; and it is supported by Eve's later apology for her proposal. The theory, furthermore, is consonant with Eve's character; that the simple and exemplary Eve who is presented in the opening scenes in the Garden would have a concrete wish, and one which would be sinless if it were not excessive, is more probable than that she would have so intangible a desire as the desire for independence, or so wicked a desire as the desire for temptation; the particular wish, furthermore, coincides with Eve's interests as these are revealed, for example, in the lament for her flowers which she makes when banished from Eden (11. 273–79). The motive, finally, is not so trivial as to be blameless, for Michael rebukes Eve for the neglect of Adam that is implicit in her attachment to Eden's flowers (11. 290–92); thus the wish can serve as the initial step in Eve's violation of her responsibilities in the personal realm.

As to the guiltiness of the conduct of Adam and Eve during their quarrel, I disagree with Empson's defenses of the pair. Empson claims, first of all, that Eve's desire for independence is laudable. He argues that Raphael's account of mankind's future elevation, with its mention of food (5. 493–500), reinforces the temptation presented in Eve's dream (5. 67–81) and induces Eve to seek "a tiny change in her experience"; "indeed," Empson comments, she "could hardly be admired if she had no impulse to react at all" (*Milton's God,* p. 150). However, even if it were granted (as it ought not be) that Eve does desire independence, and even if it were granted that Eve is influenced by Raphael's speech (and there is no clear evidence that such is the case), still the theory that Eve is acting properly would not be valid. In Eve's dream, eating the forbidden fruit is made the means of elevation; in Raphael's speech, the eating of angelic food is said to be a result of elevation, and both the condition of elevation and the inutility of seeking other means are clearly stated. Raphael tells Adam and Eve that they will be raised

> *If [they] be found obedient, and retain*
> *Unalterably firm his love entire*
> *Whose progeny [they] are,*
>
> (5. 501–3)

and he tells the pair to "enjoy" their present "happy state"—being, he cautions, "incapable of more" (5. 503–5). By seeking experience, Eve would be defying Raphael's advice and warning, and she would be perverting his account to make it agree with Satan's. She would not, as Empson claims, be innocently responding to a misleading message. Furthermore, Empson's impression of what constitutes admirable behavior is not supported by the text, since Eve in repenting pledges "never . . . to stray" from "[Adam's] side" (11. 176), repudiating an earlier defense of her conduct (9. 1153–54), and therefore the conduct itself.

Empson also claims that Adam is justified in letting Eve go. Referring to

Tillyard's argument that Adam acts from "mistaken chivalry," Empson says
that Tillyard "proves without quite meaning to" that Adam "behaves well"
(*Milton's God*, p. 151), and he states that "critics who blame Adam for
letting [Eve] go, after giving her every warning" are "preach[ing] an im-
moral moral" (ibid., pp. 150–51). He notes that Eve later criticizes Adam's
action (9. 1155–61), but argues that Milton is at this point condemning
Eve (p. 151). One trouble with this argument is that it relies upon an
overgenerous assessment of Adam's reasons for dismissing Eve. Tillyard's
claim that Adam yields out of chivalry depends upon the erroneous theory
that Eve is won over by Adam's display of authority. If—as is the case—Eve is
stubbornly bent upon having her own way, then Adam cannot be offering
a courteous compromise, but must be, as Mrs. Bell suggests ("The Fallacy
of the Fall," p. 869), capitulating. The weakness of this behavior makes im-
probable the claim that Adam is "behav[ing] well." A second fault with
Empson's argument is that it cannot be supported from the text. The fact
that when Adam repents he blames himself for letting Eve go shows that his
action is not to be approved, and though it is true that Milton condemns
Eve for censuring Adam, he condemns her for excusing herself, not for
wrongly assessing Adam's fault, and he places similar blame upon Adam
when Adam defends his conduct. As for Empson's claim that critics who
find Adam blameworthy are immoral, that charge can apply only to those
critics who explicitly use the inicident as a vehicle for the expression of
their own religious and ethical views; critics who simply wish to explain the
passage need not reply. (The issues raised by Empson's critical premises are
treated in note 8 to this chapter and in note 1 to chapter 1.)

[13] Replying to C. S. Lewis's observation that in her speech after the fall,
Eve decides to murder Adam (*A Preface to "Paradise Lost"* [London, 1942],
p. 121), A. J. A. Waldock argues that such a condemnation of Eve is ex-
cessive. He argues, first of all, that Eve's jealousy is no more serious than
the normal, everyday jealousy experienced by every man; secondly that Eve's
guilt is lessened by her ignorance as to what death is; and thirdly that any
evil in Eve's conduct is compensated for by her "impulses" of "love, heroism,
[and] self-sacrifice." As evidence of these impulses Waldock cites Eve's offer
to "renounce / Deity for [Adam]" (9. 881–85) and her claim that she
would rather "die / Deserted" than endanger him (9. 977–83) —this last,
Waldock says, a lie which is nevertheless an " 'objective correlative' for
[Eve's] feelings" (*"Paradise Lost" and Its Critics* [Cambridge, 1947], p. 63).
Arnold Stein also defends Eve, though in a more limited way. He claims
that by seeking to return to Adam, Eve is, in a "perverted" way, "affirm[ing]
the moral order," and he argues that her fall would have been more com-
plete had she not tempted Adam and thus linked her fate with his (*Answer-
able Style: Essays on "Paradise Lost"* [Minneapolis, 1953], p. 108). Neither
of these defenses is convincing.

Waldock's extenuation of Eve is weakly argued. His argument on the
triviality of Eve's jealousy overlooks the fact that Eve is not merely thinking
jealous thoughts, but is planning an action injurious to her husband on the

basis of these thoughts, an action, furthermore, which she carries out forthwith. The arguments on Eve's ignorance of death and on the nobility of her offer to "renounce / Deity" are contradicted by the text. Waldock ignores the fact that in her jealousy, Eve imagines Adam happy with a new wife while she herself is "extinct": Eve knows, thus, that death is an end of consciousness; and when Waldock credits Eve's offer, he ignores the blush which accompanies it (9. 887) and the gap between it and Eve's previous thoughts—clear indications that at this point Eve is consciously lying. As to Eve's assertion that she would rather die than hurt Adam, Waldock is right in claiming that Eve believes what she says here, for Milton attests her sincerity with his comment that she is "much won" by Adam's decision to join her (9. 990–93). If Eve is to be credited with "impulses" of "love," "heroism," or "self-sacrifice," however, there must be proof that Eve not only believes herself to be concerned for Adam, but that she is in fact concerned for him. The proof would have to indicate that Eve has reversed her initial decision to endanger her husband; Eve could, for instance, advise that he wait a while before tasting the apple. The fact that there is no such proof suggests that Eve's assertion is an " 'objective correlative' " not of her love but of her egotism.

The theory that Eve is guilty is structurally more satisfactory than Stein's theory that her decision to tempt Adam is a mixed act. The latter is a necessary corollary to Stein's interpretation of Eve's separation from Adam: if, as he argues, Eve's departure proves her desire for independence, then her return must be a repudiation of that desire, and therefore at least a partial good. The interpretation of Eve's departure is debatable (it is discussed in the preceding note), and the interpretation of Eve's return can be attacked on grounds of inadequate proof (Stein argues his theory abstractly, but the fact that Eve later refers to her temptation as a breach of her "ordained" role as Adam's "help" [11. 163–65] works against the contention that the temptation represents in some sense a restoration of Eve's rightful relationship to Adam) ; the main difficulty with the position, however, lies in its structural consequences. The theory introduces two unexplained reversals into Eve's development: after the morning quarrel with Adam (9. 205–384) which demonstrates her defection from a proper relationship to him, Eve partially restores that relationship by tempting Adam, only to revert to her earlier state in the afternoon quarrel (9. 1144–61). The first reversal is particularly incongruous if Stein's interpretation of the morning quarrel is granted. Because he believes that in this quarrel Eve displays only a prelapsarian tendency toward evil (*Answerable Style*, pp. 92–95), Stein is in fact claiming that Eve acts less evilly after her fall than before it. The alternative interpretation, that Eve's action is guilty, does not entail this sort of structural inconsistency: the act is simply a violation of Eve's wifely responsibilities, and it occurs between two other such violations; furthermore, because the act is a sacrifice of Adam, it is appreciably worse than the neglect shown in Eve's earlier decision to garden separately from her husband (that Eve's decision is to be seen as an act of neglect is defended in note 12.

5 Interrelationships

[1] My reading agrees in its basic approach with E. M. W. Tillyard's later remarks on the actions of *Paradise Lost* (*Studies in Milton* [London, 1951], p. 45). Its specific conclusions differ from Tillyard's in three respects, however. First of all, it differs in its sectioning of the plots. Tillyard divides each action into two parts, "the motives prompting revolt, and the positive lines of action afterwards" (ibid.). This division seems to me inadequate. With regard to Satan, the term "motives" misrepresents the materials of the scene referred to (this point is discussed in note 2 to chapter 2), and the term "positive line of action," since it applies to the whole of Satan's development (p. 49), does not adequately differentiate the stages in that development. With regard to Adam and Eve, the heading "motives" groups the state of innocence with the fall (this fault is discussed in note 2 to chapter 3), and the term "positive line of action," which refers only to the regeneration (p. 45), does not account for the moral status of Adam and Eve after their fall but before their repentance.

Secondly, my analysis differs from Tillyard's in the comparisons it draws between the poem's two plots. Tillyard claims that Satan's actions before and during the war in heaven are not compared with the behavior of Adam and Eve after the fall and before the repentance. The fact that the war in heaven is a reported rather than a presented action, he argues, and the fact that it concerns only God and the angels prevent the reader from connecting it with the human action, and Tillyard concludes that at this point "The virtue of the human action is not drawn on to counterpoise the Satanic action, the necessary counterpoise being supplied by the hosts of Heaven" (p. 49). The reasons which Tillyard offers are only token arguments, for despite the fact that Satan's motives are only reported and that they concern only God and the angels, Tillyard does compare these motives to those of Adam and Eve; the basis for his position lies rather in the premise revealed by the phrase "the virtue of the human action." Assuming that the actions of Adam and Eve after the fall should contrast with those of Satan, and finding that the misery of Adam and Eve does not contrast with the war in heaven, Tillyard denies that the two episodes are compared. The trouble, it seems to me, lies in the premise; if Adam and Eve are seen as like Satan before their repentance and as unlike him after their repentance, the two plots can be consistently rather than intermittently compared.

The third respect in which my analysis differs from Tillyard's is its treatment of the subject of the relation of creatures to one another. Tillyard does not separate the personal relationship of creatures from their relationship to God. For example, in applying Adam's final summary of doctrine (12. 561–73) to the action of the poem, Tillyard connects the phrase "by small / Accomplishing great things" (12. 566–67) with the personal reconciliation of Adam and Eve, and the phrase "by things deemed weak / Subverting worldly strong" (12. 567–68) with the pair's "protestation before

God" (p. 44) ; Tillyard assumes that the personal reconciliation is not only instrumental in the reconciliation with God, but that it has an equivalent religious significance. My reason for separating the two spheres is that they are treated separately at crucial points in the poem—either in separate sections of speeches, or in separate speeches, or in separate scenes; the most notable instances occur in the episodes of the fall of Satan, and of the fall and the regeneration of Adam and Eve.

² C. S. Lewis makes the standard case against the prophetic episode in *Paradise Lost:* that Virgil's use of "occasional prophecies, allusions, and reflections" is a more successful means of telling the "later results of [the] story" than Milton's connected "outline of sacred history"; that the "writing in [the] passage is curiously bad"; and that the existence of an "untransmuted lump of futurity . . . in a position so momentous for the structural effect of the whole work" constitutes a "grave structural flaw" (*A Preface to "Paradise Lost"* [London, 1942], p. 125). Though my exposition of the formal and intellectual connections between the prophecy and the rest of *Paradise Lost* touches on the three kinds of defense which have been offered for it, my purpose has been to explain rather than to evaluate; my evaluation would be only somewhat more favorable than Lewis's.

Lewis's main charge, that the episode is a long digression in a place least able to admit a digression, can be answered only by a defense on dramatic grounds—by the argument that the center of attention is not the series of historical events which Michael relates but rather the character of the hearer, Adam.

That the prophecy does have a dramatic function is suggested by the difference between it and Dryden's altered version in his *State of Innocence,* his operatic adaptation of *Paradise Lost.* When Dryden treats the events that follow the fall of man, he orients them around the doctrine of the fortunate fall, emphasizing the generosity of God rather than the regeneration of Adam and Eve (that *Paradise Lost* itself does not present this doctrine is argued in my Introduction). Dryden combines the Son's judgment of the fall with Michael's announcement of Adam and Eve's expulsion from the Garden, and he treats both from the standpoint of the lightness of God's sentence: Raphael, who delivers God's messages, opens with the announcement that the pair's punishment will be "much lighter than [their] crimes require," adding that the "All-good does not his creatures' death desire." Furthermore, Dryden places the personal reconciliation of Adam and Eve before the judgment scene; he places their repentance toward God after Raphael's announcement of God's verdict but before Raphael's relation of God's sentence, and reduces the pair's impenitence to a single complaint by Eve, a complaint which is preceded by a pious pronouncement from Adam, and followed by Adam's pious rebuke; and, finally, he places the pair's laments for Eden after Raphael's relation of all of God's punishments, reducing Eve's lament to a single line and combining Adam's lament with the admission that "Heaven is all mercy" for sentencing him to labor. Thus not only does Dryden stress God's generosity, but he avoids raising the question of whether

Adam and Eve will succumb to despair: in his version, the pair regain their piety before they are sentenced for losing it. These alterations make clear how much weight Milton places on the regeneration of Adam and Eve: after tracing the steps by which they come to accept their sentence, he brings in a second divine pronouncement, the expulsion from the Garden, and uses it as the focal point for a second series of spiritual advances.

Dryden's treatment of the prophecy parallels his treatment of the events after the fall: he uses the episode to propound the idea of the felix culpa. Compressing the prophecy into two masques and two short dialogues, he combines the subject of war with that of death, omits the other instances of sin, and converts the account of God's plan for rescuing mankind into a representation of the afterlife. His major topics, thus, are punishment and reward, and his point is that God's punishment is easily borne and that God will give the "blessed" a place which is happier than Eden, because "secure from crime." This revision points up the ways in which Milton makes his prophecy bear on Adam's development. By including a section on sin, Milton can not only suggest what sort of moral decisions Adam will have to make in the future, but can show him as making moral decisions about situations in the fallen world; and by presenting God's plan for mankind rather than merely a picture of its end, the elevation of the redeemed, Milton can emphasize the acquisition of Christian doctrine, giving Adam both the experience of mankind as it gradually learns of God's nature through history, and the experience of individual Christians as they learn by reading of that history in the Bible.

But to claim that what Lewis calls a "lump of futurity" is "transmuted" into a drama of spiritual education is surely an exaggeration. Lawrence A. Sasek makes the claim when he says that the last two books of Paradise Lost "present a drama in which the character of Adam is molded into an example of Christian fortitude" ("The Drama of Paradise Lost, Books XI and XII," Studies in English Renaissance Literature, ed. Waldo F. McNeir, Louisiana State University Studies, Humanities Series, No. 12 [Baton Rouge, La., 1962], p. 196). Sasek argues that Milton's prophetic episode contains an unprecedented amount of character interaction, that Adam is constantly responding to what is presented to him and that Michael "select[s]" incidents "for their effect on Adam" and changes in "tone and mood" according to Adam's responses. As a consequence, he says, "three elements—Michael's mission, the story of biblical events, and Adam's state of mind—are linked by cause and effect relationships" (ibid., pp. 184–85). This description, mutatis mutandis, might fit the relation between Timotheus's thoughts, Timotheus's songs, and Alexander's responses in Alexander's Feast, but it does not, I believe, fit Paradise Lost.

In the first place, Michael's choices and responses are not made prominent in the way that Timotheus's are in Dryden's poem. Timotheus is clearly shown as selecting his materials for their effect on Alexander. As Alexander weeps over the tragedy of Darius, Timotheus "smile[s] to see / That love [is] in the next degree." The smile proves that Timotheus is choosing his subject on the spot, since he would not smile to realize where the next modulation will bring him if he had planned the sequence beforehand; and the smile also proves that Timotheus is thinking of Alexander's reaction, since the reversal of mood is what amuses him. Michael's decisions, however, are not dramatized. In statements like "And now prepare thee for another sight" (11. 555), or "But now prepare thee for another scene" (11. 637), or "And now what further shall ensue, behold" (11. 839), there is no suggestion that Michael is deciding which of many possible visions to present to Adam, or that he is anticipating Adam's responses. Timotheus is shown as changing his tone according to the reactions of Alexander. When the abandoned dithyramb makes "the King gr[o]w vain," Timotheus turns to "mournful" tragedy; and that fact that here, as elsewhere, Timotheus uses in his song materials associated with Alexander keeps the relation between the singer and the listener in sight. Michael's reactions to Adam, however, are presented only intermittently and incidentally. The seven lines in which Michael tells Adam not to judge the marriage of the sons of Seth "By pleasure" (11. 603–6) and not to blame women for "Man's effeminate slackness" (11. 634–36) are responses to Adam's statements, as are the ten lines (at most) in which Michael explains that the Son's victory over Satan is not a physical victory (12. 386–95). But the prophecies themselves, the 58 lines describing (11. 556–92) and commenting on (11. 607–27) the marriage of Seth's descendants, and the 71 lines explaining Christ's mission (12. 395–465) seem totally independent of any dramatic context; a change in the reaction of Adam would produce no change in them. If, for example, Adam had condemned the daughters of Cain on sight, the first four lines of Michael's reply would be different—his speech would begin, "Justly dost thou judge" (cf. 12. 79–80)—but the rest of the description—"Those tents thou saw'st so pleasant" (11. 607 ff.)—would continue as before. If Adam had guessed that the Son was to destroy Satan's effects upon mankind, Michael would begin, "Dextrously thou aim'st" (cf. 11. 884), but after a transition like "He who comes thy Savior shall recure thee," the exposition would proceed unchanged: "Not by destroying Satan, but his works" (12. 394 ff.). The fact is, then, that Michael is only occasionally presented as a dramatic figure; emphasis in the prophetic episode is placed not upon he speaker but upon what he says.

Adam's reactions, furthermore, are not given the prominence which Alexander's receive in *Alexander's Feast*. Alexander's responses are made as colorful as the songs which invoke them; the imagined appearance of Bacchus is no more vivid than the spectacle of Alexander "thrice . . . rout[ing] all his foes," nor is the exhortation to "Take the good the gods provide thee" more vivid than Alexander's sinking upon the breast of Thaïs. But even though C. S. Lewis says of Milton's "account of Abraham [and] of the Exodus" that " 'the story cannot possibly be told in a manner that shall make less impression on the mind' " (*Preface*, p. 125), nevertheless the account is certainly more striking than the exclamation and question with which Adam responds to it (12. 270–84); and even Adam's touching lament at foreknowing his descendants' fate (11. 763–86) is overshadowed by the spectacular events of the flood which surround it. Alexander's responses, furthermore, are emphatically placed—they provide in four out of five cases the material for the climactic choruses—while in Adam's case, eight lines of reaction will be squeezed between 37 lines of description and 29 lines of explication (11. 638–711). Thus during the prophecy Adam, like Michael, is subordinated, the prophecy itself being the center of attention.

Despite the fact that it is adapted to its dramatic context, then, and despite the fact that it contains intermittent dramatic elements, the episode remains a piece of didactic exposition; the weight placed upon Adam's education is not sufficient to warrant Sasek's claim that the section is a "drama" and to answer Lewis's charge that it is an "untransmuted lump of futurity."

Lewis's lesser charges can be countered by arguments on thematic or aesthetic grounds. The argument that Milton could have conveyed the "later results of [the] story" by less obtrusive means can be met by the argument that Milton had purposes more important than merely relating the subsequent events. One version of this argument is that of John S. Diekhoff, who says that Milton uses Michael's "precepts" to "clarify and enforce" the "example" provided by the life of Adam and Eve (Milton's "Paradise Lost": A Commentary on the Argument [London, 1946], p. 135). Another is the version of B. Rajan, who argues that Milton uses the episode to expound the doctrine of the felix culpa ("Paradise Lost" and the Seventeenth Century Reader [London, 1947], pp. 82–83). My account of the thematic bearing of the prophecy supports the first of these approaches (the differing assumptions about the theme of Paradise Lost are discussed in my Introduction). Lewis's argument that the writing in the prophecy is "curiously bad" can be answered by the citation of aesthetic virtues, like the Jeremianic power which J. B. Broadbent attributes to the first half of the prophecy (Some Graver Subject: An Essay on "Paradise Lost" [London, 1960], pp. 274–75), or the formal virtues which would follow from my account of its structure.

But such defenses ought not be mistaken for total justifications. When Diekhoff says that the mission of Michael "enable[s]" Milton "to introduce . . . precepts" into the poem "with perfect narrative propriety" (Milton's "Paradise Lost," p. 135), he overpraises the episode. If the 700 lines of prophecy are primarily a didactic exposition, then the mere fact that a character rather than the author speaks them does not make them part of the action of the poem, and if they are not part of the action, then the clarification which they achieve must be weighed against what they lose in empathetic appeal, the appeal which is made by narrative (Broadbent argues this point at length, in Graver Subject, pp. 277–78). And even if, as Broadbent says, "Milton succeeds as prophet" (p. 275), and even if he uses an expository structure which is congruent with other materials in the poem, these successes must be weighed against the disadvantages of a digression that comes at an important point in the action.

Index

DATE DUE